Donald D. McMurray, Architect

'MID SUMMER'S LOVELINESS

*Is there any **beauty** as satisfying as that of a
small home skillfully conceived and executed?*

AUTHENTIC
SMALL HOUSES OF
THE TWENTIES

*Illustrations and Floor Plans of
254 Characteristic Homes*

Edited by

ROBERT T. JONES

*Technical Director of
The Architects' Small House Service Bureau, Inc.*

DOVER PUBLICATIONS, INC., NEW YORK

Published in Canada by General Publishing Company, Ltd., 30 Lesmill
Road, Don Mills, Toronto, Ontario.
Published in the United Kingdom by Constable and Company, Ltd., 10
Orange Street, London WC2H 7EG.

This Dover edition, first published in 1987, is an unabridged and unaltered
republication of *Small Homes of Architectural Distinction: A Book of Suggested
Plans Designed by The Architects' Small House Service Bureau, Inc.*, originally
published by Harper & Brothers Publishers, New York and London, in 1929.

Manufactured in the United States of America
Dover Publications, Inc., 31 East 2nd Street, Mineola, N.Y. 11501

Library of Congress Cataloging-in-Publication Data

Jones, Robert T. (Robert Taylor), 1884–
  Authentic small houses of the twenties.

  Reprint. Originally published: Small homes of architectural distinction.
New York : Harper, 1929.
  Includes index.
  1. Small houses—United States—Designs and plans. 2. Architecture,
Domestic—United States—Designs and plans. I. Title.
NA7205.J66 1987   728.3'7'0223   86-29300
ISBN 0-486-25406-2

INTRODUCTION

The man who would build a house for himself learns quickly as he works into the problem that there are many complications. He finds that technical skill and experience are necessary for the wisest assembly of material. He finds that he must choose not only the most durable form of construction but one that is not too expensive for his funds. Furthermore, he finds that the equipment of his house is not a matter to be disposed of casually. The heating, plumbing, electric wiring, all of the mechanical devices that go into the house, must be suitable and in proper relationship to the construction of the building and to his funds. The home builder quickly realizes how little he may draw from his own experience to manage the building of his home.

Then there is the planning of the house, the arrangement of rooms. How they shall turn on each other, and the size, the best arrangement of doors and windows and of the built-in equipment. The plan of the house is manifestly an essential problem, since it concerns the convenience of those who must live with it. The skill that recognizes these individual requirements of the home builder and molds them into a plan that fits his needs, is essentially of a technical order. It must be based on wide experience in handling elements of this sort.

But this is not all. The modeling of the house, the shape and contour of its walls and roofs, the selection of materials, the character of the architecture and finally of its adaptations to the specific condition of the site, are all of fundamental importance to the home builder, for they give expression to the quality of the house which he has built. If the combination of these turns out to be fine, the home builder has a priceless possession. He not only contributes a worthy share to the development of his neighborhood, but he has the comforting knowledge that he has built a sound basis for his family life. He has this added comfort, that his soundly built, well planned and beautifully designed house will conserve his investment. Many wise men who have made a study of housing have said that home builders should not count too heavily the matter of re-sale value, and yet no one can deny that there is a sense of security underlying the possession of a house that stands in the neighborhood as a monument to good taste and good sense.

Reconciling all of these complications of plans, construction and architectural form so that at the end the home builder secures the house that he wants at the price he can afford is essentially the work of the architect. No other person has the training, or the unbiased point of view that the architect can bring to it.

How is the small home builder to get an architect to help him with the building of his house? Many live where an architect is not available. To them this question is an exceedingly difficult one. To many others the fee which the individual architect is obliged to charge for his services seems to be more than they can afford, no matter how much it may be worth. For these, and for many others, who for reasons satisfactory to themselves do not avail themselves of the services of an individual architect, there must be some recourse to expert technical direction; to plans, specifications, quantity surveys, contract forms, from which their houses can be built.

It is for the purpose of service to these people that the Architects' Small House Service Bureau has been organized. It provides for this class of the small home builders—and only those who build houses of not more than six rooms in size,—house designs and other technical documents that have been prepared from a knowledge of the problem by groups of architects who have had the single purpose of placing in the hands of home builders the technical service that would at least start them on the right track.

It is not a complete service. That can only be obtained from the individual architect who is engaged to manage the home building operation from first to last. He alone is able to answer the home builder's requirements in the most worthy fashion. Yet to those who will not make direct use of this individual service, the designs presented in this book offer a partial service on which, so far as it goes, the home builder may rely with confidence.

The Architects' Small House Service Bureau recommends with all the urgency at its command that those who employ architectural documents from the Bureau organization do not miss the vital services to be obtained from having an architect superintend the construction of the house.

For each of the designs that follow in this book there are complete working drawings, and the home builder whose requirements are not of an extreme nature will find in the use of them that his house has been formed from a completed scheme, from a design that has been studied thoroughly, worked out, planned for convenience, constructed for strength, modeled for beauty.

The Architects' Small House Service Bureau stands behind these plans as a national organization with offices in many cities. It operates essentially on a non-profit basis. Its membership is made up of architects from all parts of the country who contribute their time generously to the problems of small house architecture. It operates under the control of the American Institute of Architects and with the endorsement of the Department of Commerce of the United States Government. It has no interest in furthering the sale of specific types or brands of equipment or material. Under the circumstances its work proceeds from a completely unbiased point of view.

STATEMENT

The completed houses illustrated in this book have all been built from the technical services supplied by the Architects' Small House Service Bureau. However, a few are not absolutely true to the working drawings that were supplied. Additions have been made, proportions varied slightly, the location of windows sometimes changed as well as the style of them. Some of these changes have been made for Bureau clients under the guidance of the Bureau or under the direction of architects employed by the home builder. In general, these changes have not added appreciably to the essential character of the architecture of the houses. In fact in some cases even better appearances would have been gained if the drawings had been followed faithfully.

The Architects' Small House Service Bureau is the only public service of its kind in this country controlled by the American Institute of Architects and endorsed by the United States Department of Commerce. This is your guarantee that whatever service and counsel the Bureau supplies are professional, unbiased and directly in your interests.

ENDORSEMENTS

Approved Statement

by the

Board of Directors, A. I. A.

"The Architects' Small House Service Bureau idea originated in and is approved by the American Institute of Architects, and in order that the development of the idea may retain the character of a professional service and be prevented from assuming the character of a purely commercial undertaking, the organization of the Bureau involves a certain control of its policies by the Institute.

"This control exists solely through the right of the Institute to appoint a majority of the Directors of the Bureau, such appointees being able thereby to impose policies consistent with the expressed wishes of the Institute.

"The approval of such policies does not carry with it any interest in or approval of any specific acts of the Bureau in the development of its operation, nor any financial interest or control whatever.

"The approval of the Bureau by the Institute means:

"(a) That it approves the idea only.

"(b) That it assumes no responsibility for the designs, plans, specifications or other service of the Bureau any more than it assumes responsibility for the service of individual members of the Institute.

"(c) That it assumes no responsibility for nor does it in any way presume to endorse any organization with which the Bureau may do business, nor any type or types of building construction or materials involved in houses designed by the Bureau.

"The Board looks upon an architect's work in the Bureau as primarily a contribution to the improvement of the small-house architecture of this country, involving houses of not more than six primary rooms."

Approved Statement

by the

Department of Commerce

I have looked into the work of The Architects' Small House Service Bureau of The United States with its divisions and branches and have examined its organization and incorporation papers. The complete plans, specifications, documents and bills of materials with the designs worked out for local conditions and to use stock materials and eliminate waste materially simplify home-building problems. The form of control by The American Institute of Architects should guarantee a high standard of service. It gives me pleasure to endorse this work and to assure you that the Department of Commerce will do all it can to co-operate with the Institute and the Bureau.

HERBERT HOOVER,
Secretary, Dept. of Commerce,
United States Government.

Home Built from Design 3-A-2

On an inside wall of the living room, a location recommended where economy is a serious object, is this attractive fireplace. In this case a gas log has been installed

THREE ROOMS PLUS

Exceptionally flexible in plan

Countless touches about this house take it out of the commonplace both as to exterior and plan. Ostensibly of three rooms, it may be built to accommodate either four or five, for either one or two bedrooms may be finished off in the attic. Too, the closet that opens into the living room may hold a closet bed, this to turn down into either the living room or the front porch, affording extreme flexibility of plan. All of the wanted things are included, yet the house is designed for economy in building.

Construction: Wood frame, stucco finish, shingle roof.

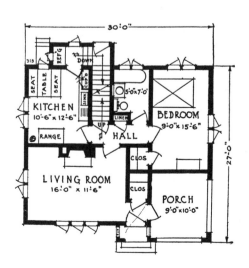

DESIGN 3-A-1

A KINGDOM OF YOUR OWN

A group of small detached homes providing apartment equipment

Charming for all their simplicity, small in size, these little houses are all large in the resources of home making. Among them we find sufficient difference in appearance and plan to meet a wide variety of family needs and desires. All of frame construction, they should prove inexpensive to build

Each of these three plans is replete with luxuries; fireplace, dining alcoves, closet bed, many storage closets—all the conveniences of an apartment in a small house, with a porch in every case for good measure

DESIGN 3-A-3

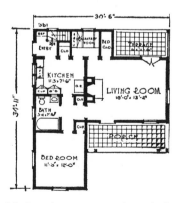

Notice the generous size of the major rooms, and the fact that all are provided with cross ventilation

DESIGN 3-B-1

How homelike these little houses would be painted white with green roofs and blinds. This is a color scheme of never-failing charm, but many others are possible. Shingles as an exterior finish would give walls of delightful texture

HOME BUILT FROM DESIGN *3-A-7*

IF YOU CAN'T AFFORD A LARGE HOUSE

*A cottage is a castle on a small scale, and in many
ways more desirable*

If three rooms meet the requirements of your family, or if they are all you can afford, why build more? Three rooms provide comfort, convenience, and fewer responsibilities as to housekeeping, advantages not to be lightly overlooked.

This house, design 3-A-7, embodies the fundamental principles of all good architecture—fine appearance, good plan, and sound construction. Its compact design, convenient room arrangement, and many comforts show expert planning. Their generous size, too, makes the rooms livable.

The house should be reasonable to build, having an almost square plan, simple type of pitch roof, and no waste in space or materials. Its beauty depends upon good lines and proportions and a few carefully studied details like the triple window in front, the pretty bay on the side, and the dignified hooded entrance. Stucco seems to be the ideal material in which to carry out this design.

The feature of the plan is undoubtedly the living room. It is a beautiful room with brick fireplace and with built-in shelves at either side of the delightful bay window. Since this room serves also as a dining room, the table may be placed in the bay window, a

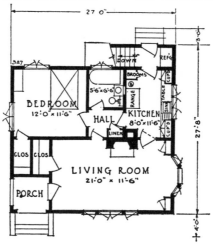

cheery, sunny place for breakfasts, or on occasion it might be placed in front of the fireplace, another delightful place for meals. Either location is convenient to the kitchen. At the other end of the room is a huge coat closet, which may contain a closet bed, thus greatly increasing the usefulness of the house.

The owner of the home pictured above added to the living room the space allotted to the open entrance porch in the plan.

The kitchen has been specially designed to lighten the work. It is provided with plenty of cupboard space. Above the sink at either side are four deep shelves. To the right below are six drawers and to the left five more of different sizes, a flour bin, and several enclosed shelves for pots and pans. A scuttle in the ceiling of the hall gives access to storage space in the attic above. The large, square bedroom is light and airy and has also a large closet.

If necessary to reduce costs, the basement may be omitted and the laundry tubs placed on a rear porch in the position now occupied by the basement stairway.

Construction: Wood frame, exterior finish stucco, shingle roof.

HOUSES FOR HERE AND THERE OR NOW AND THEN

One for mountain, woods, sea or lakeside; the other for year around use

An extensive open porch, a large living room open on three sides, simplicity of plan, and an attractive rustic exterior combine to make the house above, design 3-B-9, particularly desirable for use as a summer cottage. The ceiling in the living room has exposed rafters, the fireplace is of rough stone, all in keeping with the style of the house. The enclosed porch may be used for dining, but it also makes an ideal sleeping porch. The construction of the house is wood frame, with an exterior finish of rough sawed boards or shingles. Instead of plaster inside, some form of wallboard might be used. The foundations may be of local stone as shown here. No basement is required.

The house at the right, design 3-A-15, although small, provides many luxuries, being by no means the limited affair implied by three rooms. A closet bed and dining nook give it all the flexibility of accommodations characterizing apartment house units. A large fireplace and attractive bay window are noteworthy features. Construction: Wood frame, exterior finish stucco.

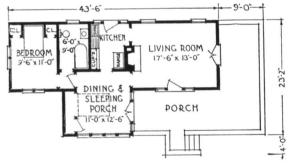

Considered as a workshop where many hours are spent during the day, the kitchen is here located at the front of the house. A table and seats beneath the front window may serve as an informal dining nook

This house would look well if the stucco were given a slightly rough floated treatment of a cream color, the roof covered with tile in variegated shades of red, the window frames, if of wood as shown, stained brown, and the sash, doors, and blinds painted turquoise blue

HOME BUILT FROM DESIGN *3-B-5*

THREE ROOMS BUT MUCH SPACE

Fine architectural character in a small house

This house, design 3-B-5, may truly be called one of Italian design. It possesses the charm and delightful proportions common to houses of this character. It has a freshness and originality rarely found in so small a house, yet it has none of what has been sometimes called "the curse of quaintness."

The roof of colorful red tile contrasts charmingly with light stucco walls, and the various units are in complete harmony. The arched openings of the porch with their simple wrought iron balustrade (wood in the illustration), the casement windows with their solid board shutters, and the general simplicity and good proportions all combine to make a home of real character. Too, it is a house that will be extremely pleasant during hot weather, for not only is a large porch enclosed under the main roof, but the living room catches the breeze from three sides.

This is a large, pleasant room well supplied with windows. A closet with a window opens from it, which may be provided with a closet bed, while a second closet makes it convenient to use as an additional bedroom if necessary. The fireplace in this room is of exceptional size.

To reduce the dimensions of the house as far as possible, the bathroom has been planned in two units opening off the bedroom.

The kitchen is rectangular, and practically all work may be performed without taking more than half a dozen steps between centers.

The living room serves also as the dining room, where, if the table is light and movable, meals may be served either before the hearth or in front of the long range of windows.

Construction: Hollow tile or brick walls, stucco finish, tile roof, steel or frame casement windows.

DESIGN 4-A-3

Construction, 4-A-3: Wood frame, exterior finish rough cast plaster, shingle roof. Brick base course, porch floor and steps brick. Casement windows. Full basement

WHENCE COMES THE BUNGALOW

Two examples which show clearly the influence of the English cottage

Construction, 4-A-7: Wood frame, exterior finish stucco, siding in gable ends, roof of slate or shingles. Space for two bedrooms in attic. Full basement

The bungalow got its name from India, but it got its style, its plan, and everything that makes it livable from our own American architects. In India it is a lightly built structure for residence, with verandas on all four sides and a widely projecting roof.

But the idea of a one-story house is by no means restricted to India. One-story houses have been built in European countries for centuries. In France and England they were called cottages. In fact, we called our own small houses by this name until recent years. Our own architects have made much of the intimacy and charm, the qualities of home, which the cottagers of the Old World put into their homes.

The bungalows on these two pages have these qualities in large measure, which is undoubtedly one reason for their great popularity among home builders.

The most distinctive feature of the two plans on this page is the location of the kitchen at the front of the house. Considering how much time the housewife spends in this room, is it not proper that it be given an interesting outlook? Not to speak of immediate and convenient access to the front door? This arrangement also permits greater quiet and privacy to the bedrooms which can be located at the rear.

Both houses afford ample proof that size is no indication of convenience and

desirability. Both have a breakfast nook, outside entrance leading to both basement and kitchen, a fireplace, ample closet space, and many built-in kitchen cupboards.

In exterior design, too, each has distinctive features that take it out of the commonplace. Half timber has been used effectively in the gable ends of the house above, and wide siding, in pleasant contrast to the stucco of the lower story, in the gables of the house shown below.

DESIGN 4-A-7

DESIGN 4-A-8

Construction, 4-A-8: Wood frame, exterior finish wide siding, shingle roof, cement finished base course. Full basement

Construction, 4-A-11: Wood frame, exterior finish wide siding, roof of wood or composition shingles. Space in attic may be finished off. Full basement

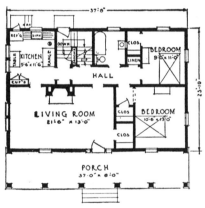

ARCHITECTURE—WHAT IS IT?

Whether in the small home or the mansion its principles are the same

Among many definitions of architecture is this one: "Architecture is putting into building certain qualities —namely, logic, strength, and beauty." Do these seem too high-sounding words when applied to small homes? Not when translated into familiar terms.

Logic means making the house convenient, livable, adaptable to both the family and the site. It means straightforwardness of plan that results in economy.

Strength, of course, means building with good materials. It means honest construction, durability, long life, low depreciation.

Beauty results from naturalness, from simplicity, and from good proportions. It depends upon careful attention to the small details as well as to the larger ones. It is the quality that makes the house a pleasure to see and to know, and to live in through the years.

These three combined make good architecture. Without any one of these a house is a mere building. It is not architecture. The bungalows on these pages show clearly that every important architectural quality that may be possessed by a larger house may also be possessed by the small house. All combine to a satisfactory degree a good plan, a fine exterior, and a sound system of construction.

Both houses on this page include large open porches, which, of course, may be screened or glazed for greater usefulness. In design 4-A-8, at the top of the page, the main roof and cornice have been extended to embrace the porch, thus giving the house an appearance of greater breadth. The entrance porch adds a desirable touch of variety, and the lattice is a delightfully decorative note. The columned porch across the front of the house at the bottom of the page, design 4-A-11, is suggestive of the fine old plantation homes of the South.

DESIGN 4-A-11

Dining space is here aplenty. A dining alcove may be arranged in the kitchen, the side porch may be used, or a table may be set in the living room

FOUR ROOM COTTAGES
With many delightful qualities

In these delightful Colonial bungalows we have again excellent proof of the fact that the small, inexpensive home can be as comfortable and attractive as many a larger, more expensive dwelling. Both of them have architectural qualities which mean not only extra beauty but extra value, for which, should their owners for any reason wish to sell, they would find a clear-cut expression in cash.

The house above, design 4-A-9, is a masterpiece of designing, so graceful and finely proportioned that the most casual observer cannot fail to notice it. Its distinction is due to the fact that the owner saw to it that the drawings were followed with absolute faithfulness. Thus all parts were as carefully proportioned as they should be.

The second house, design 4-A-10, is equally delightful in its own way with its small, latticed porch, simple pediment, finely proportioned cornice.

The plans are compact and well arranged, the living rooms generously proportioned and with attractive fireplaces. Closets are numerous and ample. Both kitchens are convenient and well arranged. In design 4-A-10, this room has an advantageous position at the front with a dining nook beside it.

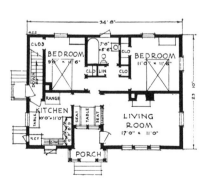

HOME BUILT FROM DESIGN *4-A-10*

HOME BUILT FROM DESIGN *4-A-14*

AND MORE OF THE SAME

Homes you will be proud to own

Even at a casual glance it is easy to understand the popularity of these two small homes. Besides providing their full quota of comforts and conveniences, they have a delightful, homelike charm and distinguished appearance. Both are finished in wide siding, giving an interesting texture to the walls; both have the so-called Germantown hood over the entrance, reminiscent of Pennsylvania Dutch architecture. Their proportions are fine and roof lines interesting.

The dining alcove in design 4-A-14 is located so that a fire on the hearth may be enjoyed there as well as in the living room. In design 4-A-13 kitchen and dining alcove are placed at the front, a location with much to recommend it. In both of these plans the sleeping quarters are definitely separated from the living quarters by a hall, thus affording them a maximum of privacy.

A stairway leads to the second floor, where an extra bedroom may be finished off when funds permit.

HOME BUILT FROM DESIGN *4-A-13*

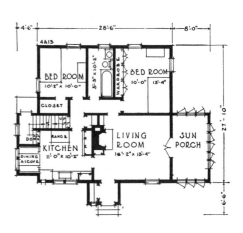

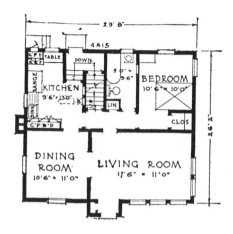

DESIGN *4-A-15*

HOUSES WITH DOWNSTAIRS BEDROOMS

One with a porch and one with a brilliantly lighted living room

In designing these two homes the watchword has been economy—economy of floor space and low cost of construction. Both aims have been achieved and this without any sacrifice of quality. In appearance both houses are charming, in plan modern and up to date and designed for our present conditions of living.

The two plans are quite similar, giving much accommodation for the money spent. They are designed, too, to grow with the family, for the attic space is sufficient to allow an additional bedroom to be finished off there when desired. Also the large coat closets in the living rooms may be converted into bed closets, thus adding additional sleeping quarters at little expense.

Even though the houses are small, the combination of living room and dining room across the front, which is nearly 30 feet in length, gives an unexpected effect of spaciousness. The wall between the two rooms can be made little or much of, as desired. A beam spanning the opening would, of course, give the best effect of large space.

Design 4-A-26 is finished in wide siding, although stucco or shingles may be used. The wide shaded porch is included under the main roof, giving the house a restful aspect.

Design 4-A-15 is also finished in wide siding, and the simple, shaded entrance, with its low platform and seat, gives a pleasant air of hospitality.

DESIGN *4-A-26*

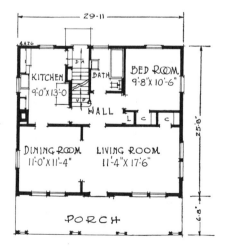

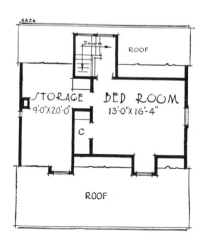

DESIGN *4-A-27*

A HOUSE DESIGNED FOR THE NARROW LOT

*Offering all the comfort and convenience demanded by home
builders, it requires only a minimum of space*

To the owner of the narrow lot, in fact the very narrow lot, this plan should prove extremely interesting. In comfort and convenience it should satisfy the most discriminating home builder, yet it can be built on even a 30-foot frontage since the house is but 22 feet wide.

The drawings call for hollow tile walls, exterior finish stucco, so that with a roof of slate or shingle tile the house would be comparatively fireproof. The many-paned casement windows are of steel construction. Brick sills and lintels accent the window openings.

Within there are four good rooms, bath, full basement, dining alcove, and commodious closets. The living room boasts an attractive fireplace at one end, with built-in, ceiling-high bookcases beside it.

The kitchen is a pleasant, cheerful room, which, with the dining alcove at one end, extends the full width of the house. Having windows on three sides, it is assured ample light and ventilation. A built-in seat extends around two sides of the alcove. When there are guests the table may be set in one end of the living room. To make a real festivity of such occasions, it may be set in front of the hearth in the glow of the firelight. This location, too, is immediately accessible to the kitchen.

In addition to the two large bedrooms upstairs, the living room may be utilized for sleeping quarters also, since the large coat closet in the hall may be built as a bed closet, the bed to turn down into the living room. Closet space is more than ample, with two large closets on the first floor and four on the second.

Construction: Hollow tile walls, stucco finish, roof of slate or shingle tile.

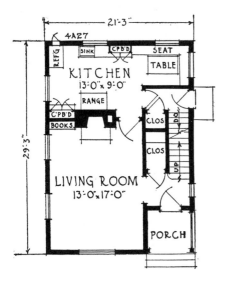

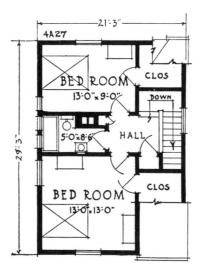

HOME BUILT FROM DESIGN *4-A-29*

A MODEL HOME IN MORE WAYS THAN ONE
Wherein the architects save space and thus reduce building costs

This house, design 4-A-29, was built as a model demonstration home designed to show how, in the midst of mounting building costs, the essentials of good living may still be brought within the reach of almost any pocketbook. It was planned to provide all the major comforts and conveniences demanded by the average family, and to be at the same time well built and fine appearing. Wherever costs could be shaved down, without injuring the house in either equipment or finish, this was done. Space was saved in every possible way.

Everything in the kitchen is planned for efficiency. Note in the illustrations the niche for the stove, double drain boards at the sink, and the raised platform and shelf under the sink.

The bedrooms are both sufficiently large for twin beds.

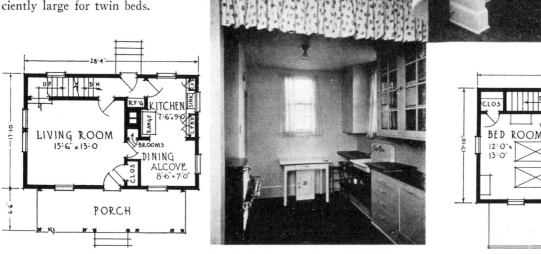

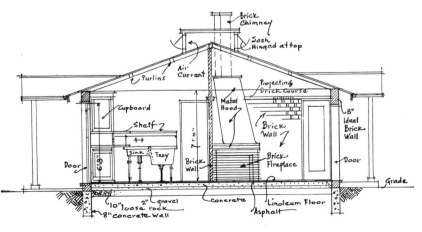

DESIGN *4-A-39*

A HOUSE THAT DOES DOUBLE DUTY

Beauty serves both economy and usefulness

For the family on a small income, to whom the cost of even the ordinary small home has seemed prohibitive, this house is ideal. There are no nonessentials, no attic, no basement. Wherever possible equipment is made to serve doubly.

The big fireplace is designed for its heating properties. Above, extending upward close to the roof, is a metal hood which acts as a radiator. The sink and laundry tray form one unit. The house heater goes behind the chimney stack under a masonry arch. The bedrooms, although of minimum size, are large enough for all necessary furniture.

The section, at somewhat larger scale than the plan, passes through living room and kitchen. From it you can see there is no ceiling to the house, the roof, too, doing double duty. At the top is a dormer. Open, it lets out the heated air, keeping the house

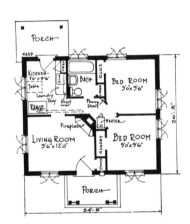

cool in summer. Closed in winter—the roof heavily insulated—all the heat will be retained. This method of using the roof for a ceiling not only affects a saving in the cost of construction but adds appreciably to the appearance. As it gives the rooms more cubic content, they are far more airy.

The floor is of concrete laid over the ground and finished with linoleum. In order that the ground may be well drained and no dampness permitted to come through the floor, there is a course ten inches thick of loose rock with gravel above, and the concrete is laid over the gravel.

These are all sound methods of building, some of them long known, some modern innovations worked out by famous architects.

Much of the interest and liveliness of the exterior comes from the hollow wall of common brick laid rowlock fashion.

DESIGN *4-A-33*

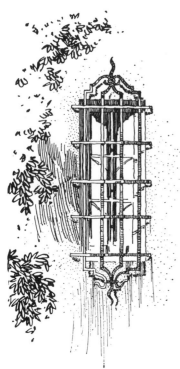

STRAIGHT FROM PARADISE VALLEY

This is the garden gate which leads to the kitchen entry. Opposite is a bit of grill work about the dining alcove window

One of the fine things about this design is that you can face it as you desire. The front may be the porch, or it may be the end, where the entrance is through a vestibule. Certainly the facing will be determined very much by the lot, but it would be well if the house could have an adequate setting. Casement windows that reach to the floor and are protected with wrought iron rails, a beamed ceiling, and a beautiful fireplace that fills one end of the room, make the living room one of exceptional beauty. Located as they are

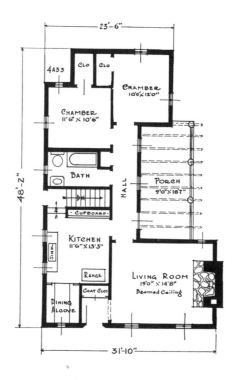

in relation to the living quarters, the bedrooms have almost the privacy of a separate apartment.

In building this house, one of the most important details to observe is the way in which it has been designed to seem very close to the ground. This effect may be accomplished at little added expense. The height of the foundation, as worked out by the architect, is an important part of the design, and should be followed with greatest care.

Construction: Stucco over hollow tile.

This is a louver. It goes over the doorway illustrated below to vent the attic space. It might have been just a series of slats, but the architect has modeled it

GLOWING WITH TEXTURE, COLOR AND VIVACITY

Bits of Architecture That Make This House Interesting

To many a window is just something to look out of. Beautifully designed it becomes a part of the decoration of the house

The most perfect piece of architecture in the world is the Parthenon. Perfection comes largely from the way the surfaces are modeled. Delicate curves are found everywhere. Note the fine modeling of the plaster work about this door

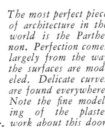

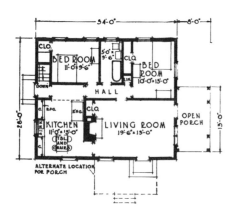

Design *4-A-34*

PORCHES FOR BROAD OR NARROW LOTS

Whether at front or side their location is in no way detrimental
to the appearance of the house

There is in reality but one house here—that is, only one floor plan. True, the exterior has been developed in Spanish style with stucco and in Colonial with wood, and there is possibly a further variation in appearance if the porch is located at the front or at the side. Essentially, however, the houses are similar.

If the porch is placed at the side, the over-all frontage will be about 36 feet, calling for a lot about 50 feet in width. If the house is placed broadside to the street, and the porch is then placed at the end, it will crowd a 50-foot lot somewhat. While the location of the porch changes the appearance of the house, it has been worked into the design so that it seems a part of it in either position. It does not appear, as is often the case with porches, like an unnatural and disfiguring outgrowth. The choice of position, therefore, depends entirely on whether you have a broad or narrow lot or a good or bad view at the rear.

In houses as small as these, every detail counts heavily in the general effect. One of the most important of small things is the blinds. They contribute greatly to the general quality of the design, make it homelike and snug with an air of domesticity, all of which is extremely desirable in small houses. The small additional cost of blinds is out of all proportion to their importance. Color is also a prime consideration.

As usual in the four-room house, there is no dining room, the kitchen being quite large enough for serving meals. Whether this room is at the front or rear depends on which way the house is faced. A table may also be set in the living room, since this is directly accessible from the kitchen. The living room although moderate in size is sufficiently large for comfort, with wall spaces adequate for all the larger pieces of furniture. Neither of the bedrooms is entered directly from the living room or kitchen but from a short hall. Here there is also a linen closet. Construction: 4-A-35, wood frame, stucco finish, tile roof.

Design *4-A-35*

TWO EXTERIORS
FOR A
FLEXIBLE PLAN

Throughout New England are many houses that look like design 4-A-36 as to exterior, with its distinctive stucco panels starting at the level of the second story windows and spreading to the corners. The trellis around the side porch furnishes a setting for vines and flowers. Houses such as this, from their very simplicity, lend themselves favorably to landscaping.

Design 4-A-37, with its quaint bonnet roof and combination of shingles and stucco siding, is somewhat English. The entrance and side porches are railed with scrolled out spindles and tapered posts. Window panes on each side of the front door and in the door itself furnish additional light to the living room, which has outside exposure on three sides.

Meals before an open fire are luxuries to most of us, for which opportunities present themselves only too rarely. Such opportunities are always present in these homes, for the living room and dining room are combined into one large room, where the dinner table may be set as near the fire or as far from it as desired.

One of the features of this plan, seldom found in so small a house, is the hallway leading directly from the kitchen to the second story, through which one may pass without entering the living room. One may also enter this hallway from either the grade entry or the side entrance and pass upstairs without disturbing members of the family in the living room.

The bedrooms are well proportioned, neither too small nor too large. Although the plans show twin beds in only one of the rooms, both are large enough for this arrangement.

In studying these designs, the thing that strikes one forcibly is the possibility for economies in construction. The contours are rectangular, the materials that go into construction and finish of the simplest. Ornamentation is limited to contrasting uses of these inexpensive finishes. Extras such as shutters and trellis may be secured from stock.

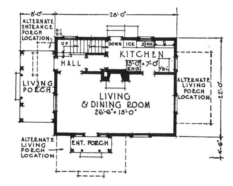

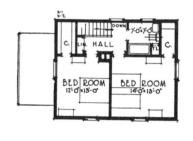

G. J. Fernschild, Architect

ROUGH TORN FINISH FOR A HOUSE WITH
LITTLE ORNAMENTAL DETAIL

There should be relationship between the architecture of a house and the texture of the stucco. The scale or roughness of the finish should be in keeping with the type of ornament on the house. If the molding and other trim is delicate, the stucco should have a fine and almost smooth surface. With little ornamentation, as in this case, a bolder and rougher stucco texture affords a desirable play of light and shadow

HOME BUILT FROM DESIGN *4-A-38*

A BIT OF OLD SPAIN
Both picturesque and efficient

This bungalow has a studio living room with vaulted ceiling and exposed beams as shown below. In this case spiral columns have been used on the exterior between windows instead of the arrangement shown in the perspective. The fence at either end was also added by the owner. Construction: Wood frame, stucco finish, tile roof.

To give the dining alcove a more intimate air, the ceiling has been dropped to eight feet. A low beam separates it from the living room. Between these rooms and the sleeping quarters the division is distinct

HOME BUILT FROM DESIGN *4-B-3*

A BUNGALOW TODAY, A COTTAGE FORMERLY

*With the simplicity that calls for a garden setting
to enhance its charms*

The direct lines and rectangular form of this little house insure economy, yet it has charm for all its simplicity. While it cannot be considered as belonging to any particular style of architecture, it easily adapts itself to any part of the country, particularly to one possessing a mild climate. It is well arranged, thoroughly practical, and excellent in outline.

The original drawings call for an exterior finish of lap siding, placed 8″ to the weather. This could be stained a chestnut brown, with a shingle roof of variegated colors, but the color scheme might also be the more usual green and white of the Colonial style. As shown in the house illustrated, however, shingles are attractive as an exterior finish. Many may prefer them, for unquestionably they give a delightful texture to the walls.

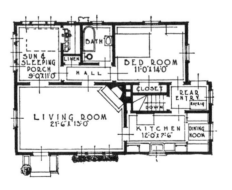

Although of only four rooms, the house contains all the necessities and many of the luxuries that the modern home builder demands. One of the usual requirements is a large living room, and certainly few would be dissatisfied with 21 x 13 feet as is this one. The fireplace, tile faced, is quite out of the ordinary in its corner location, and a fire on the hearth may be enjoyed from any point in the room. From the viewpoint of economy it is an advantageous location also, for the flue is close to the kitchen range and to the heater in the basement, thus eliminating long runs of pipe.

From the hall opens one large bedroom, bathroom, linen closet, and a combination sun and sleeping porch. This last is generously supplied with windows on two sides, making it possible to convert it into a more or less open porch in summer and a sleeping porch for night use. A large closet and a closet bed make provision for this purpose, affording in this way two complete bedrooms.

The long narrow kitchen is efficiency itself, with its working space all on one side. The dining nook at one end is not separated from the kitchen by any partition so that the combined room has air and light from two sides. The built-in seats have hinged tops.

A service entry opens from the kitchen at the rear, and here is located the stair to the basement. For reasons of economy a basement is provided under a portion of the house only. The kitchen is also accessible to the bedroom through this rear entry. Thus the sleeping quarters and bath may be reached without going through the living room. There will be occasions when this convenience will be greatly appreciated not only by the housewife, but by every member of the family. The house is thoroughly modern and well adapted to both suburban and country conditions.

HOME BUILT FROM DESIGN *4-B-6*

SPANISH IN ITS SIMPLEST FORM

With none of the elaborate ornamentation that adds to expense,
yet with innate charm and beauty

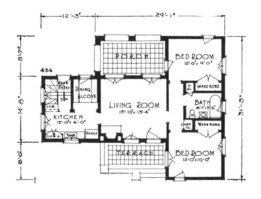

Masonry walls carry their own recommendation, for they have had man's confidence through long ages. In strength and durability, in color and texture such construction stands preeminent.

Built of hollow tile or brick, finished on the exterior with stucco and with a colorful tile roof, this house has these qualities in large measure. From the materials of which it is constructed it derives much of its charm, although in form also it is attractive. Spanish in character, it is one more illustration of the excellent results that may be obtained in small house design by following the general style of early Spanish-American architecture. Stucco of a light pink color in a trowel finish is contemplated. The woodwork should be finished in a weathered pine to give it an aged effect, with shutters of turquoise blue. The roof should be in variegated colors of browns, reds, and yellows laid irregularly.

The plan is unusual in that the living room is so placed that it serves as an axis for the entire house. Upon entering this room from the front door one will be immediately impressed with the beautiful garden view, since directly opposite two pairs of French doors open upon the porch, and this in turn upon the garden. For year-around usefulness the porch may be enclosed with glass. In this way it becomes a very satisfactory sunroom, and increases the living space of the house at comparatively little expense. Its location at the rear is one which is becoming more and more popular with home-owners, since it affords desirable privacy, and freedom from all the annoyances which passing traffic entails.

There is no formal dining room. A dining alcove, which also overlooks the garden, serves ordinarily for meals. On occasion the table may be set in the living room or on the porch. When the family becomes used to this arrangement, the dining room will never be missed.

The kitchen faces the street yet it is in close communication with the back yard. This is reached through a rear entry which also contains the basement stairs. The ice box is built into one of the kitchen walls and may be iced from this entry.

The charm of this house is its simplicity. The arched doorway, with its bit of overhanging roof, contributes the necessary element of interest and vivacity. The solid blinds, painted blue, add a pleasing contrast to the pink-toned stucco and the variegated roof.

Construction: Hollow tile or brick walls, stucco finish.

DESIGN *4-B-2*

REMINISCENT OF NEW ENGLAND

*Of direct, clean-cut outline that promises
economy of construction*

Distinctive in a quiet, formal manner, this attractive brick house is suggestive of the many charming Colonial houses to be found in the New England States. It is a house that will fit suitably into any neighborhood of small homes, and one well adapted to a narrow lot. The rear or garden side of the house is equally as attractive as the front, for the broad open porch with its square columns and balustraded balcony makes a composi-

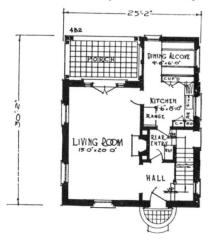

tion of dignity and repose. Windows of even size and spacing as shown add to this air of dignity, as does the front entrance of chaste design.

The plan is extremely compact, with a minimum of space devoted to entrance hall and stairs. From its very nature, however, this little reception hall gives a tone of formality to the interior of the house, and the open stairway with its simple balustrade makes an attractive picture viewed from the living room. The rear entry beyond affords communication between hall and kitchen and from the kitchen to the service door.

The living room is the pride of the house, however. Large, with light and air from three sides, it opens on to the broad porch beyond. This opening is particularly inviting, for the double French doors have tall sidelights of similar character on either side. The broad fireplace is of brick.

The efficient kitchen has its sink, working space, and china cupboards on the outside wall close to the light; and the combination china cabinet at the end of the kitchen, forming a wall be-

tween kitchen and dining alcove, is not only convenient but forms a charming setting for the alcove. This little room, too, is lighted from three sides.

The two bedrooms on the second floor are of equal size. The balcony opening from one overlooks the garden. Locating the bathroom directly over the kitchen reduces the cost of the plumbing. Wardrobes, closets, linen shelves add abundant storage space.

Construction: Solid brick walls, shingle roof.

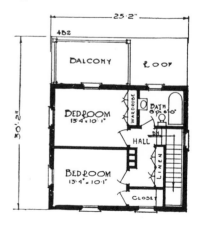

DESIGN *4-B-10*

IN THE MANNER OF AN ITALIAN VILLA

Combining in large measure the charm of foreign lands and the
efficiency common to our own

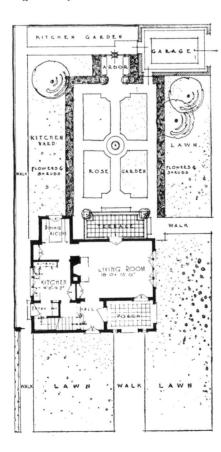

Talking over house plans with women, one is accustomed to hear them state that they want less space to take care of. And they are right! Houses must be built on efficient lines so that the accommodations will be ample, but today, when the small family rarely employs a servant, the mistress of the house is quite justified in her request that the demands on her time be minimized.

This house has been designed with this in mind, and for such reasons there is no dining room proper. The dining alcove, however, has been given far more careful treatment than in ordinary accommodations of this sort. It is larger, particularly well lighted, and has a fine position overlooking the garden. The trade entry is at the left near the front of the house but shielded by a decorative gate. Therefore the back yard will be free from the invasion of delivery and service men of all kinds.

From an architectural point of view the most notable feature about the plan is the living room. Getting a living room of this sort with windows on three sides is not easy to do in a plan that is as straightforward and rectangular as this. The usual type of house having three exposures for the living room is an L-shaped plan, which means involved construction and therefore increased cost.

The decorative quality which the house possesses is one of its finest features. Decoration has been obtained not by adding ornament, but through the happy arrangement of the parts, the use of color in the exterior, and the fine massing of walls and openings. It is a house that should make strong appeal to home builders who are interested in the Italian style.

Construction: Hollow tile, exterior finish stucco, tile roof.

HOME BUILT FROM DESIGN *4-B-8*

ATTRACTIVE BUNGALOWS BUILT OF MASONRY

*With plans offering a choice between
dining room and alcove*

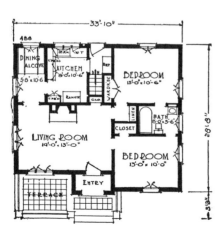

HOME BUILT FROM DESIGN *4-B-18*

*The plans of these houses are similar, but the walls of one are of
solid brick, the other of hollow tile stucco-finished*

DESIGN 4-B-9

BEAUTY IN GROUPED ARCHES

*Dignifying the Spanish
Mission Bungalow*

The simplicity of the old Spanish missions may have been due to paucity of materials and lack of skilled labor, but it is a picturesque simplicity nevertheless. More and more we see the influence of this style in home architecture, and no wonder. All other things being equal, the more direct a house the more economical it is to build, and one with as little ornamentation as found in this type has much to recommend it on that score.

This four-room bungalow, design 4-B-9, is an example of the Spanish mission type, severe in design but possessing real grace. The plan meets all of the requirements of a well-designed small home. It contains two porches, one a large covered arched porch enclosed in the main body of the house, and the other a garden or terrace porch opening out of the living room and facing the garden.

The kitchen is designed with a dining alcove which may be shut off completely from this room if desired. This alcove has a casement window opening on the terrace, and also contains a large china cabinet. The kitchen itself is compact and completely equipped, with an outside entry leading to the service yard.

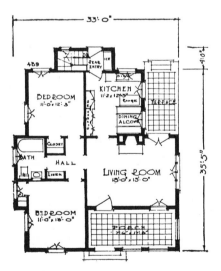

The sleeping quarters have the privacy of second floor bedrooms. Each room has a large closet, and a linen closet of ample capacity opens off the hall.

The basement, although not fully excavated, contains sufficient space for the house requirements, and includes a laundry, heater room, fuel room, storeroom, and fruit closet. The entire basement may be excavated if desired.

There is an irresistible charm about the group of arches at the front which lifts this little house above the ordinary type of bungalow. To this add the gracefully designed wrought iron railings, attractive entrance lantern, and old-fashioned tight shutters, and the whole composition is one in which the owner will long take great satisfaction. The tile "roofed" chimney, its terra cotta chimney pots, and the clean-cut gables are added features which should not be overlooked by the discriminating home builder. The simplicity of this design insures one a house economical to build and an exceptionally happy solution of the small house problem.

Construction: Hollow tile walls, stucco exterior finish, roof of shingles.

HOME BUILT FROM DESIGN *4-B-12*

A HOUSE OF MANY WINDOWS

Rooms filled with sunshine offer varied comforts and conveniences

The completely planned house, one in which every detail is thought of and thoroughly worked out in advance, is all too uncommon. Many small houses unfortunately are built by the "cut and try" method. Many others are built from plans that are inadequate so that the home builder is surprised and alarmed at the "extras" that must be added while the house is in the process of building.

Here is one of the houses, however, in which the necessity for "extras" has been completely eliminated. Every effort has been made to meet the requirements of the modern home builder, and a house of beautiful design and ample accommodations is the result. It is a house especially well adapted to city building, for the masonry construction meets the requirements of many city ordinances. Although it is rated a four-room house, it will compare favorably with many six-room houses in living area and variety of accommodations.

Seldom does a four-room house contain all that this one does: a sun porch, a dining alcove of large size, a sleeping porch, a loggia, and in addition the usual kitchen, living room and

two bedrooms. Rectangular and compact, the plan has none of the rambling tendencies and elaborate construction that add so much to the cost of building. In the house shown above the downstairs porch has been incorporated in the body of the house in a manner similar to that of the sleeping

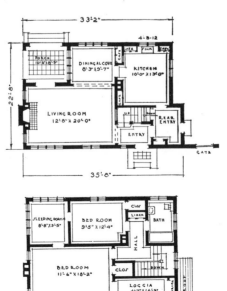

porch. In this way it becomes useful the year around.

The living room, separated from the sun porch by double French doors, has openings on three sides which help to make it the cheerful, sunny place it is. The walls of the large dining alcove are given over almost entirely to windows, eight to be exact, so that it, too, is light and airy, a delightful place for meals. In the back of the china closet in this room is a sliding panel that permits access to this cabinet from the kitchen also. The convenience of this arrangement can hardly be fully appreciated until it has been tried out.

The upstairs sleeping porch is accessible from both bedrooms, and if it is not required for sleeping will make a charming little sitting room. An upstairs room of this character is extremely cozy and often has greater charm and intimacy than is possible to achieve in the more formal living room. The loggia, which opens from the front bedroom, has a capacious wardrobe at one end and will make an attractive dressing room.

Construction: Hollow tile walls, stucco finish, roof of shingles or slate.

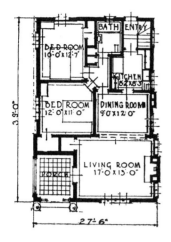

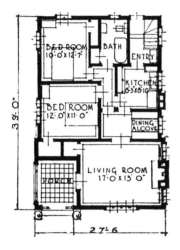

HOME BUILT FROM DESIGN *4-B-14*

The only difference between the two plans at the left is in the method of locating the partitions. One set of plan provides for both arrangements; simply specify to the contractor which way the house is to be built

BUNGALOWS WITH VARIED PLANS

Differing also in finish, both are cozy and attractive

Different as they are, the two bungalows on this page have some qualities in common. Both are conservative, yet with a marked individuality in style; both are exceptionally fine examples of the home that is all on one floor, well proportioned, and offering a good return for every dollar invested.

Design 4-B-14 in the illustration

above shows the porch enclosed. An extra room is thus acquired at little additional expense, but the porch can be left open with trellis-work for trimming. Alternate plans are presented for this design. In both the arrangement of the rooms is most livable, and they open into each other in a convenient manner. These plans take into consideration both groups of home

builders—those who consider a formal dining room essential and those who require only the small dining alcove.

Design 4-B-15 is an adaptation of the Colonial style, with exceptional charm and individuality. There is sufficient wall space to carry large window openings. The roof pitch and the small porch are well studied.

Construction 4-B-14: Brick walls, face brick or stucco exterior finish, shingle or tile roof.

DESIGN *4-B-15*

A large living room and dining alcove, convenient kitchen, and privacy of sleeping quarters feature this plan

©

DESIGN *4-B-16*

FIVE ROOMS AND A PORCH—TWO CHOICES

One bungalow showing Spanish influence, the other Italian,
both are cozy and home-like

After innumerable hours spent poring over magazines devoted to home building and excursions through the houses of your friends, you have decided a five-room bungalow with a porch will suit your requirements exactly. And after critically surveying newly built-up residential districts and prowling through as many houses as you can find in the process of construction, perhaps you have further decided that it must be either of brick or stucco.

To those of you who have arrived thus far in the process of elimination these pages and the two immediately following should prove particularly interesting. All of the houses shown on these pages are essentially alike, yet there is enough variety to make it possible even to build them next to one another without giving the impression of the deadly "row."

Designs 4-B-16 and 4-B-17, while much the same in plan, present interesting variations in exterior design. The first shows clearly the Spanish influence, the second has one detail at least distinctly Italian. This is the Pal-

ladian motif on the front wall of the porch. No matter what the name of the style, this general form of architecture has met with great favor all over the United States.

Design 4-B-16 is exceedingly prac-

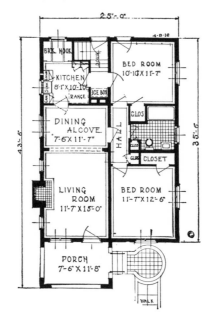

tical. The walls are of stucco on hollow tile with brick trim, and the roof is of tile. Shutters on the front windows add a delightfully "homey" touch. The plans provide for only partial excavation, and where climatic conditions permit this is one means of materially reducing the cost. The basement is still large enough to include ample laundry space and heater and fuel rooms.

Design 5-B-33, with exactly the same exterior as 4-B-16, calls for a full basement with a den below the living room. This is reached by stairs from a closet at the end of the living room opposite the fireplace. This design has a larger living room and a dining room of good size. If you like the exterior of design 4-B-16, therefore, but require more ample accommodations, design 5-B-33—shown later in this book—will very likely meet your requirements.

Design 4-B-17, while the same type of house, is still quite different in appearance. The exterior has been made interesting through the pleasing combination of tile roof, stucco finish on

The exterior of this house has been made interesting through the pleasing combination of tile roof, stucco finish on tile walls, wrought iron railing around the porch and heavy batten shutters. As shown in the perspective drawing below, the steps may be of brick

tile walls, wrought iron railing around the porch, and the colorful brickwork of the steps. Any one of a number of stucco finishes might be used to give the much desired quality of texture to the walls.

The arched entrance, flanked on either side by tall, slender openings— the Palladian motif referred to—gives

the house unusual distinction. Here also only a partial basement is provided, but ample space is allowed for laundry, heater and fuel rooms, and a large storage room.

Except for some difference in room dimensions, the two plans are quite similar. While the space adjacent to the living room bears the modest

title "dining alcove," this is really a fairly large room. Undoubtedly it will always be referred to as "the dining room." After all, the amount of space in a house is more important than the actual number of rooms, and both designs give the effect of five-room plans.

These houses can be placed advantageously on a narrow lot. They are small, compact in plan, yet of pleasing design that will look well in any neighborhood of small homes.

Construction of both: Hollow tile walls, stucco finish.

DESIGN *4-B-17*

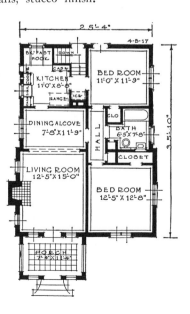

HOME BUILT FROM DESIGN *4-B-20*

EXTRAS—AND HOW THEY MAY BE ELIMINATED

*Houses developed from this design, which promise escape from
such irritations*

Probably the most irritating experience for home builders is facing the "extras" list. No one wants "extras"—architect, contractor or home builder. To them "extras" are a great nuisance. And the additional money cannot make up for the waste, lost time, and worry. We are discussing, of course, only honest building. And yet we constantly hear of them. For many it seems that home building is an experience in which one starts with the idea of spending a certain limited sum and comes out at the end having spent much more.

The home builder is certainly justified in complaining, especially when he does not have that extra money. But it is also true that this objectionable bill of extras is often the home builder's own fault. Why? Because he does not know absolutely what is and what is not included in the plans and specifications, and only assumes that he is going to get all that he desires. Or else when the building is under way he finds that he has not visualized what the drawings and specifications call for, and, not liking

what he finds the contractor is building for him, has changes made. Just one small change nearly always involves a string of adjustments in other matters, and causes "extra" charges

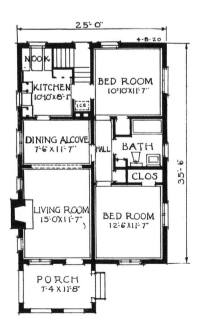

seemingly out of all proportion to the importance of the change desired.

The home builder will do well to go over the plans with greatest care, noting each one of the rooms, how it is equipped, how lighted, how it relates to the other parts of the house, the privacy that is given to the bed-rooms, the location of windows and doors, the wall spaces for the reception of furniture. In this way he will have a mental picture of the house as it will be when completed, a picture which he should have before he ever starts to build.

Here is a design which the home builder may be assured will result in a home of fine architectural character provided the drawings are followed carefully. Alternate plans are shown, giving a choice between a full-size dining room or the smaller dining alcove. Although the floor area of the living room is practically the same in either case, it is different in shape and has the fireplace in different locations. Such a choice of plans minimizes the necessity for extras even more than is usually the case with Bu-

HOME BUILT WITH SOLID BRICK WALLS FROM DESIGN *4-B-20*

Whether finished in stucco as illustrated opposite, or with solid brick walls as above, this design will stand out from the usual run of small homes that line our streets

reau plans. After deciding which plan will best meet the requirements of his family, the home builder need only specify to his contractor which way the house is to be built.

The kitchen is exceptionally convenient, small and compact and well provided with cupboards. In the built-in breakfast nook one seat has a hinged top affording extra storage space. On either side of the sink, which is located beneath the side window, are convenient cabinets. In front and to the right of the nook is another cupboard and broom closet combined.

From the rear entry stairs go to the basement. As called for in the plans, there is only a partial basement; although it is ample it does not extend under the living room and front bedroom.

The most picturesque feature of the exterior is the entrance porch with its narrow arches and iron railings.

Construction: Solid brick walls; slate, shingle or tile roof. Hollow tile walls stucco finished may be used.

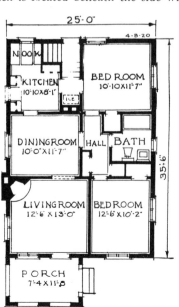

HOME BUILT FROM DESIGN *4-E-1*

RIGOROUS SIMPLICITY EFFECTING ECONOMY

*Little as to the size of the house, big in the
accommodations it offers*

With all the quaint charm of the old-fashioned vine-hung cottage, this little house yet contrives to be a modern bungalow. Perhaps this modernity is best shown in the lack of a formal dining room and the substitution of the convenient built-in breakfast nook. To have included a dining room would have meant cutting down the size of the living room, which is a far more valuable room to the family than a dining room in a house of this limited size. A table can be set in the living room when guests are entertained formally, but for the family the dining alcove will prove adequate. Set the table in front of the fireplace, so as to enjoy the fire on the hearth, then wonder why we make so much fuss over a dining room. You may be sure the luxury of a meal by firelight is something your guests will not soon forget. A table in this position, too, is as accessible to the kitchen as it would be in a dining room, so the serving of meals will present no great problem.

As a living room this is a highly satisfactory place. With five windows admitting light and sunshine it will be a bright, cheerful room, well suited to the simple furnishings and colorful cretonnes in keeping with the style of the house.

The efficiency of the kitchen, which is well arranged and well equipped with built-in conveniences, will appeal to every housewife. Windows on two sides afford the advantage of cross ventilation.

This should prove a comparatively inexpensive cottage to build, yet it has all of the elements which make a home comfortable. There are many sites to which it would be admirably adapted, many families would find it within their means. While it is designed for use the year around, it might also be built as a summer cottage—one of exceptional charm—at even less expense. In this case the basement could be omitted entirely. The exterior finish may be shingles, stucco or siding.

In the small house there are few details more important than the arrangement and type of windows. Here, as in many cases, the quality of home-like intimacy which they add depends not so much on the fact that casements have been used as on their division into small lights.

DESIGN *4-H-1*

A HOME FOR THE AVERAGE PURSE

*Materials of construction reduce costs without
sacrifice of appearance or durability*

This simple and attractive one-story cottage reminds one of some of the charming and much admired old rural cottages, the walls of which were built of stones of small size. Here, however, the walls are constructed of structural tile, a modern material. The exterior surfaces of these units have a pleasant color, and they may be had with a plain or with an agreeably textured surface. Stucco for an exterior finish is unnecessary. These tiles are set with broken mortar joints, insuring a well-insulated wall.

Inexpensive houses of this type are receiving more and more attention. Home builders who must be most economical about their homes are finding in houses of this sort a solution of their problem, one which will give lasting satisfaction. If they are to build at all, their investment must not run up such heavy charges as to represent a disproportionate part of their investment.

Although this house does answer to a certain extent the present-day question of high building costs and upkeep, it has been designed so carefully that it provides fully for the necessary requirements of space and accommodation. The rooms are of good size, well fitted out. Here, as in many small houses, we have the application of the apartment house principle to the separate dwelling—small floor area, compact equipment, no waste space, plenty of conveniences.

From the porch one enters a well-lighted living room with wall spaces designed for the placing of comfortable and necessary furniture. Beyond the door at the rear of this room is the dining alcove with its built-in seats, table under the window, china cupboard, and a useful "pantry" closet. From all this it is but a step or two to the rear to the neat, well-lighted, and efficiently arranged little kitchen. Here, within easy reach, are the stove, the sink directly under the window, a capacious cupboard in one corner, and space for the work table.

Returning to the dining alcove or the living room, one may enter the hall directly in the center of the house. This is but a step from either the front or the rear bedroom. Large linen and coat closets are located in the hall, and in each bedroom is an additional closet. In the ceiling of the hall is a disappearing stair which permits access to storage in the attic.

For the sake of economy no fireplace has been shown on the plan, but this may easily be included. A vestibule might also be added if so desired.

Construction: Texture face hollow tile walls, roof of slate, or shingles.

DESIGN *4-K-16*

A BUNGALOW APARTMENT

Apartment conveniences in the separate house

Many a family living in an apartment has often wondered why they could not have a house with the conveniences of the apartment. This house is the answer to that question, with the additional advantages of more space and more light and air than the apartment offers. The plan is both logical and livable, with all the essentials that make for pleasure and comfort.

The exterior of the house is beautifully proportioned, skillfully designed of inexpensive materials. The cast stone trim about the front window and doorway, the ornamental chimney top, and the molded ornament below the great front window give the picturesque and romantic quality that home builders appreciate. The owner will take pride in this house for years to come.

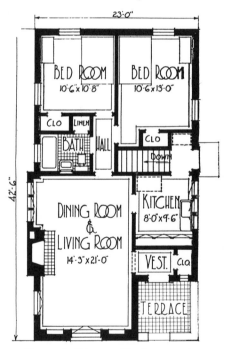

Home builders will be struck with the beauty of the interior. The sketch shows the end of the living room facing the street, with the gracefully arched niches for books

Construction: Walls of concrete blocks faced with stucco, roof of cement asbestos shingles. The floors are of reinforced concrete, although other materials may be used for both floors and roof

DESIGN *4-K-17*

WITH ATTACHED GARAGE

A house of convenience and beauty

For many, a house without a garage is not a house at all. Here it is built in, forming an integral part of the architecture, convenient and fine appearing, also made fireproof.

The large bay window in the living room has windows set at an angle to catch a flood of light and insure ventilation. The ceiling over the bay is lowered a little, adding additional charm. The handsome fireplace has a cast stone mantel. A plastered arch leading to the dining room enhances the beauty of both rooms.

In addition to the two first floor bedrooms, the attic space may be divided into three rooms well lighted by windows. Built-in wardrobe space is provided, and a stairway in the rear hall affords easy access.

This sketch gives a clear idea of the beauty of the bay window and the distinction of the square-cut entrance. Pointed gables and dormers, and picturesque chimney all contribute to the charm of the house

Construction: Concrete masonry, exterior finish stucco. The first floor is of reinforced concrete finished with wood in the living room, dining room, and bedroom, tile in the bathroom, linoleum in the kitchen. The roof is of cement asbestos shingles

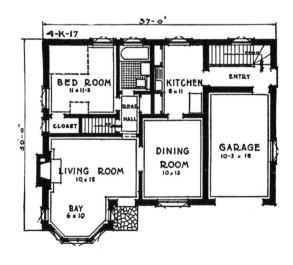

DESIGN *4-K-19*

A ROOF WITH A WAY ALL ITS OWN

Nothing new under the sun, perhaps, but sometimes pleasant variations of the old. So it is with this little house in the French cottage style, a style of which we have not yet had a chance to become weary. In design it is delightfully reminiscent of those old cottages of provincial France which, making a virtue of necessity, grew with the family.

The steeply pitched roof, the slight arch of the dormers, the rounded bay window with wrought iron ornament above, and the interesting entrance all lend distinction to the house. Much has been made of the entrance feature.

One desirable feature of the plan is that privacy is secured for every room, including the living room. The wide doorway from the entrance hall may be closed by the double doors which are ordinarily folded back against the wall in the living room, where their polished, paneled surfaces are of distinctly decorative value. As shown in the sketch, the fireplace is plain yet effective. The doors on either side lead out to the terrace, and narrow bookcases are built in beside them.

The breakfast nook is exceptionally pleasing in design, while above the window a scalloped wooden valance may be utilized as a plate rail. The kitchen, then, promises to be a gay, colorful place.

A large bedroom may be finished off on the second floor, dormer windows providing light and ventilation.

Construction: Concrete masonry walls, stucco finish, roof of cement asbestos shingles, casement windows.

DESIGN 4-K-20

A TWO-STORY HOUSE
ENGLISH STYLE

Everything changes, house designs along with the rest. And why not? Certainly we live differently today than we did years, even a few years, ago. This means requirements that should be given careful consideration in planning our homes. Many of us do not want the expense and care of a large, formal dining room, yet neither do we always want to eat in the kitchen. Here is a house that satisfactorily takes care of this problem.

The plan is intelligent, workable, and will make home building dollars stretch to the farthest limit. The house not only has an excellent plan, but an exterior with qualities of true architecture.

The bay window in the living room, the beautiful fireplace, the conveniently arranged kitchen, and the broad window in the dining alcove—shown in the sketch—are only a few of the many details making up this pleasant home. This dining alcove is not one of the built-in pullman type, but is large enough for a table and chairs.

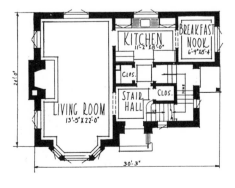

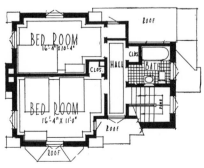

The bedrooms are very large, pleasant rooms, both suitable for twin beds. The front bedroom has windows on three sides.

The house, too, has fire-safe qualities which should mean reduced insurance rates. The exterior walls of masonry are a safeguard. The roof is of non-inflammable material, and the concrete slab that forms the first floor is a positive shut-off for any fires that might originate in the basement.

Construction: Exterior walls of furred concrete masonry, stucco finish, roof of cement asbestos shingles.

HOME BUILT FROM DESIGN 5-A-24

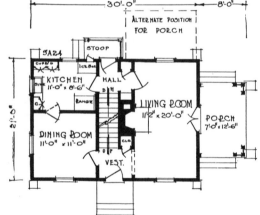

A SHINGLED COTTAGE

A plan without waste space

Passing fancies in small houses are expensive luxuries for home builders whose funds are limited. Designs like this house, because of their simplicity, architectural qualities, and good proportions, will remain in good taste as long as they endure.

The plan provides five main rooms, bath, and six closets. The living room is large and sunny, and has the two things in greatest demand by home builders—a fireplace to gather around in winter and a porch for summer comfort. This porch may be either at the side or rear.

As shown in the perspective drawing at the right, trellis may be used with charming effect about the front windows. Construction: Wood frame, exterior finish wood shingles, wide siding, or stucco, roof of shingles

HOME BUILT FROM DESIGN 5-A-27

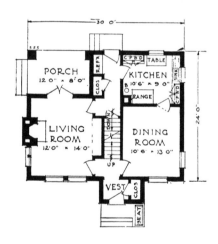

Note the numerous and varied closets and the center location of the stairs. It is a fact that no more space than is absolutely necessary has been used for hallways

HALF TIMBER, STUCCO, AND BRICK

Somewhat in the English manner

One of the restrictions with which the city dweller has to contend is the 40-foot frontage allowed him by the average lot. There are cities where lots run even narrower, in some as much as 10 feet less, but 40 feet is the average size of a lot. The owner must select a design that will meet this limitation and also allow between the lot lines the space required by city ordinances. With such a narrow frontage it is obvious that the porch is often better at the rear than at the side, so that the whole frontage of the house itself can be given up to room space.

In this house the porch is not only placed at the rear, it has been made definitely a part of the house under the main roof. On the working drawings it is shown as an open porch, but it can easily be adapted to an enclosed porch. It thus becomes part of the living room, and can be separated from it by a cased opening, an archway or double French doors.

The house illustrated above was built in one of the Eastern states having fairly cold winters, and the owner felt it was not only advantageous to enclose the porch but also to enclose the small platform at the rear which opens into the service entry.

The needs of the moderate size family, where a home of medium price is desired, have been kept in mind in producing this design. It is compact in plan, economical as possible in construction, and pleasing in appearance. The half timber treatment in the second story, the combination of brick and stucco as an outside finish, the dormers breaking into the roof line, and the outside chimney add charm and interest to what is in reality an almost square house.

There are many features to note on the plan: the alcove in the living room opposite the fireplace, the closet for cleaning equipment in the rear entry, and the two closets in each upstairs bedroom.

The living room is pleasant. While not large, the combined floor area of this room and the adjoining porch is considerable. Doors at all openings make it possible to shut off the living room from the rest of the house.

Construction: Brick veneer on frame to top of the first floor windows; second story of stucco and half timber on frame, roof of shingles.

A HOUSE WITH A SLEEPING PORCH

Simplicity enriched by grouping of windows and arch

Stairways most of us take for granted, but not so the architect. Truly they are the thorn in his flesh. Necessary they are, of course, but the amount of space they require is sometimes a sore trial, particularly in designing the small house.

In this house, rather than sacrifice the amount of floor space necessary for a liberal stairway in the main part of the house, the designer has provided space for this feature by projecting it beyond the line of the side wall. This projection not only allows space for a good stairway and side entry, but adds interest to the exterior since it relieves the square outline.

The house has a certain Spanish character due to the arched and recessed entrance, the stucco exterior, and the roof of richly colored tile, but in all other respects it is strictly American in conception. The grassed terrace before the house, the brick retaining walls and brick steps, and the lattice provided for climbing

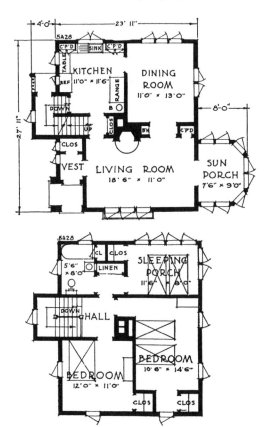

vines, which serves to balance the arched entrance doorway, all add greatly to the appearance of the house.

There are glazed double doors between sun room and living room so that the latter may be entirely shut off when this is desired. The fireplace, with its wood mantel, brick facing, and arched recess above, carries out the spirit of the general style of the house. Another interesting feature of this room is the wide cased opening between living and dining rooms. At the left of the doorway is a built-in bookshelf with glazed doors, and at the right, opening from the living room, is a cupboard.

Besides two large airy bedrooms, there is a splendid sleeping porch. The generous size of the bedrooms makes the house suitable for several persons; the first floor also promising comfort and convenience for the family of some size.

Construction: Wood frame, stucco exterior finish, tile roof.

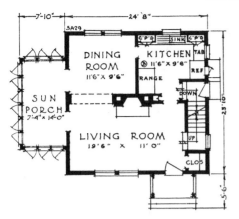

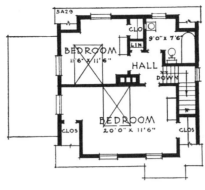

TWO COLONIAL HOMES DIFFERING IN PLAN

Translating the forms of the old Dutch farmhouse into modern Dutch Colonial gives dwellings of varied charms. The Dutch, finding the space directly under the roofs of their one-story houses useful for storage and living quarters, devised the gambrel roof characteristic of this style, but the dormer is a more recent acquisition. In modern Dutch Colonial homes the space under the roof serves all the purposes of a full second story, but the rooms often have a pleasant informality and charm not possessed by strictly rectangular rooms.

Both the houses illustrated here have five principal rooms and in addition a large sun porch. This makes them practically six-room houses. Economical to build, they are yet so expertly designed as to compare favorably with houses of far greater pretentions. Shingles may be substituted for siding as an exterior finish. The chief difference between these plans is the location of the living and dining rooms. If necessary to place the house on a narrow lot, or for the sake of greater economy, the sun porch may be omitted. In design 5-A-29 it may be located at the rear.

HOME BUILT FROM DESIGN *5-A-29*

HOME BUILT FROM DESIGN *5-A-31*

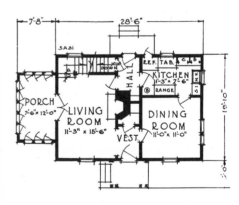

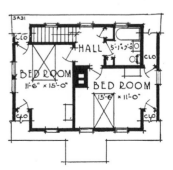

Photograph by John Wallace Gillies

Dwight James Baum, Architect

*The Architect, the Home Owner, and Nature—Which One Could Have
Achieved This Result Without the Other?*

HOME BUILT FROM DESIGN *5-A-34*

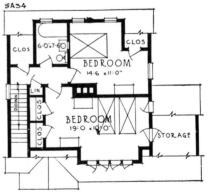

MODERN AMERICAN, SO-CALLED

*Primarily for purposes of identification
we label it in this way*

In order to make some sort of distinction among houses we classify them as to their external dress—rarely as to plan excepting perhaps as to whether they have patios or are of the center hall type. So we speak of them as English, French, Spanish, Mediterranean or Colonial. Still, there is a large group that does not readily fall under any of these classifications, and this we are in the habit of calling Modern American. Although this is rather indefinite, there is yet a certain degree of exactness in it because these so-called modern American houses do not display the distinctive national characteristics we ordinarily associate with the other styles.

One of the most striking characteristics of the modern American home is the porch. Sleeping porch, sun porch, or mere "front porch," it is a truly American feature. In general we do not find porches included in the architecture of the Old World, but if there be a porch it is never at the front or side in prominent view of the street. Such outdoor areas in English and Continental architecture are given locations on the garden. They

are placed so as to have as much privacy as any portion of the house.

In the house illustrated on this page the porch is bound in with the main portion of the house so that it is a real and essential part of the design. Perhaps the most important part played by any feature of the general design, however, is that of the roof. The high ridge pole makes possible a long sweep of roof, which, if covered with shingles in softly blended colors, will have a marked effect.

A large, well-lighted living room with a fireplace advantageously placed on the long, inside wall is a feature of the first floor. The window which lights the stair landing is really in this room, as the stairs are open. The pleasant dining room has sufficient unbroken wall space to make the arrangement of furniture a simple matter.

The kitchen is in every way the up-to-date workroom, with cupboard space, bins and drawers in abundance. The sink, with double drain boards, is located beneath one window, the indispensable table beneath another.

Only the woman who has spent much time in a kitchen with windows on only one side can realize how much cross ventilation like this means. The refrigerator, conveniently located in the kitchen, is iced from the outside.

The bedrooms are large and well-lighted, and the five closets and big storage space on this floor should content the most exacting housewife.

HOUSE BUILT FROM DESIGN 5-A-50

"‒‒SERMONS IN STONES, AND GOOD IN EVERYTHING"

*The welcome starts at the terrace.   Curving steps
and random walk lead you irresistibly toward the
white paneled door*

HOME BUILT FROM DESIGN *5-A-50*

HOMES FORMAL AND RESERVED IN CHARACTER

*The living room and a bedroom practically as large extend
the depth of the house*

Here we see the same design developed in both brick and stucco. The house is an adaptation of the Italian style, which, because of its individuality and striking appearance, is popular. The house above has hollow tile walls finished with stucco, the one below solid brick walls. This design has also been developed for frame construction with either stucco or brick veneer.

HOME BUILT FROM DESIGN *5-A-50*

HOME BUILT FROM DESIGN *5-A-52*

A HOUSE WITH HOSTS OF FRIENDS

*One that has proved inexpensive to build in many localities
because it is designed on the right principles*

Do you want an inexpensive house? Thousands are looking for one. Here is a house designed with this idea continually in mind. Countless economies have been worked out to make it yield the utmost for every dollar spent, yet at no sacrifice of quality

The house is not over-size; waste space is eliminated, stock framing members have been used throughout, the fireplace is located on an inside wall so as to save expensive facing brick. The porch may be omitted. All these are major economies

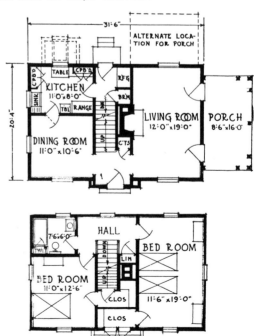

When walls are covered with such striking papers as these, the curtains and floor coverings are necessarily of plain materials in harmonizing colors

The architect, because of his training, is naturally much more critical about a house than is a layman. The home builder sees the completed house, the finished result as a whole. The architect sees not only this, but looks critically at the details also. His eyes seek out refinements, subtle proportions, the play of light and shadow, the relation of walls, roof, windows, and doors to each other, and many other details which escape the less informed observer.

It is these details that constitute an important part of every successful house design. It is their sum total that makes the result fine architecture or just another commonplace house. That is why the architect who built this house for himself permitted no variation from the drawings. The result, as the illustration shows, is a house of refinement and charm. Too frequently Bureau designs are altered and changed to meet the special requirements of the home builder, so that it is especially encouraging to have an architect build from the plans without any changes whatever.

There are many carefully thought out details here, such as bulkheads around the basement windows to give the house the effect of being close to the ground, the return of closely cropped eaves around corners, and selected designs for the various moldings.

All the doors, windows, and moldings have been taken from material dealers' catalogues so there is no expense for special millwork. As may be seen from the three illustrations of the interior, however, the house loses nothing in appearance through the use of stock details.

The plans have been designed to meet the needs of nearly every small family. The rooms are all of adequate size, well lighted and ventilated, since every one is a corner room. They open into each other conveniently, and broad entrances to the hallway from dining and living rooms create a pleasantly spacious air. The equipment of the house is sound to the core.

Simplicity is the keynote of the living room, enriched by a handsome figured wall paper and colorful floor covering

HOME BUILT FROM DESIGN *5-A-53*

A HOUSE DESIGNED FOR THE NARROW LOT

With all the desirable features of its broader neighbors

A narrow lot presents a difficult problem for the architect, but it may be solved and that very successfully. The chief requisite, of course, is that the greatest dimension of the plan be the depth from front to back. Practically the same living area may be provided as in that of the house which presents its broad side to the street, but the room arrangement will be different.

This house gives due consideration to the limitations of the narrow lot, for if the porch is omitted or placed at the rear it can be accommodated nicely on a lot 30 feet wide. If the porch is placed at the side, as shown in the house illustrated, a 40-foot lot will be necessary. The plan has long been a favorite.

Conjuring up a vision of the living room, we find it an extremely pleasant place with a sunny bay window and wide, upholstered seat, an attractive fireplace to gather around in the evening, and double French doors opening invitingly onto the porch. A window would be substituted for these if the porch were omitted. Within the archway which separates living and dining rooms is a

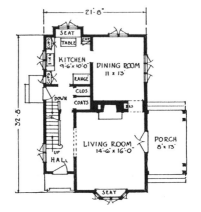

built-in case for books, but this would be an excellent location for the radio.

In the kitchen is a projection just wide enough to accommodate the built-in seat before which a table may be drawn up for meals or work. Along one wall is the sink, flanked on one side by cupboards and on the other by the refrigerator with cupboards above it. All the equipment in the kitchen is expertly disposed to eliminate extra steps.

There are two closets in the rear hall, one for coats and one for brooms and cleaning materials. This hall affords access to the kitchen and front of the house, as well as to the basement and to the outside. This arrangement is of the greatest convenience, for the living and dining rooms do not have to be crossed in order to reach the kitchen from the front door or stairway. The convenience of the second floor is on a par with that of the first. One bedroom has two fine closets, and in addition to a generous linen closet in the hall is a smaller one for towels in the bathroom.

Construction: Wood frame, exterior finish stucco, shingle roof, brick base.

HOME BUILT FROM DESIGN 5-A-58

REMINISCENT OF THE ENGLISH COTTAGE
With a plan, however, distinctly American throughout

In studying the old English cottages, you can tell from the form of each particular dwelling the fortunes of the families and generations who have occupied it. That is, when an extra room was needed, a new wing was put on, making the floor plan L-shaped, F-shaped or, maybe, eventually an H. When the owner became prosperous enough, a bay window or an oriel was added, or the tiny dormer was expanded into a gable.

This describes the floor plan upon which the modern home in the English cottage style should be built: it may be compact or rambling, large or small, according to the needs of those who live in it.

Then if you should visit the Cotswold region of England, you would notice that the old cottages, farm buildings, town houses, and shops are built of stone from local quarries. If you should journey through Shropshire, Herefordshire, and Cheshire, you would find them half-timbered. In other counties, where timber and building stone always have been scarce, you would find the majority of houses built of brick. Roofs, also, you would find of different materials—thatch, slate, wood shingles or tile according to the natural resources of the locality.

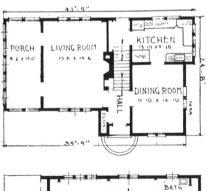

This answers the question: With what materials should the modern cottage in the English style be built? Any materials so long as they are the most easily obtainable, the least expensive, and in keeping with the nature of the place where the house is to be built.

This house is an example of the English domestic style of architecture adapted to a modern five-room home. The spirit of this style of architecture is recalled in the irregularity of the plan, the roughly stuccoed walls, the close-clipped gables, the half-timber work, and the large window openings. The plan at least is distinctly American throughout.

A feature which will undoubtedly carry a great appeal is the sun porch. This, combined with the living room, gives a large area ideal for entertaining. Each one, however, has an intimate, homelike character definitely its own. Besides the two bedrooms there is a sleeping porch generous enough for two beds, thus making the house practically one of six rooms. In contrast to the house on the opposite page, this one is designed for a wide lot, particularly a corner lot.

Construction: Wood frame, stucco finish.

HOME BUILT FROM DESIGN *5-A-59*

A LIVABLE COLONIAL COTTAGE

One which lends itself to future enlargement

The significant qualities of this design come primarily from the orderly sequence of the rooms and the reserved character of the exterior.

The plan is one long marked by the esteem of home builders. It has the virtue of narrow breadth, being suitable for a narrow lot and, in addition,

presents means for enlargement through development of the attic space.

The exterior gives an impression of repose and dignity marked by a graceful arch and column treatment at the front porch. Low eave lines and courses of wide siding make the house seem broad and low, much to its advantage.

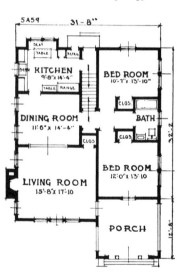

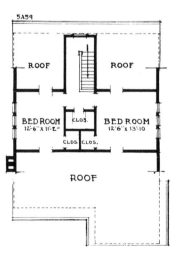

HOME BUILT FROM DESIGN *5-A-60*

A TRULY DUTCH COLONIAL EXTERIOR

Many economies practiced without lessening value

The old Dutch fathers were a canny lot, with a typically modern aversion to tax collectors. Therefore, when the authorities of their day laid a tax upon two-story houses, these resourceful gentlemen capped their homes with gambrel roofs and had thereby houses technically and legally of one story, although with still a good two-story capacity. That is one explanation of the type of roof now so inalienably connected with Dutch Colonial architecture.

Design 5-A-60 is a good example of this style of architecture. However, it shows its ancestry in still other ways than in its well-proportioned gambrel roof. The hooded entrance, the shutters at the windows, and the side lighted front door frame carry out the Dutch Colonial spirit. The brick pavement and front stoop had their prototype before many an early Dutch home.

Brick and siding for the exterior walls have been combined in a charming and effective manner, yet the house is in many ways an economical one. The economies have been made possible with no sacrifice of appearance or comfort.

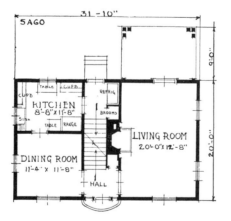

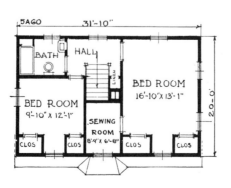

The plan is of the central stairway type, with living room at the right, kitchen and dining room at the left. The stairway has been enclosed between walls, eliminating all expense for balustrade and newel. The fireplace, in the plan, is located on an inside wall, a good position for connection with the furnace, requiring a minimum amount of face brick work. But the fireplace may be placed on the outside wall if preferred, as it was built by the owner of this house.

The living room is delightfully large, well lighted by windows. Through arched or cased openings there is an agreeable vista across the hall into the dining room.

The bedrooms are both generous in size, one of them in particular. Even the smaller room is large enough for twin beds, and the two closets in each room permit them to be used conveniently by two people. The sewing room or nursery opening from one of the bedrooms is a convenience much out of the ordinary in the small house but one every housewife will appreciate.

Construction: Brick veneer on wood frame for the first story, second story of shingles or siding, shingle roof.

DESIGN *5-A-61*

DISTINCTION WITHIN NARROW LINES

*Masonry walls lessen upkeep and well-arranged
rooms lighten labor*

This is just the design for a five-room city house where the ordinance requires masonry construction and lots are narrow. A 30-foot frontage will be sufficient in many cities. Although the roof is low, giving the house an intimate and homelike appearance, this affects the sleeping rooms but little. To all practical purposes this is a full two-story house.

Very little space has been used for hallways, a prime consideration in designing the successful small home. The entrance hall, which also takes the place of a vestibule, leads directly to the kitchen and to the side entry. This makes it unnecessary for the housewife to go through the living rooms to reach the front door. In the rear entry is a convenient coat closet and a second closet for brooms, besides the entrance to the cellar stairs.

The stairway, one of the open type, is an attractive feature of this hall, as is the wide cased opening to the living room. Openings of this width are most desirable in the small house because they give the effect of space

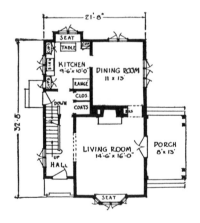

which, as it eliminates any cramped, shut-in feeling, plays no small part in the family's continuing comfort and well-being.

A bay window is a charming addition even to a commonplace room, but when made a part of a room already as attractive as this living room—a room comfortable in size and with the cozy air that only a fireplace can give—then indeed a window of this character finds an appropriate setting.

The second floor is compact, with every foot of space used to advantage. Both bedrooms are sufficiently large for twin beds, and closet space is planned accordingly. One room has two closets, the other has one of unusual capacity. The same plans with the exterior finished in stucco will be found in design 5-A-53.

Construction: Solid brick walls, roof of slate or shingles. Interior support of floor beams is on a steel girder.

DESIGN *5-A-66*

FROM THE MOUNTAINS OF SWITZERLAND

Comes this small home of interesting and distinctive design
In convenience of plan it is thoroughly American

The Swiss chalet is a type of house seldom considered among the galaxy of national styles of which French, Spanish, and English are the most prominent. As this interesting design shows, however, it is a style that bears consideration by the home builder. Here good taste and individuality have been successfully combined in a home distinctly out of the ordinary. Any change in drawings on the part of the builder could only work inestimable harm, for every detail has been carefully worked out to preserve the spirit of this particular style. Wide siding above the first story, preferably stained a rich brown, the use of casement windows throughout, and the narrow balcony at the right—which shows in the plan—are all reminiscent of the picturesque houses of Switzerland.

The details of the interior are as interesting and individual as the exterior. Archways used in place of the usual square door opening give a beautiful effect at little cost. Bookcases, a fireplace, and numerous windows make

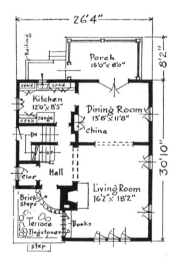

the living room a delightful place to spend one's leisure or entertain guests.

A china cupboard in the dining room, a good-sized porch overlooking the garden at the rear, and built-in seats on the stair landing and in the upstairs front bedroom all add charm and comfort to the house.

On the second floor are two desir-

able bedrooms, bathroom, three large closets, and one very large closet where the roof comes down at the left side to the rear. This opens from the bathroom. Doors lead from both of the bedrooms to the balcony.

Construction: Wood frame with stucco on metal lath for first story, wide siding or shingles above, foundation above grade of any local stone.

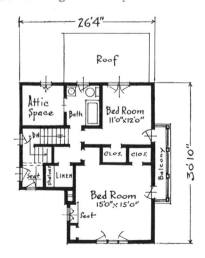

HOME BUILT FROM DESIGN *5-A-67*

WITH A DINING ROOM OF IMPORTANCE

Consider also the living room, the combination stairway,
and the convenient first floor lavatory

Texture, which means the play of light and shadow, is something all artists strive for, whether it is the portrait painter working in oils or the architect working in wood and stone. That is the quality which gives life to their work.

It is this thing, texture, which makes shingle-covered walls so satisfying, and no doubt the reason why the owner chose this exterior finish for the house shown.

The drawings call for wide siding for the walls and rubble stonework for the chimney. This, too, makes an attractive combination of materials, and it is merely a matter of personal choice.

The exterior, after all, is unimportant in comparison with the plan. The plan of this design is not even typically Colonial, to say nothing of having Dutch ancestry. It has variety, though, and livability, besides many points of real beauty. These things, which make it admirably suited to the requirements of a family to-day, we may place ahead of mere archeological exactness.

Entering the hallway there is a pleasant view of the stair curving gracefully to the right, and through the arched doorway to the living room a glimpse of the

fireplace on the far wall and of the French door opening to the terrace.

One of the plan's distinctive features is the dining room located at the rear in a wing of its own and facing the garden on three sides. The adjacent terrace, of which we get a good idea from the photograph, may be used as an outdoor dining porch.

The plan shows two conveniences all too rare in small houses. One is a lavatory on the first floor opening from a large coat closet off the front hall. The other is the arrangement of the stairs, which are so placed that steps lead to a common landing from both the kitchen and the entrance hallway. Thus one is able to reach the second floor unobserved from the living room, and every housewife knows what a convenience this is when guests are present.

Both bedrooms have uncommon features, one in particular as to its size, its many windows, and its two closets. The second, less gifted in these respects, opens onto a large porch over the dining room. This is only one story high, but a sleeping porch or third bedroom may be added above at little additional expense.

DESIGN 5-A-68

A HOUSE FOR A GARDEN

The principal rooms have been grouped about one important center—the garden

Ask any American whose means are limited what kind of a house he would like to have and he will tell you that first of all he wants a living room that is a real room—one in which there is lots of space, plenty of sunlight, a fireplace, and a feeling of spaciousness. He wants a room where his family can gather comfortably and where he can entertain a number of friends. Then he wants a dining room closely adjoining, so that on occasion the two rooms may be thrown together.

His wife will make demands in regard to the kitchen. If she is to do her own housework, she wants this room light, airy, conveniently arranged. She wants pleasant views from the windows. She spends much of her time in the kitchen and is entitled to this consideration. Almost every housewife wants an arrangement which will allow her to get to the second story without passing through the living quarters of the house. It appears that there are times when she wants to get to the kitchen without making a demonstration of it.

This design exhibits a happy com-bination of all these much desired conveniences. The living room is large, with excellent wall spaces. There is a bay window with a seat below it. Glazed doors open out on a covered

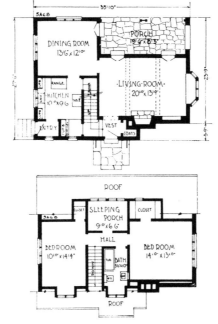

porch with slate or stone floor. Along one wall there is a beautiful stone fireplace flanked on each side by plaster archways. Through one of these one reaches the vestibule. In the other there are book shelves. The dining room also opens upon the porch, giving this room outside exposure on three sides.

The kitchen is placed along the front wall of the house. Not an inch of space in this room is wasted. From it one may go to the basement, to the side yard, or to the stairs to the second floor. The outside door to the kitchen is near the street. A table and chairs in the kitchen may be utilized as a breakfast nook, as there is plenty of space for this purpose.

On the second floor there are two large bedrooms and a sleeping porch. Each bedroom has many windows, and each an extra large closet. Very little area on either floor is devoted to halls. The sleeping porch might also be used as a sitting room or study. Construction: Brick veneer over wood frame, roof of shingles or slate, casement windows of steel or frame.

DESIGN 5-A-69

the side or the rear. To make the most of the space available, the plans include possible locations for closet beds. One is indicated on the porch, one beneath the dining room windows. In that case, of course, the porch would be built as a sun room. Both bedrooms are provided with two closets each.

Construction, design 5-A-70: Wood frame, stucco exterior finish, shingle roof.

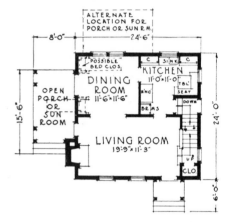

Two Inexpensive Versions
of a Successful Plan

No architectural style has a more universal appeal to the American home builder than has the Colonial. And rightly enough, for it is bound up closely with the traditions of his ancestors and exemplifies their way of living by its simplicity and straightforward dignity.

Design 5-A-69 is of this style, a house that will remain in good taste for years. Its outside chimney, unpretentious weathered shingle roof, siding covered walls, old-fashioned blinds, and checkered lattice work about the porches are all details to be found in early homes.

Of identical plan, yet strikingly different in outward appearance, is design 5-A-70. This design is somewhat after the manner of the English cottage.

The living room is open on three sides, either by doors or windows, and having also a clear sweep to the dining room windows it will catch any breeze blowing. The dining room opens on the porch, whether this be located at

DESIGN 5-A-70

DESIGN 5-A-71

A COLONIAL HOUSE OF SOUND VALUES

*Pleasantly informal, expressing the quality of domesticity, it is
planned to make the most of the money spent*

This design, 5-A-71, is an economy house. The designers have provided five rooms, each of adequate size, but no more, and have arranged them so that the house can be built inexpensively.

The rectangular plan is one of the important ways that has been used to cut costs. Something has been saved by enclosing the stairway so as to minimize millwork. Then the fireplace, put on an inside wall, effects an additional saving. This fireplace is Colonial in style, with simple wooden panels about the tile facing.

More particularly, economy arises through good use of the space. The area needed for hallways amounts in total to an unusually small proportion of the plan. Further economies can be materialized through omission of the porch.

Yet here is an excellent house of fine architectural feeling, with a plan of real convenience. Every room in the house has cross ventilation. There are windows even in two of the closets.

The drawings, particularly as to the plans, do not show how carefully the details of various kinds have been worked out. Take the kitchen, for example. The sink has been placed near the door of the dining room so that dishes will not have to be carried across the kitchen. At the side of the sink is a china and food cabinet.

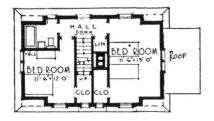

A number of shelves extend above fine working space. Below this are drawers and bins for food. Beyond is dining space.

This is in the form of a shallow alcove. That is, the kitchen table can be drawn up against a built-in seat, like a window seat, and chairs arranged along the other side. If desired, this alcove can be extended to the rear sufficiently to include the standard alcove furniture.

Near the rear entrance, but still within the kitchen, is the refrigerator, for which outside icing is provided. There is a closet arranged to go over the refrigerator, and the refrigerator itself is set on a platform to lift it above the level of the floor. In the rear hallway is a convenient cupboard and also a broom closet. In the front hallway is the usual coat closet.

The bedrooms are excellently lighted, of good size, with fine closet accommodation. A stairway in the closet of one leads to the attic where large storage space is available. The window in the hall at the head of the stairs serves to light both upper and lower halls, making them inviting.

DESIGN 5-A-74

A TYPICAL CITY HOME

An oriel window and arched entry add zest

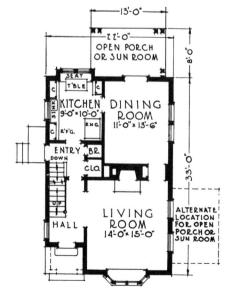

Although in exterior appearance houses suitable for a narrow lot may vary widely, in general plan most of them differ but slightly. The restrictions of such a lot offer little chance for variation, and so we find that many small two-story houses suitable for a 30-foot lot—as is this one, design 5-A-74—are built on the same general plan. The popularity of this plan, then, may have some element of necessity about it, but it is undoubtedly a fact that it offers a maximum of comfort and convenience in the area available.

The working drawings provide a porch, which may be built either as an attractive open porch or as an enclosed sun room with a sleeping porch above. The latter adds practically a third bedroom, greater accommodations than are usually found in a house of five rooms. The porch may be located at the side if the lot permits. If in the rear, the sun room will be accessible to the kitchen, affording a delightful place to serve meals in summer.

The plans are efficient and livable, with little waste space. The service portion in particular is all that the most critical housewife could desire. The side entry takes care of the cellar stairs, a coat closet and another closet for brooms, and through it there is direct communication between the kitchen and the front door.

The kitchen is arranged according to the most approved scientific principles, the range near the dining room door, the sink beneath a window and flanked by cupboards and work table. To the left of the sink, beneath a cupboard, is the refrigerator, handily equipped for outside icing. At one end of the room, out of the line of traffic, is a built-in seat with space for a table in front of it.

The second floor is amply provided with closets, one bedroom having two.

Construction: Brick veneer on wood frame, shingle or slate roof.

DESIGN 5-A-72

MEDITERRANEAN

Recalling Southern Lands

The principal difference between these two houses is the wall construction. Design 5-A-72, illustrated above, is of frame construction under the stucco finish, while design 5-A-50 is of hollow tile. Either may have a shingle or tile roof. There are other small but obvious differences in the details of the exterior. The floor plans belong to design 5-A-72. Those of design 5-A-50 are but little different. The dimensions are almost identical.

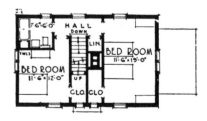

These designs, formal and severe in character—as much so as is proper for a small house—require a formal stucco finish fairly smooth in texture which will yet carry some light and shadow.

In spite of their formality, these are happy houses and should carry brightness and cheer. The roofs, whatever the material, should be in color. The tile inserts above the windows in design 5-A-50 glow with color, and the plaster medallions used similarly in design 5-A-72 are equally decorative.

DESIGN 5-A-50

DESIGN 5-A-75

Two Cottages with One Plan

*A commonly used plan
made architectural*

The floor plans of these designs are so nearly identical that only one is shown for both. Practically the only differences are in minor details; the arrangement of the rooms is exactly the same.

The architect's drawings of the exteriors show the broad side toward the street. Here the small entrance porch is placed on the broad side and the living porch at the end. The positions of the two porches, however, are reversible, making the houses suitable for a narrower lot also.

Design 5-A-75, above, traces its antecedents to the California mission dwelling. Its construction is frame with stucco finish. The roof is of tile, the windows casement type. A suggested exterior color scheme for this design is red for the tile roof to contrast sharply with the white of the stuccoed walls.

Design 5-A-76 is modern, a type of the Middle West. Either wide siding or shingles may be used as an exterior finish for the walls. This house would be most effective if painted or stained white, with green shutters and variegated green roof, red brick steps and base course.

DESIGN 5-A-76

HOME BUILT FROM DESIGN *5-B-1*

ITALIAN AND WHAT IT MEANS

*General characteristics which mark this style
are displayed in this house*

Whether it be planned after a little farmhouse or after a villa created by some master of the Renaissance, the house in the Italian style is distinctive for some degree of refinement.

Its roof is low-pitched and of tile, perhaps a blend of colors. Its walls are of stucco, brick or stone. Whichever is used, the exterior surface has a varied texture, for under the Mediterranean sun a smooth wall would be glaring and uninteresting. To avoid this the old Italian builders textured their surfaces by whatever means they could. Using stucco they wrought it into a rough palm-finish.

Although the windows are small they are not slighted. Perhaps they are simply surrounded by a graceful molding. Perhaps they are shuttered or grilled with wrought iron. Pleasantly arranged in the wall, their proportions bear a nice relation to the whole design.

Other characteristics there are of the Italian style, but knowing these it would be hard to trace this design to anything but Italian antecedents. It is a distinguished bit of small house architecture, compact in plan, beautiful in proportions. Even though the exterior is without added ornament, the general effect is decorative.

One delightful feature of this house is the number of windows. Living room, dining room, and two bedrooms have windows on three sides. Almost the entire end of the kitchen is devoted to windows, and sink and work table are placed beneath them. The arcaded porch at the rear, with access to it from both living and dining rooms, comes as nearly as possible to bringing the out-of-doors into the house.

Beside the fireplace are built-in bookcases. Directly opposite are more bookcases of equal height. These are on either side of the broad group of windows, beneath which is a wide window seat.

The kitchen, located at the front of the house, has direct access to the entrance hall and the stairway. The house illustrated has been built reversed from the plans.

Construction: Stucco on hollow tile walls, tile roof, casement windows, either steel or frame.

HOME BUILT FROM DESIGN 5-B-6

A BUNGALOW IN THE ITALIAN STYLE

*With the fireplace in a deep, cozy ingle nook; this is doubly useful
in that it also adds variety to the exterior*

In direct contrast to design 5-B-1, which demonstrates clearly how the interesting qualities of the Italian style may be adapted to the two-story house, we have here, in design 5-B-6, a beautiful example of a one-story house of Italian origin planned and designed to suit modern conditions and requirements. This distinctive bungalow, picturesque in outline and romantic in character, should have a strong appeal to the builder looking for individuality in his home. Here we have nothing of the ordinary and commonplace, nor yet anything of the elaborate and bizarre whose attractions fade in a short time. The beauty of this house will rather increase with the years as its colors soften and mellow, and a background of trees and shrubs grows up around it.

The general form of this design is delightful, particularly so as to the treatment of the ingle nook and chimney. Cozy and comfortable on the interior, this arrangement causes a break in the roof that adds interest and variety to the exterior also. Low, well-proportioned gables, a close cornice, and shutters advantageously placed contribute largely to the blending of the various units and the success of the whole.

For a house of this size the living room, 23 feet long, is exceptionally large. The ingle nook, containing the fireplace, seats and bookcases, is an outstanding feature, but the battery of windows at one end and the porch

beyond both help to make this room the pleasant place it is. This porch may be reached from both living room and dining room and may be left open for use in summer or enclosed for year-around service as the owner desires. In the house illustrated the porch has been enclosed.

The kitchen is well planned, with working space along the outside wall under a triple window. A convenient storage pantry is provided, and there is plenty of space for cupboards. The ice box stands in a niche in the rear entry. The basement stairs are accessible both from the kitchen and from the outside.

The basement is partially excavated but of ample size to meet all demands, including laundry, heater and fuel rooms, and a large store room.

Grouped around a small hallway, the sleeping quarters have much privacy. The broad wardrobe closets in the bedrooms are extremely efficient. Of the two closets in the hall, one might be used for linen, one for storage.

Good ventilation is assured in this plan. It is designed for casement windows in groups of four, three and two to an opening, and narrow arched ventilators in the gable ends supply free circulation of air under the roof.

The suggested color scheme is cream-colored stucco for walls and chimney; dull red mission tile roof; exterior woodwork stained grayish-brown.

Construction: Hollow tile walls, exterior finish stucco, tile roof.

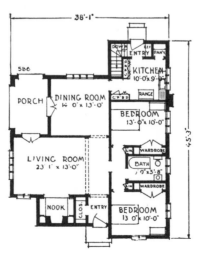

HOME BUILT FROM DESIGN *5-B-2*

A HOUSE WITH GENEROUS ROOMS

With both dining room and breakfast nook

Especially suitable for city building, this house is of solid masonry construction, has the main outlook at the front and back, and locates its porch at the rear overlooking the garden. Five rooms, breakfast nook, and bath are included, and little space has been used for halls. The stairway opening into the living room is a decorative feature, and this arrangement adds a generous effect of space to the first floor. The stairs may be enclosed and the entrance hall clearly defined and shut off by French doors if desired.

If a larger kitchen is wanted, the space now devoted to the breakfast nook can be added to this room, first

allowing for a rear entry. On the second floor are two bedrooms, bath, and seven closets. One bedroom and the bath have cross ventilation. The second bedroom has windows on three sides, and is an exceptionally large room.

The rectangular plan and compact room arrangement should insure reasonable building costs. That so much is included in the given space is due to skillful planning. The entrance, with a window box and small casements above, is an agreeable detail. Windows with both top and bottom sash divided into small lights would have been an improvement over those used above.

Construction: Solid brick walls, dormer stucco finished, shingle or slate roof.

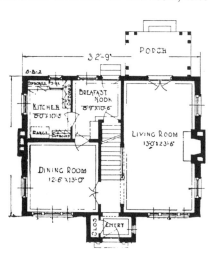

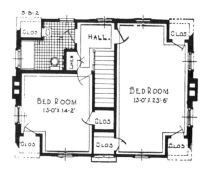

DESIGN 5-B-7

BALANCE IN EXTERIOR DESIGN

Sound style and construction minimize depreciation

As a small home of distinguished appearance, this one, design 5-B-7, would be hard to excel. The entrance porch, with its columns and pilasters, recalls the stately beauty of houses far larger and more pretentious, yet it has been designed on a scale perfectly in accord with the size of the house. The beautifully spaced windows, double hung and divided into small panes and further emphasized by slatted shutters, are reminiscent of the windows in early Colonial homes.

From the broad outside chimneys and the dormers of delicate design, to the windows and entrance porch already mentioned, every detail is in harmony. To be certain that none of the beauty of line and proportion will be lost, the drawings should be followed faithfully, the bricks should not be of too coarse a texture nor the mortar joints unduly prominent, since the house is small in size.

The plan is of the center hall type characteristic of Colonial houses. The stairway, however, is semi-open and goes up at one side of the living room. If desired, this may be enclosed between walls instead, and the entry, which is here really a part of the liv-

ing room, clearly defined as a little entrance hall.

No room that is lighted by windows on three sides, as is this living room, can ever be wholly cheerless by day, no matter what the weather. If it is not sunny, it will at least be light. Likewise no room boasting a fireplace will lack a center of attraction by night. Many home builders will prefer an open porch or sun porch in place of the terrace at the rear. This may be covered by a gaily colored awning, however, and made both useful and decorative at little expense.

Many little conveniences that tend to lighten housework have been provided, such as a broom closet in the kitchen. In the bathroom there is a built-in cupboard which contains drawers for linen below and a medicine cabinet above.

There is one especially large bedroom receiving light and air from three sides, while the blank inside wall permits the use of twin beds in this room. There is just enough cut-off to the ceiling to give the bedrooms an intimate air.

Construction: Solid brick walls, shingle or slate roof.

DESIGN 5-B-10

THE LIVABLE DUTCH COLONIAL

Large, cheerful rooms help to make it so

Do you remember the old-time parlors? There were horsehair chairs, a sedate sofa that was rarely sat upon, wax flowers under a glass case, a "what not," crayon enlargements of the likeness of the old people. There was a marble fireplace or one made of cast iron. The doors were shut, the windows closed, blinds latched; lightness, jollity, and dust did not penetrate the sacred confines of that room.

The parlor is gone, and with its passing has come the living room. When an architect arranges the details of a modern small house plan the living room gets his first consideration. It must be of generous proportions, have well-placed windows and an open fireplace. There must be spaces for furniture, room for people to move about. There may be dust in these rooms, but there is also light and life. As "living rooms" they are well named.

Here we have the up-to-date living room already described. It extends the full depth of the house and has exposure on three sides, insuring an abundance of sunshine and air. The attractive fireplace is flanked by recessed bookcases on either side.

Opposite this room, through plas-

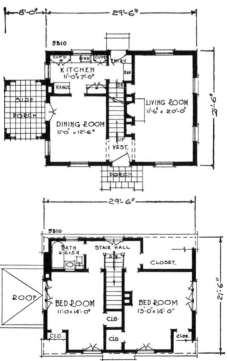

Closets are large and numerous. Placing the bathroom directly over the kitchen insures minimum plumbing costs

tered archways, is the dining room. Off this is an open porch with brick columns and trellised panels, providing not only an excellent sitting porch, but also an outside dining room for use in summer.

The kitchen is a model of efficiency, with built-in equipment and an adjoining service entry. This entry also includes the basement stairway. The second floor contains two excellent bedrooms. Both have two closets, both are large enough for twin beds, while their irregular shape makes possible attractive arrangements of furnishings.

The exterior of this house is in the Colonial style. It is marked by a gambrel roof, a charming hooded entrance, and characteristic shutters at the windows. The steps are brick; in fact, all the exterior walls of this house excepting those of the dormers are solid brick, an excellent type of construction.

The lot size required would range from 45 to 50 feet, although this house could be accommodated on a 40-foot lot if the side porch were eliminated or placed at the rear.

Construction: Solid brick walls, shingle or slate roof.

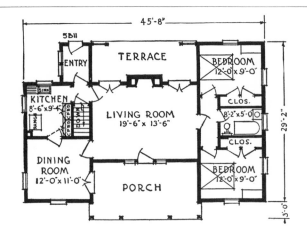

UNPRETENTIOUS

But cozy and homelike

The attractions of this living room are immediately apparent, also the privacy of the bedrooms and the convenience of dining room and kitchen. To accent its long, low lines wide siding is used on the exterior. Here the terrace at the rear has been enclosed, but left open, as shown on the plan, the arrangement is in every way charming. This is planned as a year-around home suitable for any section of the country.

HOME BUILT FROM DESIGN *5-B-11*

REAR OF SAME HOME

These interiors are not from the house opposite, but they illustrate vividly its possibilities. Early American furnishings will be quite as much at home there as in the simple cottage-like interiors shown here

In the charming breakfast room above the braided rug seems peculiarly appropriate on a floor of wide oak planks. Below, figured wall paper and a lavish display of china and silver make a plain rug welcome

HOME BUILT FROM DESIGN *5-B-18*

A BUNGALOW WITH ATTACHED GARAGE

*The home builder will have a hard time to find a small house
offering greater satisfaction than this*

From the standpoint of both economy of space in the plan and simplicity of design, this home may be considered as possessing the most utilitarian character. It is a type that has been extremely popular in the western part of the United States, but the design is one suitable for almost any region of the country. Its finer qualities will be apparent when it is placed among small homes of the usual commonplace character.

The direct lines of the stucco walls with their crown of red tile roof are beautiful in themselves, but the overhanging cornice at the e n t r a n c e supported on graceful brackets, the old-fashioned blinds, and the finely proportioned chimney with its colorful inserts give an irresistible charm to the exterior.

As for the plan, here, too, is economy, matched with fine proportions and usefulness of space. There is an open terrace extending across the front of the living room which may be covered with a gaily colored awning.

The dining room, separated from the living room by a wide archway,

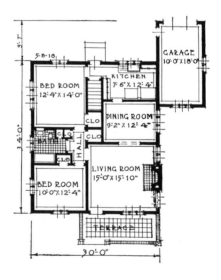

provides a pleasant vista and that effect of space which plays a large part in the livability of the small house.

The kitchen is of the most modern type, being completely designed and equipped to lighten housework. One great convenience is the connection with the rear door through a rear en-

try. The basement is reached through this entry also. Across the entry and directly opposite the kitchen is a door to one of the bedrooms, so that the housewife may pass from the kitchen to the sleeping portion of the house without entering the dining room or living room. Both bedrooms are plentifully supplied with windows, both have large closets.

The garage, although it does not open into the house, is immediately accessible. It may also be heated conveniently without too long a run of pipe.

The color scheme suggested is cream stucco and red tile roof, with colorful tile inserts in the chimney. The stucco should not appear to be artful. The roughness should seem to come from a lack of regularity rather than from artificial working over of the finished plane. The tile roof, of a dark red mission type, should have only moderate variations of color. The exterior woodwork will look well if it is of cypress stained dark.

Construction: Hollow tile walls, stucco exterior finish, tile roof.

Home Built from Design 5-B-20

STURDY AND SUBSTANTIAL

Yet with sufficient vivacity for interest

This design shows something of the Old World character that has become so much desired in recent years. The form and mass are borrowed from the Mediterranean. The plan is strictly American. The house is equally out-standing whether finished with brick as above or with stucco as shown in the drawing below.

Seeing the informal massing and apparent irregularity of the exterior of this house, one would hardly expect a plan of such directness and order. Yet here is the utmost in simplicity, the effects of which will appear in economies in construction and in household management. The house, with its picturesque exterior and splendidly worked-out plan, is designed especially for a small family, and includes in its accommodations practically everything that is to be found in the modern small home.

The porch offers a splendid opportunity for extensive use. It will serve as a pleasant dining place in summer. Glazed, it may be used as a sun porch.

The living quarters are separated from the sleeping quarters by a hall-way, thus conforming to good practice in bungalow design.

The original working drawings call for solid brick walls with stucco finish, roof of tile. The owner of the house illustrated above faced the wall with interesting brickwork. An extra sheet has been added to the drawings, giving a typical wall section for stucco over frame construction, a less expensive method.

DESIGN 5-B-20

The house as originally designed for stucco. Whether the walls are of masonry or wood, the effect would be about the same, though with masonry construction deeper recesses could be obtained at the windows

HOME BUILT FROM DESIGN *5-B-22*

LOW LYING AND COMFORTABLE

Masonry construction promises few repairs

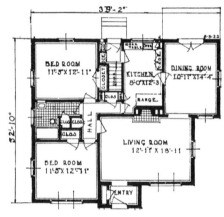

In designing a brick house an architect has the comfortable feeling that he is not being extravagant. Even the more expensive bricks are relatively cheap in the end, considering their durability, and some of the cheaper kinds are as effective when rightly used as some of the costlier varieties. Properly made brick is practically indestructible either by fire or weather. However, its greatest appeal to the architect lies in the possibilities for decorative effects. No other material offers anything like the variety of color, texture, and pattern possible with such simple means.

The house illustrated above is typical of brick construction. Below is another house built from the same plans but with solid masonry walls finished in stucco. In both houses a door in the front outside wall of the dining room was substituted for the window shown on the plan. French doors at the rear open on the terrace, and a broad window at the side in addition makes this room exceptionally light and airy. The living room is of comfortable size, with a recessed fireplace which takes up no valuable floor space.

The room arrangement is fine. Sleeping quarters and bath are along

one side and separated from the living room by a small hall. Privacy is thus assured to both sections. The kitchen is compact. The rear entry is equipped with a package receiver, broom closet, and space for the refrigerator.

Construction: Solid brick walls, left plain or stucco finished; shingle roof. The working drawings provide also for a tile roof which may be substituted if desired.

HOME BUILT FROM DESIGN 5-B-23

A HOUSE OF MANY GABLES

With a glorified breakfast room

The low, rambling style of this bungalow gives it the appearance of size even though the house is a small one. As illustrated, the design may be developed in brick alone or in brick and stucco combined. Both houses are distinctive.

In the brick house there is no orna-

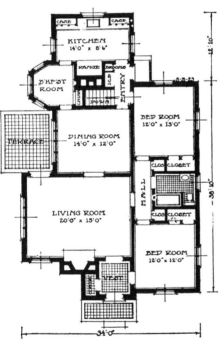

mentation in the strict sense of the word yet each unit—gables, chimney, windows, entrance—is so designed and so well combined that the whole is extremely pleasing. The house above gives the appearance of greater elaboration from the very nature of the contrasting materials and the stressing of

HOME BUILT IN BRICK FROM DESIGN 5-B-23

openings and corners by outlining in brick. Choice of materials is a matter of personal taste. The paved terrace may be covered by awnings.

The plan has much to recommend it. Note the breakfast nook dominated by a great bay window, and the kitchen flooded with light and sunshine from three sides.

Construction: Solid brick walls, stucco shown in one case above level of window sills; steel casements; roof of tile, slate or shingles.

Frank J. Forster, Architect

BEAUTY IN BRICK

*A combination of brick walls and slate roof of rare refinement
and beauty. The slates are graduated. "Swept" valleys unite
the dormers with the main roof*

AGAIN THE ENGLISH COTTAGE

*Making effective use of sharp gables and colorful
brick and tile*

One plan serves for both these designs. It will be seen that the built-in equipment is extensive. In the living room there are bookshelves at each side of the fireplace. This is tile faced. Just above the bookcases are small circle-headed windows. In the breakfast nook are built-in seats and table. A china closet extends completely across one end.

One of the architectural details that adds exceptional beauty to these houses is the high ceiling of the living room. The arrangement of the roof makes this possible, giving the room additional dignity. The ceiling is covered.

There is a glass partition between the living room and the sun room, which has the double virtue of separating these apartments and yet giving them the effect of one long, continuous area.

In the dining room is a projecting bay with a great battery of windows of the casement type. Excellent ventilation is thus assured, and the brilliant lighting afforded by these windows will make the room extremely inviting. The basement plan provides for a den or game room running the full width of the house.

Construction, design 5-B-21: Hollow tile walls, stucco finish, brick trim; design 5-B-26: Solid brick walls.

HOME BUILT FROM DESIGN *5-B-21*

HOME BUILT FROM DESIGN *5-B-26*

HOME BUILT FROM DESIGN 5-B-25

A Plan Worth Study

This small house provides five conveniently arranged rooms and a bath. Only 33 feet wide by 31 feet deep, the floor space is efficiently planned to give maximum accommodations.

An arched recess in the dining room may be used for bookshelves or for a buffet. A recess in the kitchen provides space for the range. The sleeping quarters, accessible only from the small hall, have complete privacy.

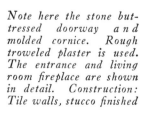

Note here the stone buttressed doorway and molded cornice. Rough troweled plaster is used. The entrance and living room fireplace are shown in detail. Construction: Tile walls, stucco finished

HOME BUILT FROM DESIGN *5-B-27*

FIVE SUNNY ROOMS OF GENEROUS SIZE

*The English cottage has set the precedent for much that makes
this exterior picturesque*

Here is a home that should appeal to the apartment dwellers or young married couples who are seeking home ownership yet who, for obvious reasons, do not desire a large establishment. Houses are shrinking in size in this servantless age, yet the successful small home must meet certain definite requirements. True, the economic problem makes it necessary for us to build on a smaller scale than was common formerly, yet we have learned to make the best possible use of such space as we have.

This design illustrates in a practical way a modern solution to the housing problem, but it does not show the most rigorous application of present-day schemes for minimizing space. While the floor area is comparatively small, there is still a certain generosity about it. A full-size dining room such as this one is not included in the smallest apartment cottages. Neither would such a cottage boast two regular bedrooms and a kitchen of such size as we find in this plan.

The colorful roof with its many gables, the small-paned windows, and the low chimney with its picturesque chimney pots are all features for which we find a precedent in the English cottage. The front entrance door is a solid affair of ten panels, with the two at the top of glass. It is of the so-called

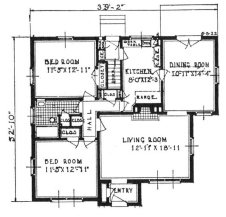

"Dutch door" type, divided in the center so that the upper half alone may be opened.

In addition to the interesting exterior, we have here an admirably worked out plan. The arrangement for communication between the rooms, by which passage through the living room may be eliminated entirely, will be of particular interest to the housewife. Not only the two bedrooms, bath, and kitchen open from the hall, but also several closets of varied uses.

There are two linen closets, one close to the bathroom door and one opening into the room. Around the corner in the hall is a second many-shelved closet, a clothes chute, and a recess for the telephone with a seat beside it which slides into the wall out of the way. Near the door to the kitchen is a closet for pots and pans. In the rear entry is a space for the refrigerator; beside it is a narrow broom closet with space below which may be opened from the outside and is therefore available to delivery men.

The two bedrooms are exactly the same size and shape. Both have cross ventilation, capacious closets, and the long, unbroken wall spaces so necessary for large pieces of bedroom furniture.

Construction: Tile walls faced with brick and stucco; shingle, slate or tile roof.

DESIGN 5-B-30

THE ORIGIN OF THE PATIO

A bungalow Spanish in origin but twentieth-century American in convenience

Imagine—if you can—that our country was invaded by foreigners of strange race, religion, customs, and standards of morals. Would you feel comfortable to live in a house with unbarred glass windows in the ground-story floor, to let your children play in an unfenced yard, and to have your wife and daughters freely walk the streets? Hardly!

That is just what happened to the Spaniards some 1,200 years ago. Mohammedans swarmed across the Mediterranean Sea from North Africa, defeated the Spanish armies, and ruled the land for about 700 years. It was not until the reign of King Ferdinand and Queen Isabella—who about the same time backed up Columbus on the voyage that discovered America—that the Moors were driven finally from the kingdom.

One result of these bitter years in Spanish history was the creation of the patio. Instead of setting a home in the midst of a yard, the Spaniard set a yard in the midst of his house. That is, he built the house in the form of a hollow square with an open court in the center. Within this he and his family spent most of their time in pleasant weather. Thus the house itself formed a great protecting fence around the patio.

There are other reasons why the patio became part of the ancient architecture of Spain. During the Middle Ages cities had to be walled to prevent invasions. So the ground available for building was limited. By

building a house around a garden, the home owner of those days assured himself of a little bit of natural beauty.

Patios became a part of the American home design for the same reason that they first came into existence. The early Spanish settlers in Mexico, California, and our other Southern states needed protection, not against Mussulmans, but against Indians. So they followed the traditions of their homelands and built their ranches and their missions around the four sides of patios.

Hence it is that the real Spanish or "Southern California" style of home, built in any part of the United States today, must have a patio if it is to be true to form. Even now we find the patio useful in many delightful ways.

The garage has been utilized in this case to form one side of the patio so that, being an important part of the design, it is doubly useful. The fireplace is of an informal type suited to this style. A partial basement is provided, large enough for laundry, storage and heater rooms.

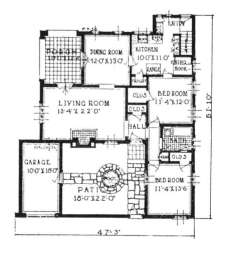

One of the most satisfactory things about this plan is the circulation between rooms. The front entrance opens into the living room at the left and the bedroom hall at the right. The rear bedroom opens directly into the kitchen, which the housewife will find a great convenience. In the kitchen is a dining alcove and large storage pantry, also ample cupboard space.

Construction: Hollow tile walls, stucco finish. An alternate detail provides for stucco over wood frame.

DESIGN 5-B-34

ROMANCE FROM THE SOUTH AND WEST

*Stamped with the character of sectional architecture in boldness
of color, form, and construction*

In this design the purpose of the architect has been to create a house which, although modern in the accommodations it provides, shall be as charmingly as possible reminiscent of the romantic architecture of Old Mexico and southern California. From general scheme to smallest detail the design has been carefully and studiously wrought to insure the house being built consistently Spanish-American throughout.

Boldness of color, form, and construction were outstanding characteristics of this early American-Spanish architecture. Strength and durability rather than refinement of detail were chief considerations of builders of that day.

The entire plan centers around the walled patio with its flagged walk and pool—a pleasant out-of-door sitting room amid flowers and shrubs. The loggia, wide and cheery, may serve as a sun room during the cooler months —as a breakfast room through the entire year.

Important features of this design are the beamed ceiling and corner fireplace in the living room; the loggia opening rooms on a different level from that into the walled patio; the sleeping of the living quarters.

If the architects who planned this home for you were personally to superintend its construction, they would have the exterior walls finished in a rough troweled stucco of a pinkish gray or light buff color. The woodwork would be painted dull blue. The cor-

ners of the building would be rounded rather than left sharp and true, as is generally the practice in other styles of house architecture. The roofing tile would be of the mission type, red in color, and laid in random lengths.

Inside the house the architects would use the simplest of materials. The floors would be pine, laid in random widths and lengths. The woodwork, beams, and doors would also be pine. All of these would be stained dark, or a weathered pine effect. They would have the fireplace built of hard-burned red brick. The soffits of the beams in the living room would be painted in bright colors. The walls would be plastered in a sand finish, colored to suit the individual taste of the owner. The hardware for the doors and windows would be black, either rustless iron or hammered iron, depending on the amount of money to be spent. Bolts would be used for all interior doors in place of locks and keys.

In short, the treatment of the materials and the choice of them, would correspond with the character of the architecture, thus unifying all.

Construction: Hollow tile walls with stucco exterior finish, tile roof. Frame construction for metal lath and stucco may be substituted. Details for this type of construction are furnished with the plans. This is an especially fine house for a corner lot. The basement, excavated beneath bedrooms and bath, provides space for heater and fuel rooms and a laundry.

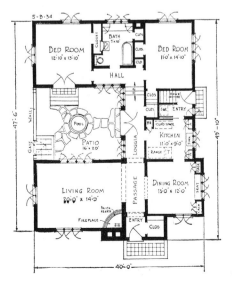

HOME BUILT FROM DESIGN *5-B-31*

FROM THE ARCHITECTURAL MELTING POT

Two charming little houses built from the same design

Small house architecture in America has a quality of its own. We do not always call it American, but when we have done with the designing of a house having details taken from the Spanish or English or Italian, so much has been added to meet the requirements of home life in this country that the final result is truly American.

Design 5-B-31 illustrated here is typical of what happens to an Italian cottage after it has been transformed by American designers. It is really American, but we do not hesitate to borrow the Italian's close-clipped eaves, his roof of tile, the casemented windows, the arched entrance, and the plain stucco walls. The result is a home of charm and individuality, with a beauty of line and proportion and a plan of

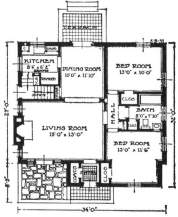

HOME BUILT FROM DESIGN *5-B-31*

The mantel in the living room is copied from an old Italian fireplace. It is made in cement and molded while moist by the workman's hands. Painted a light buff color and then overglazed with blue, it produces a pleasing two-toned effect

such direct convenience that any nation might be glad to call it its own and be proud of its craftsmen and designers.

Tile is used freely throughout. The roof is covered with tile in variegated reds and tans. Large red quarry tiles ornament the vestibule floor, and the bathroom floor is laid in tiles of black and white. Dull red tiles in the hearth of the fireplace add color to the living room.

Opening off the living room is a flagstone terrace which in summertime may be covered with an awning. The living room may be entered from this terrace or through the vestibule. The ceiling of the living room is higher than that of the other rooms, giving it the proportions due a room with so large a floor area. A wide arched opening separates living and dining rooms. The vista from the front carries through these rooms and on to the rear across another open terrace.

The kitchen is scientifically small, with everything within easy reach and stepping distance. The range is set within a recess so that it does not protrude into the kitchen, and above it is provided a hood to carry off the fumes and odors of cookery. Adequate cupboards flank the sink. Into the corner

Kitchen entrance, garage, and garden gate of the house opposite. The small door below the kitchen window is a package receiver. The casement window at the right of the entrance is one of the pair shown in the drawings on either side of the living room fireplace

cupboard is built an outside door for keeping foods chilled in cool weather. There is also the built-in china closet in the dining room, the linen closets in both hall and bathroom, the recessed bathtub, the niche for the telephone in the hall between the bedrooms, and the coat closet off the vestibule.

The exterior walls may be finished in white stucco, tan, light gray or gray green, with a roof of variegated

tiles in harmonizing colors. The doors should harmonize with the roof.

The illustration below shows how house and garage may be tied together by means of an arched gateway. The result is a pleasant effect of unity which is missing when house and garage are entirely separate.

Construction: Solid brick or hollow tile walls, stucco finish; outswinging casements either steel or frame.

HOME BUILT FROM DESIGN *5-B-33*

A STRAIGHTFORWARD PRACTICAL PLAN

*Providing many comforts and conveniences
with space for recreation*

One of the most interesting features of this five-room bungalow is the ample provision for leisure and recreation. Not only is the living room large and attractive, but there is also a den or amusement room in the basement. This is reached by a flight of stairs at one end of the living room, so that guests will not have to be taken down by the service stairs in the rear entry. If the owner prefers to omit this feature, the working drawings give details for an alternate placement of the front porch and for a long window seat and closet in the living room in the space here utilized for the basement stairs.

The kitchen contains a number of conveniences that will be appreciated particularly by the housewife. One of these is a California cooler or cold air box, which is a device to keep food in storage at low temperature by passing a current of outside air through apertures in the wall into a closed container built into the wall—at great saving in the ice bills. When hot weather comes the refrigerator in the rear entry would be used. A cozy breakfast nook and the ever desirable broom closet complete the accommodations of the kitchen. The rear entry permits the bedroom side of the house to be reached conveniently from the kitchen without passing through the dining room or living room on the way.

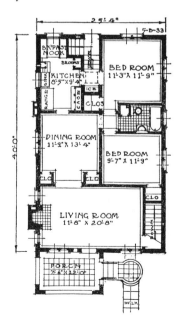

The two bedrooms are of good size and well lighted. Although reduced to the absolute minimum in size, the hall serves to give the desired privacy to the sleeping quarters.

A wide archway connecting the living and dining rooms adds to the beauty of both rooms. This archway provides space for two china closets in the dining room, which may be as decorative in character as desired.

The drawings call for heavy batten shutters at the front window, which add character to the house. The owner of the house illustrated added the room at the right, which is not shown in the plans.

In design 4-B-16 much the same plan arrangement will be found with an exterior identical in design. There are the same number of bedrooms in both plans, the chief difference lies in the living rooms and the size of the dining room, which in design 4-B-16 is reduced to a moderately large dining alcove. Both designs offer large accommodations at moderate cost.

Construction: Brick or tile walls, stucco or brick exterior with tile roof. Wood frame with stucco may be substituted, and a shingle roof used.

HOME BUILT FROM DESIGN 5-B-28

A GAY LITTLE HOME FROM THE WEST

*Glowing with color on the exterior, and beautified with
architectural detail on the interior*

It would be hard to find a more delightful example of the California type of bungalow than this home. Not only is the exterior attractive, but the plan is an excellent example of what the one-story dwelling should have in the way of rooms and conveniences and the manner of their arrangement to be truly successful and livable. The same plan has been developed in the spirit of the English cottage in design 5-B-27, so that between these two styles a large number of families should find the solution to their home building problems.

The plan calls for five major rooms, all of good size, all light and sunny and well ventilated. There is an abundance of closet space, many built-in conveniences, and in addition the rooms are so grouped about the hall as to afford the maximum of privacy to all portions of the house.

The color scheme suggested for this exterior is cream color stucco either in a floated finish or dashed and rodded; gray for sash and doors; light brown brick sills; and variegated tile for the roof. A less expensive roofing may be used, however. The wrought iron railing at the side of the steps and terrace and the gaily striped awnings add greatly to the picturesque appearance of the house.

The front door is of heavy matched

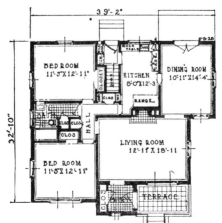

boards. From the entry a plaster archway leads to the living room. The fireplace is located on an inside wall, a situation in many ways to be recommended. Built of brick, perhaps its most distinguished feature is the wide, slightly recessed arch above the mantelshelf.

Double French doors at the far end make the dining room a particularly pleasant place. These open out upon a grass terrace. This room, although it has abundant wall space for the arrangement of furniture, has outside exposure on three sides.

The bedroom hall contains a roomy closet above the basement stairs, a clothes chute to the laundry with telephone closet above, and a linen closet adjoining the bath. A scuttle in the ceiling of the hall leads to the attic space above. Louvers at either end of this space provide ventilation.

In the kitchen a cabinet beside the sink provides for four capacious drawers and deep shelves. The cupboard at the right is also provided with many shelves and several drawers. The drawings call for a full basement.

Here the owner provided a door in the front outside wall of the dining room instead of the window shown in the plan.

Construction: Brick walls faced with stucco, tile or shingle roof.

Wide pine boards sheath this enchanting liv-
ing room. The ceiling beams are hand hewn,
the floor is of oak planks of random widths.

Books, draperies, and gay china glow with
color against the mellow background. The
great fireplace has been wrought by an artist

C. B. Straus, Architect

HOME BUILT FROM DESIGN 5-B-35

WITH AN INGLE NOOK

The entrance bids you welcome,
the fireplace entices

In this cottage the brick chimney with its leaded glass window and quaint projecting flues, the arched entrance with its little square grill and wrought iron hinges, the brick rowlock trim just under the eaves of the front gable, the brick quoins at the corners, the clean-cut lines of the roof, are all interesting features. The plan is compact and convenient, the interior as charming as the exterior.

Construction: Solid brick walls trimmed with stucco; slate, shingle or tile roof; casements steel or frame.

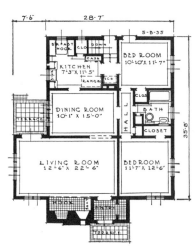

ENTRANCE OF HOME BUILT FROM DESIGN 5-B-35

DESIGN 5-B-37

THE ENGLISH COTTAGE TO THE FORE

Here with a high ceilinged living room and great window

Just what are the characteristics of English cottages? This is a question often asked but difficult to answer, for in England the cottage follows closely the life and manners of its occupants, and there are almost as many different modes and ranks of life as there are counties.

There is nothing stereotyped about the picturesque cottages from which we derive architectural inspiration. That is one of their essential charms. Nearness to the source of supply dictated the choice of building materials, hence their variation in different localities. Convenience dictated the size and shape of the plan. As the cottages were occupied for several generations, each in turn made additions, sometimes merely of a door or window, sometimes of one or more rooms. If the cottage finally became large and rambling, it was for logical reasons.

In the cottage illustrated here, the floor plan is compact, convenient, and comfortable. Just as the plans of cottages in England reveal the manner of life of the families who occupy them, the plan of this design expresses the efficiency, orderliness, and love of beautiful surroundings that characterize the American family. You will find the plan used in this book with practically every type of house architecture, so that among them should be an exterior to suit every home builder.

Although the plan is typical of the best five-room bungalows, the ex-

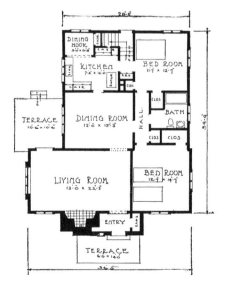

terior inspired by the cottages of old England is handled with such distinction that it is anything but typical in appearance. The informality of the massing is accentuated by the happy combination of materials. The wrought iron lamp at the door, the diamond-paned leaded glass in the door and the entry window, the heavy wooden beams over the windows at the side, are all items which add in no small measure to the charm and interest of the exterior.

The architects have given the living room a sloped ceiling following the rafters. The great window at the end insures floods of light; the beautiful fireplace is recessed in a cozy ingle nook; the door opening upon the terrace affords a view of the garden beyond. Altogether this is a beautiful room indeed.

In addition to the large dining room, there is a convenient breakfast nook. This is larger than the usual built-in affair, and may be equipped with a small table and chairs. With these gaily painted, brilliant china and glassware on the shelves of the china cabinet at one side, the effect will be wholly delightful. The kitchen is replete with space-saving equipment scientifically arranged. No doubt the direct entrance to the rear bedroom from the kitchen will be appreciated.

Construction: Wood frame; exterior finish stucco with brick at the front; shingle or slate roof; wood or metal casements.

DESIGN 5-B-38

A BUNGALOW OF SPANISH INHERITANCE

The living room bright and sunny all day

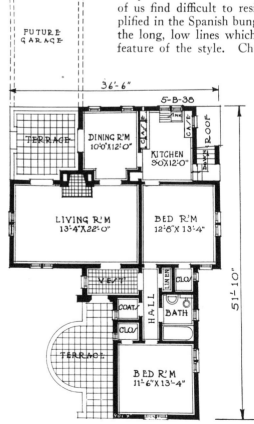

Spanish architecture has a charm that most of us find difficult to resist, a charm best exemplified in the Spanish bungalow. This design has the long, low lines which are such an attractive feature of the style. Characteristically, too, interest centers particularly on the openings—the picturesque doorway and the windows with their distinctive and striking shutters.

Beyond the vestibule, which becomes here a virtue from an artistic as well as a practical standpoint, one enters the long living room. Casement windows on two sides and double French doors upon a third mean light and sunshine throughout the day. The fireplace, interestingly designed, promises to be the center of attraction on many an evening.

Construction: Solid brick walls, stucco finish.

"THE BEAUTIFUL RESTS ON THE FOUNDATIONS
OF THE NECESSARY"

DESIGN 5-B-39

UNUSUAL REFINEMENT IN SO SMALL A HOUSE

*Sketches of the entrance, the large window at the right,
and the fireplace are shown on the opposite page*

Those who should know tell us that the most intensely Spanish houses are found not in Spain but in America. This is not so much to be wondered at, considering the American propensity to excel at anything undertaken—from athletics to architecture. The fact is that this style is particularly well adapted to our needs. In many parts of both Spain and America the winters are severe, the summers blazing hot. The necessity, then, is for houses that will conserve the heat in winter and retain coolness in summer. The old-time mud and adobe plastered walls served this purpose admirably. True, following the beacon of efficiency, America has substituted concrete, hollow tile, and stucco for these primitive materials, but the essentials of the design itself have been retained.

In this house we have an excellent example of the Spanish style. The broad, flat wall surfaces, the well-designed openings with their deep reveals, the wrought iron balcony, and the delicately turned balusters screening the window have all been skillfully combined herein.

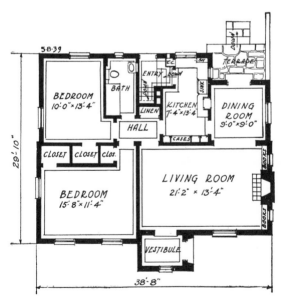

The plan resolves itself naturally into two sections: living quarters on one side, sleeping quarters on the other. The hall necessary to provide passage from one section to the other is reduced to the minimum so that no valuable space is lost. This division allows the utmost quiet and privacy to the sleeping quarters, almost as much as in a two-story house.

Closet space is ample, and in the kitchen are innumerable built-in cupboards and conveniences of every kind.

In the long living room ample wall spaces make the arrangement of furniture, even of large pieces, a simple matter. French doors opening on to the small balcony, and narrow, small-paned windows above the bookcases, are equally decorative. These bookshelves on either side of the fireplace add to the beauty of the room, as does the wide opening to the dining room which affords a delightful vista across the terrace. This, with its low flight of flagstone steps, tends to tie house and garden together. Construction: Brick walls with stucco facing, tile roof.

DESIGN *5-B-40*

SPANISH FROM THE GROUND UP

With a choice of plans for your approval

So charming is this bungalow, so studied in detail, form, and mass that no slightest change in the exterior would seem permissible. To eliminate such necessity, yet make it available to the greatest number of home builders, alternate plans are presented. One has but two bedrooms, the other three, thus meeting family needs. A study of the plans will reveal other differences, particularly in the kitchen.

Construction: Hollow tile walls, stucco finish, tile roof.

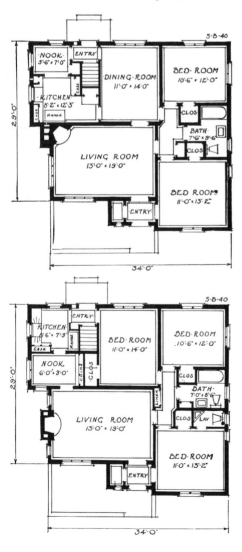

Two corners that are full of suggestions. The size of the furniture is especially adapted to the proportions of the rooms. In the illustration below the tall screen makes a gorgeous background for the grouping of table and chair. Note also the excellent grouping at the left

Photographs from Mattie Edwards Hewitt

A FIVE-ROOM CALIFORNIA BUNGALOW

Alternate plans present two arrangements for the kitchen

Casement windows, an arched entrance, a tile roof, stucco covered walls, and a judicious use of ornamental detail make up this delightful California bungalow. The house illustrated has been built with garage attached, but so skillfully handled that the design of the house is not impaired. Also, the brick terrace indicated in the plans has here been extended to the end wall of the house.

The vestibule opens either into the living room or into the front bedroom. This makes it possible to reach the rear of the house without passing through the living room.

The living room is admirable in size and proportions, with ample unbroken wall spaces. The fireplace is informal in design, of tile and plaster, and without a mantelshelf. A large dining room is provided in both plans, and in the alternate plan a cozy breakfast nook is also included. This necessitates a rearrangement of the kitchen and service entry, but otherwise the two plans are identical.

The basement, under only the rear portion of the house, is quite adequate for all the usual purposes, including laundry, fuel and heater rooms.

Construction: Wood frame, stucco exterior finish, roof of variegated mission tile, casement windows.

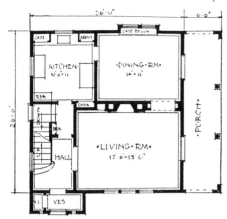

HOME BUILT FROM DESIGN 5-C-10

TWO BEDROOMS OR THREE

A choice of plans to fit special needs

There are three main things to remember if you want to keep down the cost of your home. First—limit requirements to those things that are actually necessary. Second—use inexpensive but sound materials. Third—eliminate waste in materials and labor.

The house illustrated here was a prize-winning design in a competition for a small five-room home of frame construction. It deserves careful study, not only because of its architectural beauty, but because it gives an unusual opportunity to put into practice the three principles mentioned above.

Perhaps the only space in this plan that is not entirely useful is the vestibule and even that is debatable. The arrangement of the living room and hall is such that one may pass directly from the front door to the kitchen without going through the front part of the house. The rooms have a natural sequence, are open, airy, well lighted. The living room, comfort-able but not so large as to add unduly to the cost of construction, is one of excellent proportions well adapted to furnishing and decoration. The dining room is of generous size, a wide recess affording space for a buffet.

In the second story practically all the area has been converted into useful rooms. What little remains of floor area restricted by the slope of the roof, becomes entirely useful storage space.

The splendid porch, which stretches the full depth of the house, can be glazed or screened. The kitchen is large enough for a table and chairs beneath the side window to serve as a breakfast nook.

The attractive main entrance shown at the right is simplicity itself.

Due to its excellent plan, and the careful adaptation of Colonial details, this is a house that will not go out of style. Its resale value is therefore stabilized, an important consideration.

Without increase of size, the second story may be divided into three bedrooms

DESIGN 5-C-9

WHEN A DINING ROOM IS NOT NEEDED

Other corners make pleasant dining places

How pleasant is a large, well-proportioned living room, and what a luxury it becomes for the small home builder, for few of the small and inexpensive homes have them. In design 5-C-9 illustrated here, the fine large living room is obtained not by increasing the outer dimensions of the walls, and thus the expense, but by omitting the dining room. Meals for the family

may be served in a sunny corner of the kitchen or in the fernery, a delightful little room with windows on three sides. Or if there are guests, what could be more charming and informal than a table set in one end of the living room with a fire blazing cheerily in the grate?

Another convenient feature of this house is that the first story is complete in itself. If funds are limited and the family is small, the second story need not be finished. There is a bedroom on the first floor and a hall that leads directly from the bedroom to the bathroom and linen closet. Moreover, the bedroom and bathroom are so separated from the living room and kitchen that there will be privacy. If the second floor is finished, it offers two bedrooms each with good closet space and cross ventilation, a lavatory with a large linen closet for second-story supplies, and two huge storage spaces under the roof.

The basement makes provision for laundry, furnace, fuel room, and storage space.

The exterior is exceedingly simple. It has been designed for the family who wishes to keep costs as low as possible.

But it has a good deal of charm. The proportions are essentially fine. The lines are easy and have a "just right" feeling. The house is low and set close to the ground, as all small houses should be, in a homey fashion. Then for trimming there are the shutters across the front and the latticed entrance. The small dormers are perfectly in keeping with the size of the house. This is of the greatest importance, as larger dormers would destroy much of the beauty of the house.

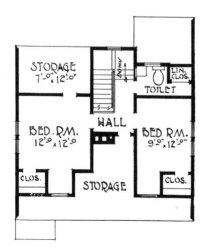

DESIGN 5-C-13

RECALLING CONNECTICUT COTTAGES

A house that will do honor to its owner's good taste

People have been building homes for no one knows how many tens of thousands of years. Architects have been doing it for several thousand. By this time, it seems, we ought to know just exactly what to do to get the best effect, the most accommodation at the least cost.

But happily we do not know. There isn't any best. If we knew which one was the very best there probably would be so many houses built just alike that we would feel that the modern urge for standardization had gone too far. The best piece of architecture, like the best tune and the best bit of sculpture, is relative. All depends on the point of view. But we do arrive, to a certain extent, at two or three types of plans for five-room houses that are the most logical, most efficient, especially from the economy point of view.

One of these is the type that has the living room running across the front, dining room and kitchen to the rear. Here in design 5-C-13 we find a skillful handling of this program of rooms. Even though this house is built on a thoroughly established scheme of planning, it is by no means commonplace. Happily in small house archi-

tecture so much variety is possible in form and detail and in color that, even though we do set up a recognized type of room arrangement, the treatment can make it entirely distinctive. One of the most important features about this house is the entrance.

The stairway is open and because of the wide opening between the living room and hall it can be seen from the living room. Dining alcove and living room are almost one because of the wide doorway between them. In

cold climates, where it is necessary to shut up rooms to conserve heat, it would be possible to use French doors between the hall and living room.

In the dining alcove there are built-in corner cupboards for china, the French doors lead to the porch. This may be either glazed or screened.

The kitchen has an exceptional amount of cupboard and drawer space, and in addition two convenient storage closets. By means of the window above the sink, the door in the adjoining entry, and the dining room windows, it is always possible to keep the room cool.

HOME BUILT FROM DESIGN 5-D-1

BUT BUNGALOWS GO ON FOREVER

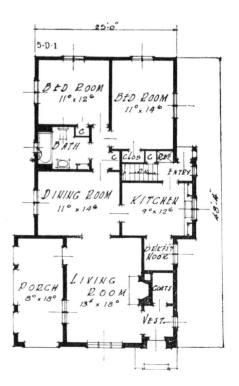

Styles in houses come and go, but bungalows go on forever. Here is one that many will like. There is justification for it. It has an efficient plan with the wanted things, and an exterior for which the present-day home builders have shown a preference.

There is a beautiful living room with fine lighting and a handsome fireplace. In addition its wall spaces provide place for all required furniture.

The exterior speaks for itself. The great window in the front lights the living room. The wooden lintel above this window and the ornamental shutters lend a delightfully domestic quality. The front entrance of heavy planks with iron hinges, lighted by a pleasantly formed wrought iron lamp, is balanced on the other side of the house by the porch. This is shown in the sketch above. Its openings are attractively modeled, the wrought iron railing decorative in design.

The construction beneath the stucco finish is wood frame.

HOME BUILT FROM DESIGN *5-D-25*

FIVE ROOMS AND AN INGLE NOOK

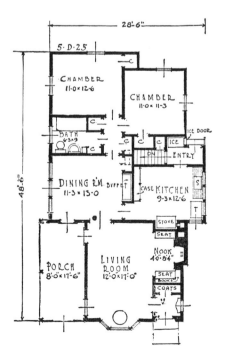

In this house the living room stands by itself, with a great bay window at the front to command the view and with the fireplace in a deep ingle nook where people around it will not be in the way of others passing.

The dining room, lighted by three large windows, opens upon the side porch shown in the illustration above, which makes it possible to use it as a dining porch in fine weather. There is a recess for a buffet, or one may be built in, with a china closet to the left.

In the kitchen a recess is provided for the stove.

One of the finest things about this plan is that every room has cross ventilation. It is extremely rare to find this in a five-room bungalow, where ordinarily at least one room has windows on one side only. Cross ventilation in the kitchen is assured by placing one window at the front and giving practically one entire wall over to windows. Storage space is ample, with two closets located in the hall.

DESIGN *5-D-26*

A HOUSE WITH A STUDIO LIVING ROOM

*Although the exterior appears large, the plan is really compact
and economical to build*

The man or woman searching for a five-room bungalow of originality and charm, a home with an unusual arrangement of rooms, and different in appearance from the average commonplace shoebox bungalow, will appreciate this design. It is a mission type bungalow with adaptations to suit the climate and other conditions of the middle west and east.

The designer has made skillful use of architectural refinements to increase the apparent size of this house, where, as a matter of fact, the cubic content is unusually small. He has done this mainly through the use of relatively low roof lines and compactness of the plan.

Since the exterior finish of the walls is of stucco, much depends on the way in which this finish is handled for the proper carrying out of the design. In fact, the refinement of this design is such that all the details should be carried out with rigorous faithfulness to the drawings in order to attain the results desired.

The chief feature of the interior is the change in floor levels, which makes possible a living room with a fine high ceiling. Entering the front door through the entrance porch, one steps into a small vestibule. This contains the coat closet, so essential in the well ordered home.

Descending two steps, to the level of the living room,

the visitor will find himself in an impressive, beautiful room of generous proportions, with a high vaulted ceiling. This is made possible by lowering the floor level and raising the ceiling of the living room above that of the other rooms.

The family who has acquired the porch habit may object to the absence of a covered porch in this design. Opportunity for providing such a porch is afforded, however, at the rear of the house, opening off the dining room. The drawings now provide a paved terrace in this position. This terrace could be roofed without detracting from the general effect. Covered with an awning, perhaps screened, this area would make a very satisfactory outdoor sitting room in summer. In winter, however, the awning down, no light into the dining room would be obstructed as would be the case with the covered porch.

The two bedrooms and bath are arranged like a suite of rooms at one side. They are on the same lower floor level as the living room.

The dining room and kitchen are on the higher floor level corresponding with that of the entrance hall. In the kitchen there is a space that can be used as a breakfast nook, or used for cabinets and counter room.

Construction: Frame, with stucco finish, shingle roof, casement windows.

HOME BUILT FROM DESIGN 5-D-29

THE IMPORTANCE OF SIMPLICITY

Utterly without ornament, yet with a quaint and appealing charm

The design shown here is distinctly in the English character. Our architects have worked it out in such a way that it has a high degree of individuality. One does not see houses like this in all our streets. We wish there were more of them. Undoubtedly the character of this house comes about from the way in which the plan elements are massed—the shape of the walls and the contour of the roof.

But this effect does not come first by making an interesting exterior. In order to be sound architecture, it must first of all have a good plan. This one is unusual in the fine accommodations it affords. It is unusual also in the way in which the rooms turn on each

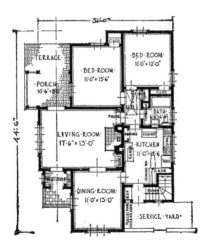

other. Circulation between them is direct and eliminates unnecessary steps.

For example, the dining room is placed at the front, as is also the kitchen and its service yard. The living room is given a more private setting with a view at the side through broad casement windows and to the rear over a terrace or porch. Any part of this may be enclosed.

The kitchen, dining room, and living room, which comprise the living quarters of the house, are entirely separate from the sleeping quarters, which are reached through a hall to the rear. The position of this hall is a mark of good planning.

The main entrance and the service entrance are widely separated and each is so treated that there can be no mistake as to which is the principal entrance of the house. The screening of the service entrance and yard assures the necessary degree of privacy. One can easily visualize the convenience of this kitchen entrance, in which is placed the refrigerator with outside icing, and the stairway to the basement.

The living room is of good size and well proportioned. Beside the fireplace are shelves for books. An insignificant detail, but one which home builders appreciate, is the special nook for the telephone in the center of the arch at the other side of the fireplace. This is only one of many comparatively unimportant details with which the house is replete, all of which go to show how carefully the plan has been studied to make it a satisfactory one. The bedrooms, located as they are at the rear, have all the quiet and privacy possible, almost as much, in fact, as sleeping rooms on the second floor.

The dining room facing the front has a battery of casement windows along the front wall and a high window along the side wall, under which may be placed a buffet or other dining room furniture. There is direct connection to the kitchen.

Construction: Stucco over wood frame, shingle roof.

HOME BUILT FROM DESIGN *5-D-28*

The texture of the stucco walls and the play of color in the roof planes give this house much of its architectural distinction. The house is entered through a covered portico

A HOUSE WITH A LICH-GATE

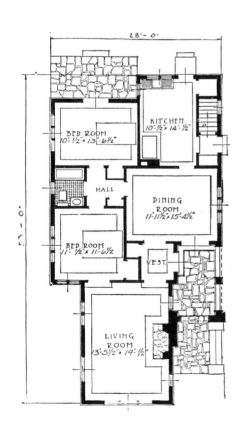

The fireplace, not over-refined w i t h molded woodwork, is especially well designed in relation to the high ceiling of the living room

In spite of its many English details, this house is American because its scheme of plan is wrought from traditions of American home life. One will hardly find a single plan like this in all England. Of course, the designer borrowed a number of details from England. One of them is the great window, another the lichgate, and perhaps the peaked g a b l e s and the glorified chimney. Disregarding the name, however, it is enough to realize that here is a beautiful little house with a first rate, convenient plan.

T h e h o u s e is entered through a covered portico, which, if the owner is lucky, he has paved with stones. At the right of the vestibule is the dining room, at the left the living room.

The living room has much of the English character. In the first place there is the high ceiling, the lines of which follow to some extent those of the roof. Then there is the gorgeous window, which was never invented in America. It did not come from the English small home either but from the English mansion. The room has exposure on three sides, a little trick borrowed from Europe. The fireplace has a cosmopolitan nationality, its general style common to all nations with cold climates. Being off by itself gives the living room a virtue which has great merit with many.

Across the vestibule is the dining room, with a triple window at one side and French doors opening on to the terraced portico on another.

This home is an example

of what may be done with a house that has its long axis corresponding with the long axis of the lot. Here we see how well this principle may be made to work—how pleasantly situated are all the rooms.

The construction is wood frame, which is almost exclusively an American way of building. The wall covering is of stucco, the roof of shingles. To give the best effect the stucco should be a little rough—but not too much so—and a little warm as to color. This is as inexact as a formula can be, but about as exact as it is possible to give. A middle ground permits the house to speak for itself, and not as an exhibition of plaster.

A view of the great window at the end of the living room which shows the coved ceiling also. The divided glass insures privacy without obstructing the v i e w from within

DESIGN *5-D-31*

A DEMURE AND FRIENDLY COTTAGE

Pity the person who would not enjoy his meals in
such a dining room

If the time ever comes when we take our meals strictly in tablet form—as science predicts we undoubtedly will —and dining becomes truly one of the lost arts, as epicures count it even today, why, then the owner of this house might see fit to change the idea of the plan somewhat. The dining room might become a study or, more delightful still, a library.

However, dining still plays an important part in the general scheme of things, and so the most prominent room in this house—and one of the most charming—continues to be the dining room. Pity the person who could not find pleasure in meals in such a light, airy room, with sunshine undoubtedly flooding it the greater part of the day from one side or the other of its three exposures.

If the living room seems deficient in size, it has other compensating features on the credit side. There is here, also, the matter of light, air and sunshine from three sides. There is the attractive brick fireplace which dominates one end of the room. There is also a cozy alcove in one corner, with boxed-in seats for extra storage. These

might hold a supply of wood for the fireplace. Just off this room, also, there is a roomy covered porch which looks out over the garden as the best behaved porches are doing today.

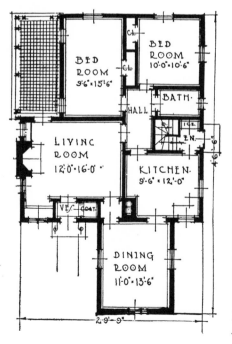

The pleasant bedrooms carry their own recommendation, for they have size, light, cross ventilation—all the virtues of sleeping quarters.

The large triple window under the front gable is reminiscent of early Colonial homes, as is also the front entrance with its paneled transom, two small top lights of glass, and its brick paved stoop flanked by wrought iron railings. The long flower box under the wide front window and the old-fashioned blinds add pleasantly picturesque touches.

Siding is the exterior finish used, and wide siding in particular would effectively accentuate the long, low lines that are the most distinctive feature of the design. Shingled walls would also be effective. The chimneys, either painted or whitewashed, would be brought into closer harmony with the general color scheme and with the general style of the house. Brick was frequently treated in this manner in Colonial times.

Painted white or light gray, with roof and shutters a moss green, the house would present a picture of a real American home.

HOME BUILT FROM DESIGN *5-D-32*

REMINISCENT OF EARLY COLONIAL TIMES

The bungalow is an American institution. To be sure, it has a long ancestry of Old World cottages, but the American family has made such distinct demands as to plan that our modern bungalows bear little resemblance to the small houses of England and Europe.

Here is a good example of the American bungalow of five rooms. The exterior is characterized by the charm and simplicity of the homes of our forefathers built during the Colonial period. The combination of plan and exterior is simple, honest, and straightforward, characteristic of the best spirit of our American civilization, hence its long-lived charm.

Beauty is gained through skillful spacing of the different parts that make up the walls rather than through the addition of decorative features, such as columns, benches, blinds, and hooded canopies. The living room is provided with a doorway at the side of the fireplace for access to the garden. The fireplace itself dominates the living room, and is located in such a position that people sitting about it are not disturbed by those passing from the vestibule to the dining room. A stairway from the hall leads to the attic, while close by is a large storage closet.

THE KITCHEN AT THE FRONT

Designs for small houses come and go
Here is one which will not go

HOME BUILT FROM DESIGN *5-D-33*

The architect's drawing of the front entrance. Vines trained over the trellis will effectively conceal the service door behind it

Five-room bungalows 24 feet wide are common. Usage and practical common sense have made them so. Here, however, is a distinctive five-room bungalow of this type. Although it has the 24-foot width and the arrangement of bedrooms that is typical of this sort of plan, the location of the kitchen at the front and the massing of the walls have resulted in an exterior of fresh and unusual interest.

The kitchen at the front of the house will upset the ideas of a good many people, accustomed as they are to having this room at the back. Others, however, believe that the logical position for this important room is at the front. This permits the bedrooms to be located at the rear, and gives them the pleasant outlook and the quiet and privacy they should undoubtedly have. It also means greater privacy for the garden.

The living room is of good size, light, cheerful and well proportioned. For the sake of economy a fireplace has not been shown in the plan, but this may be built between the windows in the longer wall, or at the end of the room. The dining room is also large, and with its deep bay window should be a delightful place indeed. One unusually long, unbroken wall space will serve admirably as a background for the buffet. A door between dining and living rooms gives privacy to both, and makes a definite distinction between the two areas.

Intercommunication between the rooms is so arranged that it is possible to pass from the kitchen to the dining room and on to the sleeping quarters without going through the living room.

Although the disposition of the kitchen overshadows all other details of the plan, the real stroke of genius on the architect's part is what he did for the exterior. The monotony that might have come from an unrelieved rectangular floor plan, he overcame by the offset along the front kitchen wall and by the projecting bay of the dining room. The offset at the kitchen made possible the setting in of a second gable end, adding interest, life, and vivacity. The front wall being somewhat lower gives an impression of hominess. The roof treatment, nevertheless, is simple and direct, without hips and valleys, thus insuring economy of construction.

The shingle walls of this house are a weathered gray, with ivory trim, the blinds a rich olive green, the roof a blend of various tones of green. Wide siding could also be used for the exterior walls.

A RAMBLING COTTAGE

With features from both the Old World and the New

HOME BUILT FROM DESIGN *5-D-35*

We find in this design much that is reminiscent of the small stucco houses which dot the countryside in both France and England. From such it derives its appealing charm and simplicity, from our own country its efficiency and convenience.

Every detail of the exterior has been planned with an eye to the effectiveness of the whole. This, of course, is as it should be. The sturdy lintels above the doors and windows, the grouping of the windows and the small diamond-shaped leaded glass in those of the dining room, the terra cotta chimney pots, even the down spouts add a bit of beauty to the exterior. As shown in the plan, there is a side gate with a roof top separating the front yard from the service entrance, and this too is in keeping with the cottage-like qualities of the design. In the house illustrated, the drawings have been followed faithfully, so that no iota of charm is lost.

There are innumerable plans for five- and six-room bungalows, but two arrangements in particular have been found most satisfactory, particularly where economies are in order. In one of these arrangements the living quarters of the house are separated from the sleeping quarters and bathroom by the hall that runs down the center from front to back. Thus living room, dining room, and kitchen are arranged on one side, with bedrooms and bath on the other. The second scheme is to have living room, dining room, kitchen in front and two bedrooms in the rear. Both of these are old, well-established plans.

This design is the second of the two schemes described, but its arrangement complies with that formula only in the most general way. Changing the direction of the living room, for example, appears to give an entirely new plan scheme. The arrangement is quite sound. There is the separation between living quarters and the more private quarters of the house which should be possessed by every bungalow.

Undoubtedly the most distinguished feature of this design is the living room with its high ceiling, of which the rafters form a part. This makes possible the use of a large window in the front wall, and adds a sense of luxury at nominal expense. The room is further marked by the arrangement of the bookcases. These have been built at each side of the fireplace in line with the mantel, and with it form a band of decoration across this end of the room. A generous opening at the rear affords an enjoyable view of the garden.

In the dining room is a built-in cabinet, its glass doors divided into small square panes behind which china may be attractively displayed. To its windows, however, the room undoubtedly owes its greatest beauty.

The kitchen opens into the grade entry and also into the hall, which affords direct access to the bedrooms.

Construction: Wood frame, stucco exterior finish, roof of shingles.

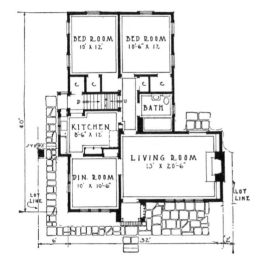

The sketch below shows a side elevation of the house; that at the left is a section through this showing the high-ceilinged living room

The fireplace with its broad, high chimney breast and a line of bookcases at either side decorates one entire end of the room

The simplest kind of stucco house can be made a dwelling of personality and charm through a careful use of color. In these designs it is suggested that the walls be of white rough troweled stucco with roofs of variegated red tile

The close-clipped gables, the severity of line and mass, the tile roofs, and heavy porch posts give these two houses a Spanish mission character. The drawings provide for frame construction under the stucco finish. Design 5-D-41 uses double hung windows; design 5-D-40, casements

DESIGN 5-D-41

A GROUP OF BASEMENTLESS BUNGALOWS

These illustrate one way by which the cost of home building may be most materially reduced

If you are planning to build a home of the most inexpensive type, costing, let us say, not to exceed $4,500, you may be interested to learn that one of the most certain ways to reduce costs is to omit the basement. In this way you may be able to save as much as 15 per cent of your total building cost.

The first cellars in American homes were provided in districts where rigorous winter weather demanded insulation of the first floor against the penetrating cold air. The most feasible method was realized to be the provision of at least a shallow air space beneath this floor and, as excavation was also necessary for foundations, it soon became customary to provide full cellars, which were also found useful for storage and partial refrigeration purposes.

The advent of central heating plants, including hot air, steam, and hot water systems, all coal burning types, was the next step in the establishment of the cellar as a fixed habit in home planning. For the heating plant was located there with the fuel supply.

In recent years the high cost of building materials and labor has forced home builders as well as investment build-

ers to consider ways and means of reducing the cost of building. Rooms have grown smaller, ceiling heights have been lowered, hallways cut down, beds and furniture built in the walls and even the dining room is now being classed as an unnecessary room.

On first thought a cellarless home seems to be a radical departure from the accepted principles of home construction, but this idea is by no means a new one. In fact, the complete basement, which we have installed in most of our modern small homes, is a rather recent development.

It will not do at all to build a cellarless house without taking into consideration matters of ventilating the space underneath and removing the top soil and following out other principles of sound building. When a cellarless house is built as it should be, the results are satisfactory. Often home builders think that a home must have a cellar to be comfortable in every way, but a home built properly without a cellar is dry and warm. Also, since many a fire starts in the basement, where it may gain great headway before it is found, a cellarless house is less in danger from fire than a house with a basement.

DESIGN 5-D-40

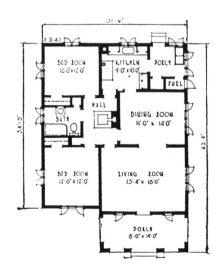

DESIGN 5-D-42

The construction of design 5-D-42 is frame with an exterior finish of stucco. It is suggested that the stucco be worked out with sweeping trowel marks, but not overdone, and that a roof of tile in variegated colors be used

The construction of design 5-D-43 is of frame, exterior finish wide siding—shingles may be used. It is suggested the siding be rough sawn, stained white. The shutters would be effective stained blue-green, with green or variegated shingles for the roof

BOTH STUCCO AND WOOD REPRESENTED

Four bungalows suitable for warm climates which may also be made comfortable for severe climates

A cellarless house also may be beautiful, for being built close to the earth, it hugs the ground and gives an air of shelter and protection. Certainly to the prospective home builder who must build inexpensively, cellarless houses will appeal for their low cost of construction.

As to the necessity of providing a place for the house heater, there are on the market various forms of ground floor heaters which heat five or six rooms comfortably.

It is not intended that these statements shall be of a sweeping nature. The idea of the cellarless house is simply presented for careful thought to those who must build at the least expense. The answer as to whether or not the basement will be used depends very much on the particular case. Certainly it will not be satisfactory to everyone, but before you pay out money for a cellar, prove to yourself first that the cellar is worth what it costs.

The two bungalows opposite and the two on this page are designed for mild climates. They do not have basements and the plans do not provide for them. The heat-

ing plants are located on the first floor. However, basements could be arranged to accommodate central heating plants. In any case, if the walls, floors, and ceilings were thoroughly insulated, as they should be in every home, these houses may be kept warm in cold climates and cool where it is sultry. There is no reason why these bungalows could not be constructed in any section of the country.

Provision has been made in the plans, of course, to accommodate the necessities ordinarily located in the basement. Laundry trays are placed either on the porch or in the kitchen. Each plan shown is adapted to the two exteriors on the page with it, so that for whichever plan best suits him, the home builder has a choice of two exteriors.

These bungalows lack nothing except the basement. In beauty and convenience they are the equal of any homes of their size, and the superior of many. While the rooms are of moderate size, they are large enough for comfort. Larger rooms would mean greater cost of construction, and the purpose of these plans is to save the home builder's money.

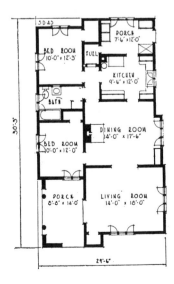

DESIGN 5-D-43

HOME BUILT FROM DESIGN *5-E-1*

BEAUTY WHICH ENDURES

A Colonial bungalow which will outlast passing fads

It is amazing how much the quality of the small house depends upon the little things. The architect works over them with the greatest care so that the result will be fine, and it is hardly possible to pay them too much attention in building. Of course the plan must be right, and the construction sound enough to withstand the elements for years. Without excellence in these matters the house does not have real architectural distinction, but the things which appear to count to an even greater extent are the minor details—the shape and projection of the cornice, the position of the windows, the proportions of the entrance. The whole effect of individuality and architectural excellence may be lost if these details are not carefully studied.

In this Colonial bungalow such details have been worked out accurately. They are combined with a fine plan and substantial construction in such a way that the house may be classified as real architecture.

From the standpoint of everyday living, the plan is still the most important element. Unless this works out well with the way in which the family desires to live, it is better to choose some other arrangement. No matter

how much one might be pleased with the exterior of a house, he should not allow this partiality to overcome his best judgment about the suitability of the plan, for this is the part of the house that has to be lived with day after day.

The plan of the house illustrated above is a model of convenience. Each room is provided with large windows, and light and ventilation there are in plenty. The fireplace in the living room is of brick with a wood mantel and generous hearth. The broad groups of windows which are such a pleasant feature of the exterior also beautify the interior of this room. The wide opening into the dining room frames an attractive view of the room and of the garden beyond.

The kitchen has been planned to provide cupboard space where it will fall most conveniently to hand. Both the sink and the range have been placed to economize steps and labor.

Besides the commodious closets, there is also storage space in the attic. Stairs to both the basement and the attic are accessible directly from the kitchen.

The exterior is Colonial in spirit, a

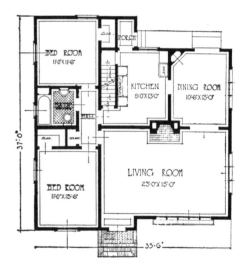

style that outlasts passing fads and fancies of a more spectacular character. Simplicity dominates everywhere, and yet there is an interesting quality about the arched entrance doorway, the proportions and grouping of the windows, the wide shutters, that gives it an air of distinction. The entrance is particularly charming, with the simple trellis at either side and with the glass of the door divided into small lights in the same manner as the windows. Houses of such character are seen too rarely in our residential districts.

The shingled walls should be stained or painted white and the blinds green. Wide siding may also be used as an exterior finish.

HOME BUILT FROM DESIGN 5-E-3

HOMES FOR BOTH CITY AND FARM

Each designed definitely for one location or the other

The bungalow above will be perfectly at home in the city. It owes its attractive appearance to its excellent proportions, well-designed porch, and the size and placing of the windows. It is attention to such details that gives a small home character.

The rectangular plan means economy in building, and also permits excellent room arrangement. Grouping the bedrooms about the hallway gives them highly desirable privacy, a factor not always given sufficient consideration in the one-story house. The fireplace in the living room is the finishing touch to this pleasant room.

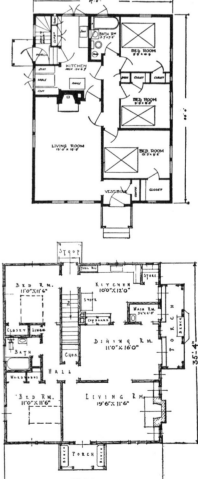

DESIGN 5-E-5

A MODEL FARMHOUSE

This little bungalow has been designed especially for farm use, and with a thorough knowledge of the problems presented by farm life. It includes large kitchen and dining accommodations, storage space for food, wash room, and a bedroom for hired help accessible from the rear entry, all desirable features.

HOME BUILT FROM DESIGN 5-E-4

AN INTIMATE COTTAGE

Its charm lies in its simplicity

Straightforward in design, inexpensive to build, this bungalow is excellent both in plan and in exterior. The walls, openings, and roof are interestingly combined, but these forms are not elaborate in themselves. The living room is 20 feet long, a larger room than ordinarily found in the small and

inexpensive house. The fireplace, shown in the illustration, is tile faced and has a delicately modeled wood mantel.

The plan makes the most of its five major rooms, while a dining alcove and small porch at the rear add greatly to the family's convenience and comfort. In the attic is space for a third bedroom of large size and for much storage space. A stairway from the hall makes this easily accessible. It need not be finished off until funds permit.

The exterior finish may be of shingles, or stucco if preferred.

HOME BUILT FROM DESIGN *5-F-14*

A STYLE FOR THE MODERATE INCOME

Dutch Colonial that bears the approval of generations

The time will come when we will recover from jazz architecture. There are indeed signs of recovery now. The change is marked by the desire for less flashy homes, types in which forms are simpler and little money is lavished on extravagances. The simpler architecture need not be Colonial, by any means. From all of the architectural styles we can develop small houses that are dignified, in which good taste abounds and which will retain these qualities through generations. However, because Colonial architecture has stood the test for so long, it is easy to see that it will continue to hold its own.

In this house we have a splendid example of this style. It also offers further proof of the fact that beauty and economy can go hand in hand, for here almost nothing has been added merely for the sake of appearance. The house is straightforward, without pretense or elaboration. Yet so finely balanced are all the larger parts, and so excellently proportioned are all the smaller ones, that real beauty has resulted. Its fine character is the result of correct proportions

and harmonious details. The cost of these is practically nothing in comparison with the higher resale value they bring to the property and the immense satisfaction the owner will take in his home.

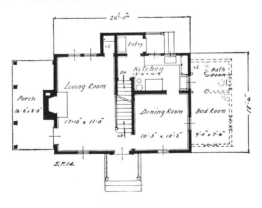

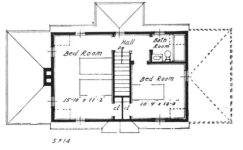

Although this house is small it is really quite roomy, for it has been planned so that no space is wasted. Comfort and convenience have been the aim in planning the rooms. Space has been saved in the overall width of the house by turning the stairway directly into the living room. With the fireplace at one side and the stairway at the other, this room achieves exceptional character. A French door leads to the open porch, which runs the depth of the house. Dining room and kitchen occupy the opposite side of the house.

At the right of the main mass of the house is a suggestion as to how the house may be extended to include a downstairs bedroom and bath or sun porch.

On the second floor are two substantial bedrooms. The corners of these rooms are encroached upon by the roof only to a slight extent.

Careful study of this design will bring out its superior qualities. There is here a refinement in line and mass, and when, as in this design, inexpensiveness goes with distinction the desires of many home builders are met.

DESIGN 5-G-1

FIVE-ROOM CAPE COD COLONIAL

Snuggling close to the ground as though
it had grown up with the trees

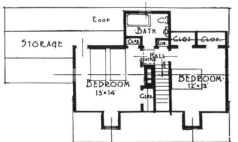

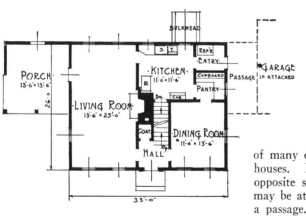

Imagine the charm of this house set in an expanse of green turf with trees about it. No one could pass it without admiration.

The partially enclosed porch at the left suggests the ell of many of the early Cape Cod houses. Balancing this on the opposite side is a garage which may be attached to the house by a passage.

The beauties of this house are not by any means limited to the exterior. Inside we have a plan with most delightful rooms. The arrangement is c o n v e n i e n t. There is no waste space.

The living room is exceptionally large, and recessing the fireplace gives it even more space. A French door leads to the porch. On the other side of the house are dining room, kitchen, and entry.

One likes to think of such a house finished with white clapboards, or with weathered gray shingles and white trim. Either of these schemes would make a lovely background for shutters lively in hue—green, green-blue, or perhaps golden brown. If the finish is as suggested above, the chimney would be charming painted white with a black band at the top.

DESIGN *5-G-2*

A COTTAGE WITH TWO BAY WINDOWS

*One lights the living room, one the dining alcove. The downstairs
bedroom with lavatory meets many home builders' needs*

The exterior of this charming cottage, with its finely modeled walls, roof, and openings, carries its own recommendation. The interior shows good planning. The central stair hall gives access from the front door to all quarters of the house. The dining alcove is large enough for table and chairs. Set in a bay window, it will be an agreeable place in which to dine.

The porch, which may be placed at the left side, or omitted, would have access from the living room through French doors in place of the window shown on the plan.

Construction: Wood frame, exterior finish stucco, rough siding on gable ends, shingle roof.

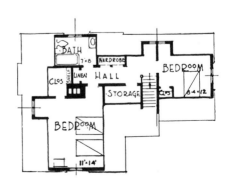

The living room is beautified with a well-chosen mantelpiece over the fireplace, with book shelves at one side of the mantel, with a broad window at one end, and with a graceful bay window in front

DESIGN 5-H-4

WHERE FIRST COSTS WILL BE LAST

*At least for a long time, perhaps long after
the home is paid for*

For those of us who must, as it were, keep a watchful eye on the right-hand side of the menu when ordering a home, design 5-H-4 offers many advantages. Economies there are in plenty, but without sacrificing anything in the appearance of the exterior or in the comfort and livableness of the interior. Houses which one can afford, which are really within one's means, are more often than not poorly constructed, cheap in appearance. Any economy in the original cost is more than made up for in constantly recurring bills for repairs and replacements.

Not so 5-H-4. In the first place, it is made of texture face hollow tile. This we might almost call an all-in-one building material. No facing is required, as the tile comes in a wide range of colors and textures. The plans also call for a slate roof, so the house adds fire resistance to its other desirable features.

Well-designed lattice work and a simple balustrade about the porch, the window box beneath the front windows, and the curving brackets which support the little canopy over the side

entrance, all add a decorative note to the appearance of the house without requiring any considerable outlay. Double hung windows divided into small lights have been used. Such windows add immeasurably to the

charm of a small, inexpensive house.

The plan is simple and compact with none of the built-on and built-out features which may appear picturesque, but which always add so materially to the cost. Yet nothing has been omitted which might make the house more pleasant and livable. The rooms are of good size, the windows are numerous and well placed. The fireplace in the living room is distinctive in that it is designed for surfaced tile.

There is a plaster arch between the living room and dining room. At one side of the entrance to the dining room is a roomy built-in china closet.

The kitchen is a long room, well arranged for work. The sink, with double drain boards, is located close beside the window, therefore well lighted and ventilated. Above it are shelves for dishes, and another built-in cupboard is located against the opposite wall. In the back entry there are also shelves, so storage space is adequate.

The bedrooms, identical in size and shape, are pleasant rooms large enough for twin beds.

DESIGN 5-H-5

BEAUTY IN MASONRY WALLS

*This house has a fine, large living room
with views on three sides*

For a house comparatively small in area this offers an enormous amount of usable floor space, while considering its textured masonry construction the cost is by no means prohibitive. This is explained in the compact square plan, always the least expensive, and by the material of which it is built.

This material is a modern structural tile which offers all the benefits of hollow tile construction. It is supplied in a variety of colors and textures, making possible many beautiful effects. No facing is necessary, a saving in labor and material. The roof is of slate, although it may be of shingles.

The method of handling the fireplace is shown in the sketch. On occasion the rear portion of the living room may be used for dining. Making this one large room affords a maximum of beauty and interest to the living room, while by no means eliminating the utilitarian purpose of the dining room. A dining alcove serves ordinarily, a desirable economy in labor.

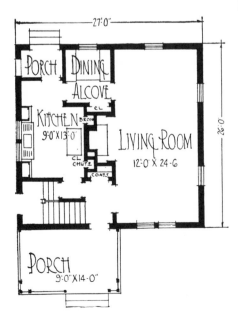

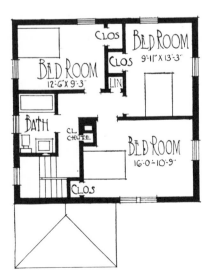

DESIGN 5-K-17

CONCRETE FROM FOOTINGS TO ROOF

*The exterior is in the English manner with
close-clipped eaves and peaked roof*

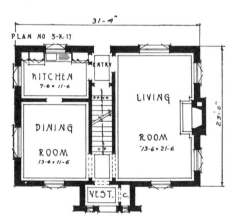

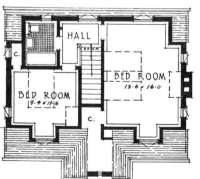

The foundations and walls of this house are of concrete blocks, the exterior is finished with cement stucco, and the roof covered with cement asbestos shingles. In addition, the home owner may choose between having the first floor a reinforced concrete slab finished with the usual floor coverings, wood or linoleum, or having it the standard wooden joist construction. The cross walls of the basement are of concrete masonry. The window sills are of precast masonry. Reinforced concrete beams span the windows, which are metal casements.

The fire-safeness of the house will appeal to many. The furred exterior walls will be dry and warm.

A view of one of the bedrooms which shows the effect of a dormer window—an attractive feature not only of the exterior but of the interior as well

DESIGN 5-K-18

FORMALITY TEMPERED BY NICETY OF DETAIL

*Here is a house not only distinguished in appearance
but commodious in plan*

For usefulness of space and economy of construction the center hall plan is difficult to improve upon for the small house. As shown here, the rooms are of generous size with excellent wall spaces. With the living room extending from front to back, as in this case, the most is made of views at both front and rear.

The stair hall is eight feet wide. Separated from the other rooms by plaster arches, it gives the house a desirable breadth of floor space from side to side.

Construction: Exterior walls concrete masonry, stucco finish; roof of cement shingle tile; first floor slab of reinforced concrete, wood finish.

A view of the living room showing the fireplace, with cast stone trim and brick in pleasant combination. Four windows, two of them shown, light the room

DESIGN *5-K-19*

ROMANCE AND SOUND ARCHITECTURE

A combination rarely found in small houses

French doors lead from dining room and living room to the patio. Over this gay canopies may be arranged

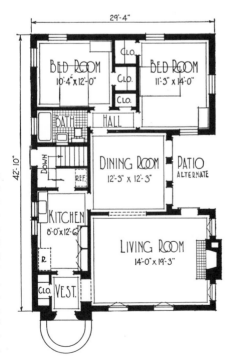

Out in California people have built countless attractive little homes, full of sunshine, light and airy. Many of them are bungalows. They have brought a new meaning to the term. Happily a great many of the qualities they have wrought into these little houses are just as suitable for more rigorous climates.

Design 5-K-19 shown here is in the California manner, picturesque, a little gay, and including in a sound architectural way some of the romance that marks the modern small home.

The character of the architecture is determined by the plan itself and is delightfully carried out. The forms are simple and straightforward to keep down the cost of construction, yet there is a decorative quality to the whole that will not be missed. The illustrations here cannot show the interesting color effects that are obtainable—textured wall surfaces, tile on the roof, and heavy wooden shutters at the windows.

The construction is of concrete masonry, the exterior finish stucco, casement windows either steel or frame.

DESIGN 5-K-20

MASONRY—SYMBOL OF QUALITY

This house will make a host of friends

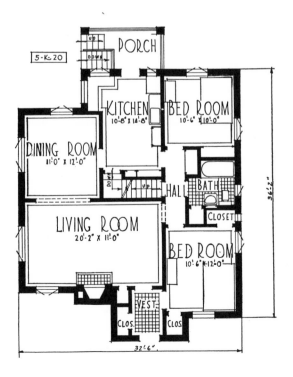

There are still some people who, not knowing what the architect can do for them, think they can get along without him in their home building. This house, design 5-K-20, illustrates eloquently why they cannot. The beauty of the exterior and the convenience of the floor plan represent many hours of study and planning by the architect. In order to achieve these qualities in the house, the drawings must be followed carefully. The sketch shows the effective treatment of the fireplace with its ornamental cast stone trim.

The construction of the exterior walls is of concrete masonry, with stucco finish, field stone trim and brick chimney stack. The roof is of cement asbestos shingles and the floor of concrete with wood finish. Other materials may be used for either roof or floor.

DESIGN 5-K-16

GRACEFUL COTTAGE OF GOOD PROPORTIONS

*To be built with concrete masonry walls with one of the
attractive stucco finishes available today*

Five-room bungalows have long deserved wide popularity. They are economical to build, give much accommodation, and are in better scale with the cottage idea than bungalows of larger size, which necessarily must spread out more extensively.

The home builder will wisely consider all the details of the plan, noting the way the rooms are arranged, the large number of windows, the amount of wall space, and the equipment afforded. In this way only can he visualize the particular advantages of this house.

Taking up each room by itself, we find first of all the vestibule. Here is a lavatory, which, though extremely convenient, may be omitted if necessary to economize. Immediately beyond the vestibule, in the living room, is a coat closet. The living room, 20 feet long and 14 feet wide, is of good size. The uninterrupted wall spaces are ample for large pieces of furniture. At one end is a handsome fireplace, flanked on both sides by bookcases. At the front is a broad window opening with four casement sash.

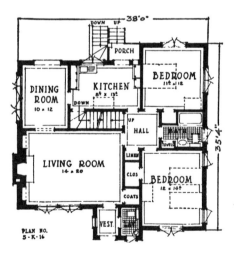

PLAN NO. 5-K-16

Through a plaster arch we pass into the dining room. This room is 10 feet wide, 12 feet long, and is bountifully lighted with four casement sash along the side and with French doors opening to the garden terrace at the rear.

A swinging door opens directly into the kitchen, which is equipped in modern style for greatest efficiency. Immediately inside the door is the china

closet. Below are drawers for cutlery and below these bins for food. Immediately at the right is the sink. This is placed directly under broad casement windows, insuring for the working center excellent lighting and a minimum amount of moving about for the person who must work here.

Passing from the kitchen to the bedroom hall we find at the front a bedroom 12 by 14 feet, in which may be accommodated twin beds. Three window openings light and ventilate this room and there is a generous closet.

To the rear is the bathroom with a recess tub, towel closet and the other usual fixtures. The rear bedroom is also of good size, with broad windows to insure cross ventilation.

The exterior speaks for itself. It is gracefully designed, beautifully proportioned, having the qualities of concrete masonry for which it was designed. These include clean-cut lines and forms. The contrast of color between walls and roof, the interesting texture of both give it lasting beauty.

Construction: Exterior walls of concrete, stucco finish, tile or slate roof.

DESIGN 5-K-21

A HOUSE WITHOUT EXPENSIVE HABITS

Its masonry construction insures fire-safeness, permanence, and low depreciation, with a minimum of expense for upkeep

The design of this house speaks for itself. The illustration above and the drawing of the doorway show it a design not subject to changing taste. Fifty years from now it will be in as good taste as today. The plan is equally fine.

Note particularly the downstairs lavatory, the well-arranged kitchen, fine closet space in the bedrooms, and the convenient sewing or dressing room opening from the smaller bedroom. A closet bed can easily be accommodated in the smaller bedroom.

Construction: Exterior walls concrete masonry, stucco finish. Roof of cement asbestos shingles.

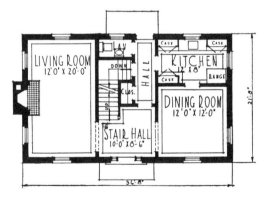

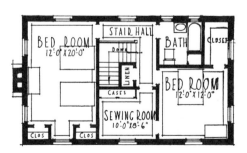

The beautiful doorway opposite is in the Georgian style, handsomely trimmed in cast stone with wrought iron balustrade and lamp

DESIGN *6-A-2*

VIVIDNESS IN WHITE STUCCO AND RED TILE

The exterior walls are of hollow tile construction

FIRST FLOOR

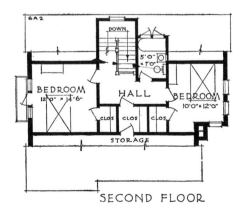

SECOND FLOOR

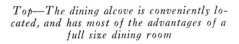

Dining alcove, balcony, arched openings—a few of the inexpensive details that contribute to the fine appearance of design 6-A-2

Top—The dining alcove is conveniently located, and has most of the advantages of a full size dining room

The richly colored tile roof, the recessed porch, the iron balcony are only a few of the picturesque features

Spanish mission style is suggested rather than literally followed. This makes it a home suitable for almost any section

The simplicity of the Colonial house was relieved chiefly by its decorative entrance.   On this was lavished all the knowledge and skill of the designers of that period, and it was ordinarily as ornamental and beautiful as the owner could afford.   Above is a fine modern entrance done in the same spirit.   Delicate fluted pilasters, paneled door, and a graceful pediment broken by a slatted fan light recall the houses of yesterday

HOME BUILT FROM DESIGN *6-A-5*

LONG, LOW LINES AND PLEASANT PORCHES

The cornice line ties the various parts of this design together

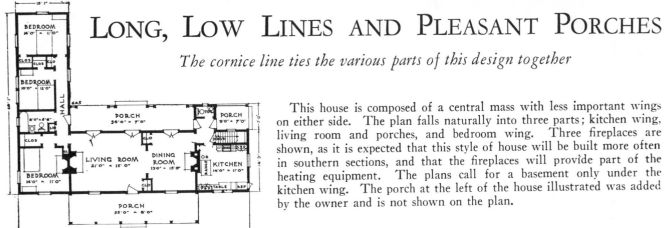

This house is composed of a central mass with less important wings on either side. The plan falls naturally into three parts; kitchen wing, living room and porches, and bedroom wing. Three fireplaces are shown, as it is expected that this style of house will be built more often in southern sections, and that the fireplaces will provide part of the heating equipment. The plans call for a basement only under the kitchen wing. The porch at the left of the house illustrated was added by the owner and is not shown on the plan.

DESIGN *6-A-5*

OPEN AND AIRY ROOMS

A cottage which permits the outdoors to come in

This bungalow of English antecedents has three bedrooms, sleeping porch, living room, sun room, dining room, kitchen, many closets and a bath, all on one floor. In addition it has a generous, well-lighted and ventilated attic reached from the hall. Plans provide for a partial basement.

A pleasing feature of the exterior is the brick terrace before the house. Both vestibule and sun room open on this terrace, and a hospitable seat is placed against the wall. The cheerful, sunny interior is a delightful place. Sun room and living room are arranged to count as practically one great room. While this bungalow offers splendid accommodations, its simplicity should keep it reasonable in cost.

Construction: Wood frame with stucco finish, shingle roof. In the sleeping porch and sun room siding is used up to the window sills. Drawings for the same design in brick rowlock construction may be obtained. The number of the brick design is 6-A-93.

HOME BUILT FROM DESIGN *6-A-11*

SHOWING WHAT CAN BE DONE WITH BRICK

A beautiful exterior which in no way belies its delightful interior

There should be no difficulty in realizing that a story and a half house, for the amount of room enclosed within the walls, is less expensive to build than a bungalow of the same accommodations. The story and a half house has just one-half as much foundation wall, basement and roof as would be necessary for a bungalow of the same size. Both are popular but the man looking for economy in building will do well to study the advantages of the story and a half house.

Bedroom ceilings will be cut off, to be sure, but in the house that is skilfully designed there is always sufficient head room at the wall line so that there is no interference with furniture. The cut-off ceilings give these rooms a quaint, old-fashioned air that is charming and restful, more so, oftentimes, than that of rooms with level ceilings.

This six-room house is practically a bungalow as far as the first floor plan goes, but under the roof it has two bedrooms and bath, giving it three bedrooms in all. A feature of the plan is the first floor bedroom and lavatory. This bedroom is an attractive place with windows on two sides and two

closets so arranged that a mirror or dressing table can be placed in the wall space between. The one-story wing at the left in the house illustrated was added by the owner and is not shown on the plans.

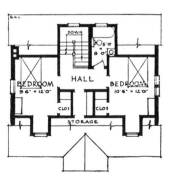

Living and dining rooms are really one large room, separated by a wide opening that can be square-cased or arched or provided with double French doors. In a small home this arrangement has many advantages, for it gives a long uninterrupted space across the front that is ideal for entertaining purposes. A fireplace may be built at the end or on the inside wall of the living room. One has been added in the house shown above, and chimneys at either end of the house carry still further the perfect balance which is so essentially a part of the design and which gives it such a restful quality.

This is a compact, economical, and livable interior with a very trim exterior. Looking at the house from the outside, one's attention centers upon the attractive entrance vestibule, with its pointed roof and rounded doorway set off by patterned brickwork. The wrought-iron side lights, the partially glazed door and transom, are in keeping with a certain quaint trimness, which is further heightened by the solid shutters at the windows.

Construction: Brick veneer on wood frame, roof of slate or shingles.

HOME BUILT FROM DESIGN *6-A-17*

A STANDARD OF GOOD TASTE

Containing maximum equipment within a minimum of space

With shade trees, a well-kept grass plot, and colorful flower gardens as a setting, this dignified Colonial home will appear to advantage in practically any section of the country. Outwardly it differs little, if any, from the accepted Colonial pattern which has been popular in this country for nearly three hundred years. The interior, however, with its numerous conveniences and fine room arrangement, shows the hand of the skilled modern designer.

Early Colonial houses were for the most part built of wood, though brick and, to some extent, stone were also used. This home follows the Colonial tradition of frame construction, having wide bevel siding, shingle roof, brick base, and brick chimneys. The windows are double hung except those in the dining room bay, which are of the casement type.

The graceful, hooded Colonial entrance shelters a small vestibule with coat closets on either side of the door. The plans provide for another less elaborate treatment of this entrance. There is also an alternate detail for glazing the porch.

The house has really two living

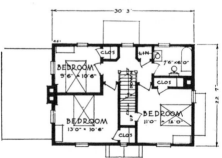

rooms, for the wide, roomy porch will be used extensively in the summertime. French doors open onto it from the living room. The living room is not darkened perceptibly by the porch, for it has windows at both ends as well as on the porch. A finely proportioned

Colonial fireplace of b r i c k with wood trim ornaments this room. Opposite the fireplace is an alcove eight feet long with lights on either side, thus providing a splendid location for piano or lounge.

In the dining room bay is a specially built-in buffet above which are three short casement windows. The kitchen is well lighted and carefully planned to route steps, lessen labor, lighten housekeeping. In the rear entry is a broom closet and niche for the ice box, with provision made for an outside icing door. The basement stairs lead directly down from this entry.

All bedrooms have corner exposure, each with a closet and windows on two sides. Attic storage space is reached by stairs leading from the closet in the right-hand front bedroom. The second story rooms are of full height, not clipped by the rafters as is common.

This is a home that will give one full value for the money spent, for its rectangular plan and ridge roof make it economical to build. It is a home, too, that will remain in style for years and one that will therefore have a good resale value.

HOME BUILT FROM DESIGN *6-A-18*

WITH FRONT PORCH AND SLEEPING PORCH

In spite of the long, sloping roof there are two full stories

If no one will take it seriously, we will call this a Dutch Colonial home. No other way of describing it will do so well. Even so, it isn't Dutch and it isn't Colonial, but it is clearly modern American. A better label to give it would be "A House with a Front Porch." This is a good definition because houses of that type bear a character which distinguishes them. They have become something of a rarity. Now that you think about it, how many generous front porches have you seen built in recent years?

Probably one of the important reasons for the vanishing of the front porch has been its cost. There are others. One is the automobile. But for many a home lover a front porch is the outdoor living room of the house, and is just as important a part of the scheme of living as any other department in the house proper. Much has been written about the necessity of making the porch belong to the house, and here it will be seen that this principle has been kept in mind and the porch handled with expert nicety. The porch floor may be paved with tile or brick, or less expensively finished in cement.

As for the plan of the house, it is

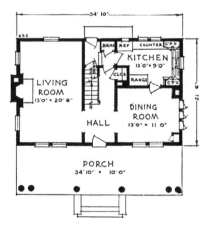

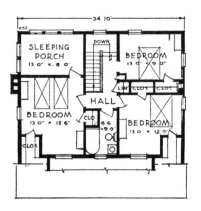

the kind known as the central hallway type. The house is divided by this center hall, from which the stair to the second story arises. On one side is the living room, on the other a dining room and kitchen. The hall serves many uses. It provides direct communication between kitchen and front door. In summer it insures good circulation, making the house cool and fresh. It gives a pleasant air of spaciousness to the house. A full basement is provided.

In the second story are three large bedrooms and a fourth area to be used as a sleeping porch. The latter is large enough to accommodate four or five standard cots. This may be reached, if desired, from the landing of the stairway.

The shape of the roof and the broad dormer are responsible for giving this house its Dutch Colonial classification. The way in which the roof comes on gives the appearance of cutting into the second story rooms, but this it does not do. The sleeping porch and bedrooms at the rear are full story in height. The bedrooms in front are also constructed in this way, but in order to make this possible large closet spaces have been arranged at the sides of the dormer.

HOME BUILT FROM DESIGN *6-A-20*

A PLAN OF THE CENTER STAIRWAY TYPE

This permits worth-while economies in construction and generous rooms

Styles in houses come and go—most of them go. When they go their market worth goes down. Everyone is familiar with well-built old houses of twenty-five or thirty years past. They are not wanted, principally because they do not look well. Yet there are a few houses many times as old as these that still command a high resale value and are treasured as examples of fine architecture. The passing fancies in small houses are expensive luxuries for the home builder whose funds are limited.

The house illustrated above is of a type that has stood the test of time for scores of years. While it cannot accurately be called Dutch Colonial, it is yet reminiscent of the homes of the old Dutch colonists. The rooms on the second floor of their homes were distinctly attic rooms, with low sloping ceilings, and windows only in the end wall. Here, however, we have what is essentially a full two-story house. Only the corners of the upstairs rooms are cut away by the roof, and dormer windows, a modern solution to the lighting problem, make the bedrooms bright and cheerful.

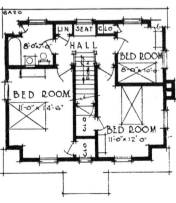

Here, as in all good architecture, the plan has been given first consideration. The problem, of course, was to get the greatest amount of livable space into the house. On looking over the plan you will find this has been accomplished. There is no waste hall space, every foot of floor area is useful. The plan is a really fine example of the typical servantless American home, where convenience is of first importance to the housewife. The kitchen is efficiently planned to save steps; very desirable as to size so that sink, cupboards, and working space on one wall are easily accessible to range and refrigerator.

The living room with its large windows and Colonial style fireplace will be an attractive gathering place for the family.

On the second floor are two fine bedrooms. The third, although not so generous in size, is still a corner room with cross ventilation. Closets and window seat along the outside wall of the hall eliminate all waste space in this area. The drawings provide for a porch at side or rear, which may be added if desired.

HOME BUILT FROM DESIGN *6-A-43*

MODIFIED PENNSYLVANIA COLONIAL

Compact in plan, attractive as to exterior, reasonable in building costs

Luxurious economy. At first sight these two words appear to conflict, and the ideas they convey seem as far apart as the north and south poles. Today, however, modern mechanical genius and human daring are lessening the inaccessibility of the poles, while modern planning is bringing a luxury of convenience to the modern small, economical-to-build home that was undreamed of a few years ago.

This six-room home was primarily designed for economy of construction, and to give the home builder a great deal of house for his money. A study of the floor plans will reveal that comfort and even luxury have been provided generously.

One real luxury is the sense of roominess. By that we do not mean a reckless and extravagant use of space, but the fact that, through careful planning, there is everywhere plenty of elbow room. Particularly is this true of the living room. No space has been taken off for a stair hall, for the open stairway leads directly from one end of the room. This becomes, then, a part of the decoration of the room. The fireplace might be classed as a luxury.

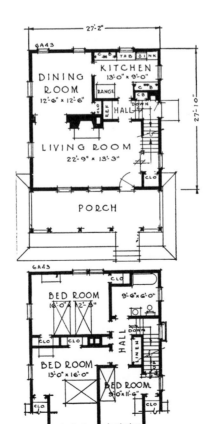

We can get along without it, but few of us want to.

As to closets, there are enough in this house to satisfy any housewife. There is a coat closet on the stair landing, a china closet in the dining room, in the side entry a special closet for brooms and cleaning material. Two bedrooms have two closets each, and on this floor also is a broom closet. The linen closet is of exceptional capacity; two feet deep and over five feet long, it has four adjustable shelves above and five drawers below. A stairway from the third bedroom leads to the attic where storage space is available.

The photograph shows the exterior so well it hardly needs more than a word or two. Of frame construction, the exterior finish may be shingles, siding or stucco as preferred. The style is a modified Pennsylvania Colonial, of plain, straightforward, simple construction. Common materials are assembled uncommonly well, and the result is a home of good taste and good values. As an essential feature of the design, the front porch avoids the appearance of being stuck on, which characterizes many less well planned.

DESIGN *6-A-37*

A HOME OF NEW ENGLAND ANCESTRY

*A square plan and inexpensive forms keep
building costs comparatively low*

This house is a monument to the common sense of the American home builder. It is one of the most popular small house plans, and justifiably so, because it is expertly designed and economical to build. If the plans the architect has made are followed faithfully, good architecture results, giving the home builder substantial reason for happiness in the comfort, fine appearance, and sound construction of his home.

The first floor plan is remarkable in that it contains practically no unused areas. There are no wasteful halls or other extravagances of planning, yet the rooms are of good size and their arrangement is such that the greatest convenience is obtained.

The porch at the side may be inclosed. It is even possible to put a sleeping porch above it if necessary.

The kitchen will reward study. Here sink, cupboard, work table, range, and refrigerator are so placed as to minimize a housekeeper's work. The

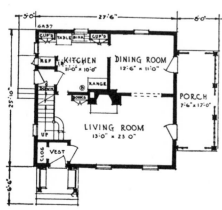

The working drawings show several different types of entrances for the home builder's choice. The houses opposite show two of these entrances on homes built from this design

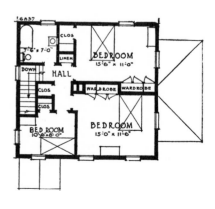

The entrance porch is in keeping with the side porch

dotted lines show where the ironing board may be hung. A dining alcove may be arranged in the space now occupied by the refrigerator and cupboard at the left of the kitchen.

In the second story are three excellent bedrooms, two of them much more commodious than usual for a house of this size. There are six closets, two of these being of the wardrobe type, but, if desired, these may be made into ordinary closets. A stairway can be arranged from the front bedroom or from the front hall to give access to the attic for additional storage space.

The architecture of this house is of the New England type. All the details—cornice, porch, doors, blinds, and the design of the windows—have been skillfully worked out so as to keep the spirit of the old architecture.

Here the entrance shown in the perspective drawing has been used

HOME BUILT FROM DESIGN *6-A-41*

TWO STORIES AND AN ATTIC

With an exterior somewhat English

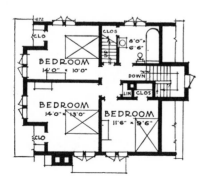

This combination of hooded bay window and flanking chimney is picturesque, after the English manner. A built-in seat nestles comfortably into the chimney corner. The porch may be glazed or else enclosed as part of the living room, both methods being illustrated. As the photographs show, either stucco or shingles may be used as an exterior finish. Both were built reversed from the plans. Construction: Wood frame.

The interiors shown here are found in the house at the top of the opposite page. Like the exterior, the arrangement and plan of the interior departs somewhat from that of the ordinary six-room house.

The recessed window with the wide arch above adds greatly to the beauty of the living room. Low radiators are concealed beneath the window seat. Fireplace and hearth are of small hand-made tiles, with here and there a patterned tile. The closed door leads to a big coat closet, and beyond is the entrance.

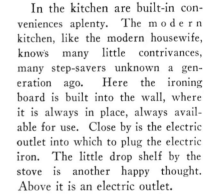

In the kitchen are built-in conveniences aplenty. The modern kitchen, like the modern housewife, knows many little contrivances, many step-savers unknown a generation ago. Here the ironing board is built into the wall, where it is always in place, always available for use. Close by is the electric outlet into which to plug the electric iron. The little drop shelf by the stove is another happy thought. Above it is an electric outlet.

Below is the graceful open stairway which leads from one end of the living room. The woodwork is birch with ivory finish. Stair rail and treads are mahogany finished. As these illustrations show, finely finished woodwork adds immeasurably to the charm of an interior.

The attractive built-in corner cupboard above was not part of the original plan. It was selected from stock mill work. Beside it are the French doors leading to the large porch which the owner added at the side of the house. All the moldings, doors, and window casings are of the simplest.

Home Built from Design 6-A-45

A Colonial Home That Bespeaks Hospitality

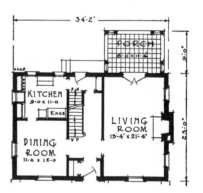

This is a beautiful example of the Colonial style carried out in the small home of brick. It would be hard indeed to find one more satisfactory either in plan or design in a house of similar size. The fine old trees on the lot were carefully preserved during construction, so that the house, although comparatively new, appears mellowed and softened, an effect seldom obtained until after many years.

A graceful broken pediment adorns the front entrance, iron grilles fence the brick steps, and the windows have long, quaint blinds with slats below and solid wood above. While the house retains the exterior charm of the early Colonial dwelling, the interior provides those modern improvements which make home keeping more enjoyable.

The fine appearance of this house is fundamentally dependent on such details as the proportion of the walls and roof, the window spacing, the width of the eaves, the moldings, the entrance, and the height of the first floor above the finish grade. Any deviation from the drawings in these respects is almost certain to have a bad result. The windows are divided into small lights by narrow muntins, which give interest and scale to the exterior.

Above: Wide archways throw living room, dining room, and stair hall together, thereby creating the effect of spaciousness. The beautiful open stairway is typically Colonial

Right: French doors at one end of the living room lead to the large screened porch beyond. The woodwork throughout the house is finished in ivory

Below: The living room is large and well proportioned. The fireplace, like other details of the interior, follows carefully the best Colonial architectural traditions

The second story windows across the front, it will be noticed, break through the cornice line and form small dormers. This is an interesting treatment, but if, in the interests of economy, it is desired to raise the cornice line above the tops of the windows so that the roof will be unbroken, the working drawings show how this may be done. When this arrangement is carried out, the second story windows should be equipped with shutters.

Refinement of detail is of prime importance on the exterior. It is equally so on the interior, as the views on this page show. The plan offers large accommodations.

This house has been planned to take advantage of all reasonable economies in construction, the use of sound building methods with stock materials.

Construction: Brick veneer on wood frame, slate or shingle roof.

DESIGN 6-A-46

SIX MAJOR ROOMS AND ANOTHER

*A Colonial home which adds to its ordinary accommodations a
dining nook and a sewing room*

Do the majority of home builders give first consideration to appearance and cost? Real estate men claim they do, but should not the plan be given equal, if not first, consideration in selecting a design? It is conceivable that one could live comfortably in a homely house that had an excellent plan, while it might be most irritating to live in a poorly planned house no matter how charming the exterior.

This house has been carefully designed to give it as attractive an exterior as possible considering its reasonable building cost. It is almost square in plan, which means economies in building, and the details have been kept unpretentious yet refined.

The economy of the square plan is continually stressed in this book, and it might be well to explain why. Plans for a square house are always more simple, more easily understood and read. In building there is a larger number of parts uniform in size. Although these things seem unimportant, they show up clearly in the final cost of a house. Every home, no matter how small, is a combination of many hundreds of

items. Each must be listed in size and quality and appear in the plans and specifications. It is easy to see that the simpler the house the less work is required, not only in building but in "taking off" the items and measurements by all the workmen employed on the job.

Perhaps the most potent factor in lower cost for the square house lies in the labor bill. When the contractor sees a plan all turns and angles, he knows that his mechanics must also do much turning and angling. There will be measuring, cutting, fitting, and adjusting of parts. This takes time, costs money. If you are interested in keeping down building costs, it is worth while to follow the square plan. Here the shutters relieve what might otherwise seem a severity of exterior.

Among the conveniences here we find a breakfast nook in the kitchen, sewing room on the second floor, clothes chute, built-in bookcases, ample closet and cupboard space. A stairway from a front bedroom leads to the attic. Construction: Wood frame; siding, shingle or stucco exterior.

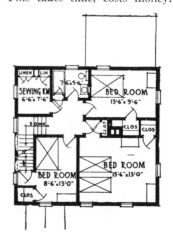

HOME BUILT FROM DESIGN *6-A-48*

A DISTINCTIVE STORY-AND-A-HALF HOUSE

A downstairs bedroom makes it possible to finish the second floor
when this becomes convenient

Homelike in appearance, convenient in plan, here is a house that offers real accommodations at a reasonably low price. If funds are limited, there are a number of ways in which the cost of building may be reduced. A bathroom can be made of the first floor lavatory, and the second story left unfinished for a time. The porch may be screened instead of glazed, left open, or omitted entirely.

The lavatory is so placed with respect to the bedroom and all other rooms of the first floor that it is not necessary to pass from one room through another to reach it.

The dining room and living room are separated by a wide arched opening which makes of them practically one large room. The fireplace, situated at the end of the living room, can be enjoyed from both rooms. French doors on either side lead to the sun room. In the kitchen a built-in seat with a table before it serves as a breakfast nook.

On the second floor are two good bedrooms, one with wall space for twin beds. This room, in addition to a large closet, has immense storage space under the eaves. The shape of these bedrooms offers possibilities for attractive furnishing. The location of the stairs at the rear has made it possible to reduce hall space to a minimum on both floors, an important consideration in the small house.

Wide siding, shingles or stucco may be used as an exterior finish.

HOME BUILT FROM DESIGN *6-A-50*

DUTCH COLONIAL OF FRAME CONSTRUCTION

A sewing room on the second floor solves many problems for the
busy housewife

If you are interested in building a small home and at the same time enjoying a large amount of accommodation, you will be enthusiastic about this Dutch Colonial home. As far as possible stock materials are used throughout, thus reducing building costs.

There are three bedrooms, each with cross ventilation and its own individual closet. The attic is reached by stairs leading from the smaller front bedroom. The sewing room is a useful addition to the house. Every housekeeper likes to have a little room set apart for her sewing, where she can leave her work undisturbed and go back to it next day just where she left off. There are built-in cupboards along one wall so that sewing materials can be put away if desired.

On the kitchen plan you will observe in one corner provision for a breakfast alcove—a convenient built-in seat in one corner to which a table may be drawn up. In the side entry

there is a big closet. In the doorway between the living room and dining room are built-in cupboards affording storage for books, china, or phonograph records.

Perhaps you like the plan of this design, but prefer a full two-story exterior instead. In that case you may find in design 6-A-46 what you desire. That design has a New England Colonial exterior, but the plan is nearly identical with that shown here.

If the porch is placed at the rear as indicated, a 40-foot lot will be sufficient. If it is placed at the side, a 50-foot lot will be required. This increase in the breadth of the house gives it a fine appearance. The exterior finish may be siding or shingles.

The second floor porch as shown is merely an uncovered balcony. This space, however, might be more usefully employed as a sleeping porch. This, together with an enclosed sun porch on the first floor, would greatly increase the livable area of the house.

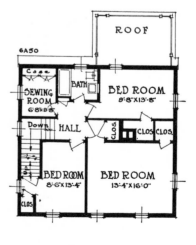

HOME BUILT FROM DESIGN *6-A-51*

IN THE ENGLISH MANNER—FOR A NARROW LOT

*Rooms which may be shut off from one another, a large porch, and
numerous closets distinguish this house*

Again the narrow lot comes into its own. Build upon it a house such as this, and its lack of width ceases to be a fault and becomes almost a virtue. While this house is only 22 feet wide—suitable for a 30-foot lot—it contains within its four walls the comfort, convenience, livability and charm that grace the successful home of far larger size. Besides its narrow width, it is of all masonry construction, which makes it still more suitable for a closely built-up neighborhood.

The narrow hood above the group of windows in front, the recessed entrance, t h e long slope of the roof and the twin gables at the side are picturesque details which have been skillfully combined to produce a house of distinguished appearance.

As the plans show, there are six fine rooms, a dining alcove, bath, and porch. If a sleeping porch is desired, this can readily be added above the porch at the rear, where it will have all possible privacy and quiet.

The living room, although not extremely large, has many features to recommend it. It

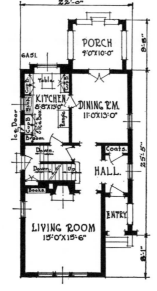

has windows on two sides, including the broad group of three at the front, and an attractive brick fireplace. The fact that it can be shut off from the remainder of the house makes it all the more desirable. The doorway to the hall is balanced by a recess of similar size and shape on the other side of the fireplace, this containing shelves for books.

French doors lead from the dining room to the open porch beyond. In the kitchen we find an exceptional amount of cupboard space, the room itself being as conveniently arranged as science and skill could make it. For the large front bedroom on the second floor, the plans give an alternate arrangement of the closet at the right, showing a closet bed installed.

This makes it possible to use this room for other purposes also; as a study or an upstairs library or sitting room. Having windows on three sides as it does, the room is a particularly bright, cheerful place, admirably suited for such uses. The o t h e r bedrooms, although smaller, are of comfortable size.

Construction: t i l e walls, stucco finish.

DESIGN 6-A-49

FOR A VERY WIDE OR VERY NARROW LOT

*Skillful handling of the design makes the house appear
to be larger than it really is*

This house may be placed on lots of various widths and facings. If the broad side is next to the street, as shown in the illustration, it will require a wide lot, at least 60 feet frontage. If the porch is placed in the alternate location at the end of the living room, the lot may be 10 feet narrower. But best of all, it has been especially designed for a narrow lot, 35 feet or slightly less in width, by placing the narrow end toward the street.

The windows are arranged in an informal manner that lends variety and interest to the exterior. The entire house, plan and exterior, should appeal to the home builder looking for a six-room house with marked individuality, one that will stand apart from others in the neighborhood because of its distinguished design.

On the second floor there are three bedrooms, a bath room, a linen closet, and an extra closet in the hall for vacuum cleaner or household supplies. Each bedroom has two closets. The smaller corner bedroom has a charming little built-in seat between the two closets.

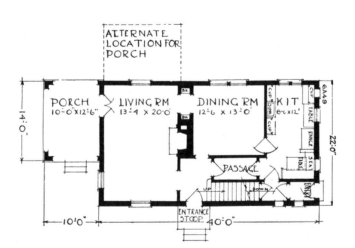

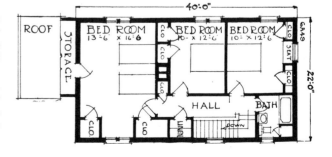

The entrance at the side leads to a small hall, on which open the stairs, living room, dining room, and passageway to the kitchen. This passageway will also serve as a coat closet and storage space.

In the kitchen is a built-in seat before which a table is drawn up for meals or work. Ample cupboard space is provided.

Construction: Brick veneer over frame; roof of shingles or slate.

DESIGN *6-A-53*

SUGGESTIVE OF NEW ENGLAND COLONIAL

*Six big rooms, a broad porch, and two closets for each bedroom
make it suitable for the larger family*

Ordinarily we think of a house in the New England Colonial style as being perfectly symmetrical, with similar windows equally spaced on either side of the center door and a hall in the exact center of the house. That this is not necessarily true, however, is shown by the house presented here. While it is unmistakably reminiscent of New England homes, it is also unsymmetrical.

A study of the first floor plan shows that it would be practically impossible to plan a house with greater privacy for all rooms. A hall gives direct communication between the kitchen and the front of the house.

At either side of the wide archway between living room and dining room are narrow built-in bookcases. These could also be used for china. The fireplace is of brick, with an attractive wood mantel.

The kitchen is amply supplied with built-in conveniences. The refrigerator stands under a cupboard in one corner, where provision is made for an outside icing door. One end of the

room serves as a breakfast alcove.

On the second floor there are three bedrooms, a bath, linen closet, and an extra closet which will be useful for storage. There are in all eight closets on this floor. In two of the bedrooms the windows are set back in the space between the closets, and the recess is slightly arched, making a charming and decorative feature. This plan is similar to that of design 6-A-49.

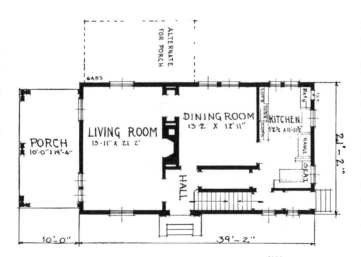

FROM DESIGN *6-A-45*

AN ORDINARY WINDOW, BUT THE ARCHITECT
HAS MADE IT BEAUTIFUL

The beauty of the exterior depends not alone upon the windows, but if the windows are not correctly designed the exterior is ruined. In Colonial houses one would not use casements but double hung windows. In any style of small home *they should be well proportioned and carefully placed. They should not be too large, and the panes should be small. They should suggest snugness and comfort within. Large windows with wide expanse of glass do not give this effect*

HOME BUILT FROM DESIGN *6-A-54*

STATELINESS IN BRICK

*A house which upholds the prestige of the
Colonial style*

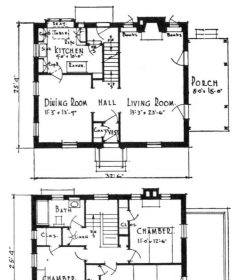

Those familiar w i t h house plans will recognize here an arrangement of rooms that has been employed t i m e s without number. If the prospective home builder should make this his choice, he may do so fortified with the knowledge that there must be good reason behind such extensive use of this plan. There are, in fact, many good reasons. The arrangement is orderly. The use of space is economical. The size and shapes of the rooms are fine, easily accommodated to furniture.

As to the exterior, great leeway permitted by Colonial architecture has allowed the designer to create interest and vivacity. He has done this without using expensive forms of ornament. The qualities are there because of fine massing, skillful uses of the simple decorative elements, careful placing of windows. The ornamentation of wood accentuates the lively color of the brick walls.

Construction: Wood frame, brick veneer, roof of shingles or slate.

HOME BUILT FROM DESIGN *6-A-55*

DESIGNED TO GROW WITH THE FAMILY

*The second floor may be finished later. The space is always
at hand ready to be utilized*

This six-room house, in the English cottage style, is designed for future enlargement. The second floor can be left entirely unfinished for the time being if the family is small and if funds are low. The bedroom and bath provided on the first floor make this possible without serious inconvenience.

One of the most delightful parts of this house is the sun room. Equipped with casement windows, and surrounded in the summertime with the gay color of well-filled flower boxes, it imparts to the house a cozy, homelike air. The outside chimney shown in the house above has been added by the owner who desired the enjoyment of a fireplace. For the sake of economy this was eliminated from the plans.

The first floor has complete bungalow equipment. Living and dining rooms are thrown together by the wide opening between so that both rooms get the benefit of light and air from two sides, besides from the front. The sun porch, by reason of the narrow openings from

these rooms, retains a definite personality of its own. The fireplace suggested by the chimney on the house illustrated would occupy the end of the living room.

The first floor bedroom, a corner room, has cross light and ventilation. The stairway's location in the rear hallway has several advantages. No valuable living space is taken up in the front of the house. It also makes possible the use of simple and inexpensive construction.

The second floor bedrooms are of ample size, both have storage space under the roof in addition to the usual closets. The plan suggests a lavatory in each bedroom, a great convenience since no other provision is made on this floor. However, it would not be difficult to install a bathroom opening off the hall in the space marked "storage."

This house will appear to good advantage even when neighboring houses crowd it closely. A 40-foot lot will be required.

Construction: Wood frame, exterior finish stucco, brick base course, roof of shingles, casement windows.

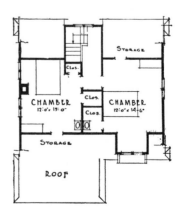

HOME BUILT FROM DESIGN *6-A-57*

COLONIAL WITH A CENTRAL HALL

Not only a center stairway, but a hall that runs the depth of the
house, a hospitable style and a convenient one

Standardized architecture would be an enormous bore. At the same time there are qualities about certain of the architectural styles that are generally recognized and therefore may be given a standard value. One of these styles is the Colonial. The merits of this type of architecture are universally appreciated, so that they are evaluated and given something of a market price. Stated another way, we may say that Colonial architecture applied to small homes commands a ready resale. The article is staple and well known in the market.

Here, then, is a house having the virtues of this type of architecture, the kind of house that has been in style for 200 years and bids fair to remain so indefinitely. The plan is of the central hall type, one that has proved by test of long years to be satisfactory. Not only does it

afford a certain generosity of space not often found in small houses: it produces an orderly sequence of rooms that comes from the position of the stairway; it permits immediate circulation from the front door to the back; it realizes to the full the decorative possibilities of the stairway itself. In this design, also, there is such a straightforward plan of construction that building costs will be lower in consequence. The plan is not new, not original in layout, yet it is one of the most livable arrangements that has been worked out for a house of its size. Many windows and fine wall spaces in every room make furnishing and decorating an easy matter.

The front wall in the second story is planned for a panel of plaster or for grooved boarding. Overlapping siding, however, may be used for the entire wall.

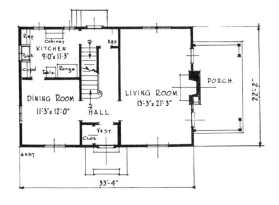

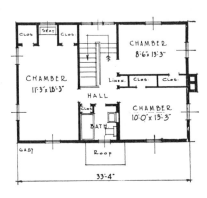

HOME BUILT FROM DESIGN 6-A-58

THE SUN ROOM COMES TO THE FRONT

Masonry construction and a compact plan make this a
suitable house for a city lot

One feature of home planning which builders should give careful study is salability. Oftentimes t h i s is not given proper consideration, because the owner decides in his own mind that this, being perhaps the last home he will build, must serve only his own personal requirements and those of his family, irrespective of whether these meet the needs of others who might wish to buy. It is, nevertheless, good business to incorporate as far as possible the equipment and features that give a house resale value, since circumstances may arise which make it desirable or necessary to sell.

It has been thoroughly demonstrated that a house with three sleeping rooms, a dining room, living room, kitchen, and a practically square plan is a type which finds a ready market. The exterior, of course, must also present an attractive appearance.

The brick house illustrated here is such a house. In order to keep costs at a minimum every available foot of floor space has been devoted to actual living quarters, and the necessary halls

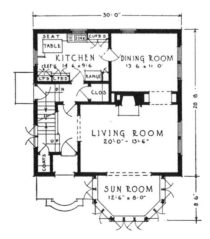

have been confined to a small area.

The distinguished appearance of the house is achieved not through the use of elaborate and expensive ornamentation but through a fine disposition of forms and materials. With the living room and sun porch across the front, the house is particularly advantageous for a site where the principal view is to the front.

The plan includes a coat closet on the first stair landing, a breakfast nook in the kitchen, and a grade entry at the side.

Construction: The house may be built of solid brick or with brick veneer on wood frame. In ordering the drawings please state which type of construction is desired. The roof may be of shingles or slate.

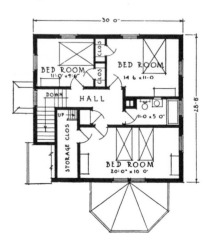

HOME BUILT FROM DESIGN *6-A-62*

SPANISH FOR THE TWO-STORY HOUSE

*A studio living room, two different floor levels, and a downstairs
bedroom make this distinctive among small houses*

The design presented here incorporates much of the charm of the Spanish style. The living room is spacious and is handsomely executed, having a lofty beamed ceiling and exposed rafters. High above the broad fireplace is a small wrought iron balcony which opens from the second floor hall. At either side of the hearth are tall arched recesses for book shelves. Opposite the entrance door is a broad archway leading to the dining room. This is two steps above living room floor level. Beyond this archway are French doors leading to the terrace. A high transom above, divided into small lights as are the doors, brings this opening into scale with the size of the room. The windows on the other two sides of the room are also on the same generous scale.

An attractive dining room, an efficient kitchen with cupboard and drawer s p a c e in abundance, several closets, and a bedroom with a lavatory opening from it complete the first floor. Two bedrooms, a bath and six capacious closets make up the second.

The exterior makes a distinguished appearance from e v e r y standpoint. The size, character, and spacing of the

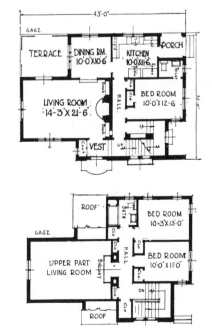

openings give life and vivacity. The rich colors of the tile roof contrast superbly with the white stucco walls. The tall, narrow arched windows at the front are those which light the stairs, while the window to the left of the entrance door is that shown at one side of the living room. Above the latter is a broad band of gay tile, and similar bits of color have been used at other points to ornament the exterior.

Planned for a lot 50 feet or more in width, the house may also be turned with the narrow end to the street and be accommodated on a 40-foot lot. The owner of the house illustrated built the one-story structure to the right, also the high wall which surrounds the area in front of it. This makes, in effect, a patio. There is no basement under the living room, but the remaining space is sufficiently large to include the usual laundry, fuel and heater rooms, and an ample storage closet for fruit and vegetables.

Construction: Hollow tile walls, stucco finish, tile roof.

HOME BUILT FROM DESIGN *6-A-60*

DUTCH COLONIAL IN SHINGLES

With a living room noteworthy in size

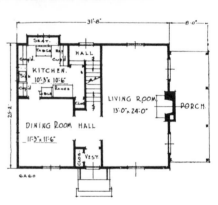

In the so-called D u t c h Colonial house there are three things in particular to be reckoned with if the potential beauty of the style is to be fully realized; the height of the walls must be in accord with the proportions of the roof; the dormers must be delicately designed so they do not appear to weigh heavily on the roof; the foundation should be low so that the house appears to lie close to the ground.

This design meets all these requirements in splendid fashion. The cornice line is brought just above the level of the first story windows so that the house appears broad and low. The low stoop and the front door raised only slightly above the level of the walk give it a pleasant air of hospitality. The dormers are not, as they are

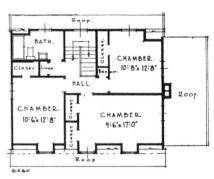

often found, either bulky or cumbersome. The three small dormers illustrated at the top of the page are recommended as being superior in appearance, but the home builder may choose.

The plan, equal in merit to the exterior, has all the desired comforts and convenience, with six good rooms generous in size. The exterior finish may be either siding or shingles, the outside chimney of common brick, whitewashed.

HOME BUILT FROM DESIGN *6-A-60*

C. B. Straus, Architect

A Bedroom Finished Like an Attic

Bedrooms do not need to be elaborate. What a wealth of charm there is here with the barest simplicity. The architect has used the most elemental of materials for finishing—pine boards for the walls, iron for the hardware, exposed beams and rafters, paints and

stains to give a mellow tone to the wood. The floor is painted a dark pumpkin yellow. The secret of the room's personality lies in the fitness of the architect's selections, rather than in large expenditures of money. Early American furniture is particularly appropriate

DESIGN *6-A-61*

FOUR ROOMS NOW AND SIX ROOMS LATER

*A house complete on the first floor. The downstairs bedroom will be
most convenient even after the second story is finished*

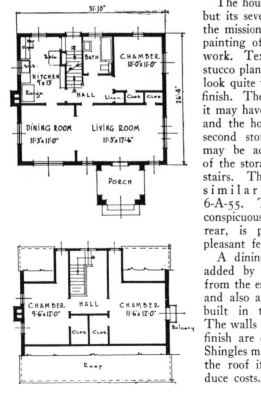

The house pictured above is essentially a square type, but its severity is relieved by a happy play of color in the mission tile roof, in the stucco walls, in the bright painting of the woodwork, and by the wrought iron work. Texture also lends vivacity to the design, for the stucco planes may be roughened. However, they would look quite well if the stucco were troweled to a sanded finish. The plan is the kind that can grow, for it may have only four rooms finished at first, and the house will be complete. When the second story is finished a bathroom may be added, occupying a portion of the storage space at the side of the stairs. The plan is q u i t e s i m i l a r to that of design 6-A-55. The stairway, inconspicuously located at the rear, is partially open, a pleasant feature of the hall.

A dining alcove may be added by projecting a bay from the end of the kitchen, and also a fireplace may be built in the living room. The walls beneath the stucco finish are of h o l l o w tile. Shingles may be employed on the roof if necessary to reduce costs.

Below is a section of the eave trough to catch the water from the roof. Supported by interesting brackets it becomes an engaging bit of architecture

The balcony at the gable end is also gracefully bracketed. The wrought iron work will not be expensive, yet how much it counts in the final effect

AND HERE ARE THE DETAILS
*Close-ups of the Little Things
That Make This House
Big in Architecture*

The window could be just a window and nothing more, but when an architect pierces the wall he thinks not only of lighting the room but of adding beauty

Here you can see how fine the entrance porch truly is. The wrought iron rails and the heavy wooden beams lend distinction

DESIGN *6-A-63*

QUALITY IN THE ENGLISH STYLE

*High-pitched gables, fine proportions, and a distinctive
entrance make for beauty*

If the word "English" is mentioned in connection with the style of a house, there are many who think of half timber. Contrary to this quite general idea, however, all houses of half timber are not English nor, on the other hand, are all English houses half timber. To this fact the house pictured here, design 6-A-63, bears witness.

Both as an example of what can be made of even a small home when built of brick, and as a house skillfully designed in the English spirit, this is exceedingly fine. While it gives the impression of solidarity, of sturdiness, yet it has also grace and beauty. Since there is nothing artificial about it, no gingerbread ornament to detract from it as the years pass, time will only serve to mellow and increase its charm. Those things upon which it depends for favor are integral: the trim angles of the high-pitched gables, the curve of the roof over the front entrance, the fine proportions of the dormers, and, not least, the soft blend of colors in walls and roof.

The windows, too, add distinction to the house. Many in number, they make the interior light and cheerful, yet as they are varied in treatment and well spaced, they give none of the spotty appearance noted in houses less ably handled.

The recessed entrance, located at one side, adds great dignity, and as the arch of the doorway has been repeated over the window which lights the upper stair landing, this portion of the house ties together in a pleasing manner.

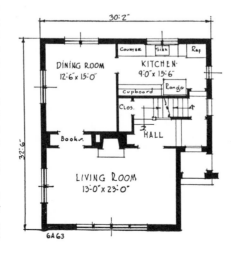

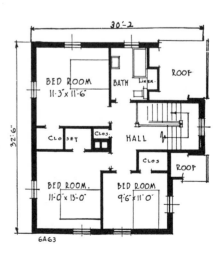

ment purposes as well as for family use.

The kitchen is convenient and well arranged, an extremely practical workroom. Countless steps will be saved by the location of refrigerator, sink and work table in close conjunction.

From the rear entry off the kitchen steps lead to the basement. This entry also opens into the front vestibule, giving direct communication between kitchen and front door. The front hall proper is one step above the level of this vestibule.

The three bedrooms are all light and airy and provided with commodious closets. A disappearing stairway in the hall leads to storage space in the attic.

With all these advantages, the house is not unduly expensive, since the drawings call for brick veneer over wood frame construction. The roof may be either of wood or slate.

The curve of the roof above, the arched doorway, and the small recessed porch all combine to form an entrance of charm and dignity

Another example of the skill which has gone into the design of this house is in the economy of the plan. While it is delightfully roomy it is compact, so that it may be built in cities where lots are comparatively narrow—even as narrow as 40 feet, providing, of course, the city ordinance permits. Its contour is such, too, that its appearance will be good even t h o u g h closely flanked by neighboring houses.

The long living room with its six large windows is of satisfying size and of a shape to set off attractive furnishings to the best advantage. Whether in the daytime with the windows—colorful drapes at either side—admitting a flood of light and sunshine, or at night in the glow of the lamplight and with a fire on the hearth, the living room is always certain to be a delightful place to spend one's time.

Opening from it, through an archway flanked on either side by narrow, ceiling-high bookcases, is the dining room. This is somewhat above the average size for a six-room house, and will be quite adequate for entertain-

The bookcases in the archway between living and dining rooms are ceiling high

The fireplace is simple yet attractive, a combination of wood and face brick

HOME BUILT FROM DESIGN *6-A-64*

ELIZABETHAN AS INTERPRETED TODAY

Designed for stucco and half timber, this house recalls both the informality of the English cottage and the dignity of the manor house

Generally speaking, the distinguishing characteristic of English architecture is its picturesque informality. The plan is irregular; the rooms are not symmetrically arranged; windows and doors locate themselves largely where they happen to be convenient. The exterior is also irregular, with steep roofs, sharp gables, large chimneys, and varying combinations of materials.

Naturally such informality lends itself sympathetically to our inborn notions of what a home ought to be. Skillfully done, such houses have a "homey" quality that is irresistibly appealing, but the rich possibilities of the style impose a corresponding degree of restraint. Because a great variety of features is possible, it does not mean that all should be used on one house. Informality and picturesqueness may easily degenerate into restless and ineffective complexity. The saving grace of English homes is often their simplicity.

The house presented here, for example, has comparatively few features of design. Its effect depends chiefly upon the overhanging gable, the chim-

ney, the bay window, the doorway; and there is only enough variety in the use of materials to enhance these few principal features.

Neither has the Old World charm of the exterior been achieved at any sacrifice of convenience in room arrangement. In the plan will be found all the essentials of modern living. Every effort has been made to keep the plan simple, the house economical in construction, although the exterior design is of a type often seen in more expensive residences. Six generous rooms, a breakfast nook, bath, and ample closets comprise the plan.

In building great care should be taken that the drawings are followed accurately, for a change in dimension or a variation in the use of materials may produce an unexpectedly unfortunate result. The stucco should be fairly rough—not too much so—and warm in color. The wood of the gable should be rough sawed and stained—not too dark.

Construction: Wood frame, exterior finish stucco, half timber and wood in gable, native stone trim, shingle roof.

ENTRANCE OF HOME BUILT FROM DESIGN *6-A-66*

Above is a beautiful doorway which may be used as a substitute for that shown on the next page. Both are used with design 6-A-66

Left—The corner cupboard was added by the owner of this house, and is not shown in the plan of this design. Beautiful examples may be chosen from dealers' catalogues at comparatively little expense

Right—The fireplace is one of Colonial design, with fluted pilasters supporting a plain cornice. This, like the rest of the woodwork, is finished in ivory

ENTRANCE OF HOME BUILT FROM DESIGN *6-A-66*

*Colonial---Yesterday, Today and Tomorrow.   The style has been the standard of good taste
for generations, and bids fair to remain so for as many more*

HOME BUILT FROM DESIGN *6-A-66*

BEAUTY IN SIMPLE THINGS

In shingles, shutters, and straight lines

If you want a central stairway house with a long living room, and Colonial architecture appeals to you, you will hardly be able to find a better plan than this or a more beautiful handling of the exterior. The plan has been tested and found satisfactory by thousands of home builders because of its convenience and the straightforward simplicity of its planning, and because of the beautiful effects that are obtained both inside and outside the house. The exterior with its beautifully vaulted stoop at the entrance has distinction obtained without extravagance.

The plans include a vestibule, coat closet, fireplace, an open or enclosed porch, a dining alcove and broom

closet in the kitchen, and a grade entrance to the rear and basement.

The bedrooms are practically equal in size and importance. They have long wall spaces for twin beds, capacious closets, and cross ventilation, as bedrooms should have. An attic stairway may be arranged over the main stairs, giving access to large storage space. An even simpler arrangement would be a disappearing stairway in the ceiling of the hall. Broom and linen closets are provided.

Living room, hall, and dining room may be thrown together by large cased openings, or the rooms may be shut off by French doors. Wide siding may be used on the exterior walls if desired.

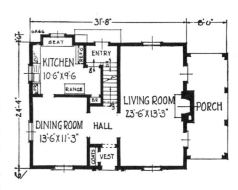

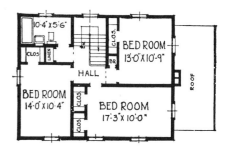

HOME BUILT FROM DESIGN *6-A-67*

QUALITY IN HOME BUILDING

*A straightforward design treated in a truly artistic
and genuine manner*

Ruskin's eloquence may have at times led him into exaggeration, but his insistence on a home that was secure, permanent, beautiful, and that fittingly symbolized the character of the man who built it rings true to the last word. Aside from the deep-lying urge to build a house worthy of himself, there is also a simple, practical reason that ought to appeal strongly to every man who is beginning to think of build-ing a home. That is economic value.

Not because a thing is cheap is it economical. Cheapness in the end often means extravagance, and at the same time only offers what is always unsatisfactory. This is especially true of a house, where cheap materials and labor result in quick depreciation and large repair bills. Ordinarily when a family builds, they live in the house for a long time. They are judged by its character, and it is important that it represent them worthily in the community.

The handsome Colonial home illus-trated here may be built of brick veneer, design 6-A-67, or with solid brick walls, design 6-A-68. It provides a satisfactory room arrangement and innumerable conveniences. In addition to its six major rooms, all generous in size, the plan includes a breakfast al-cove, sewing room, six closets, and an attic for storage purposes. This is reached by a stairway leading from the smaller front bedroom. The porch may be built at side or rear and either open or enclosed.

The bedrooms, it may be noted, are longer than they are wide. The long, narrow room has an advantage over the square room, for although both may contain the same amount of floor area, the longer room gives greater space at the sides of the bed than does the square room.

Here the bath is located at the rear immediately over the kitchen, so there are no long, expensive runs of pipes.

GOOD TASTE

IN

INTERIOR DESIGN

The interior of this home displays the same degree of refinement and architectural distinction as is found in the exterior. The architect's aim has been to produce an interior in fine balance and to provide well-proportioned rooms interestingly arranged. Thus the home builder has a background for furniture, rugs, pictures, and draperies that will set them off to the greatest advantage.

The wide archways between living room, hall, and dining room frame attractive vistas. That from the living room into the hall showing the Colonial stairway is particularly fine. Cabinets for books or china are inserted at either side of the entrance to the dining room.

HOME BUILT FROM DESIGN *6-A-69*

CLEAN-CUT AND STRAIGHTFORWARD

The first as to exterior, the second as to plan. Note the flat stucco
walls and cornice without overhang

Among the many definitions of architecture there is one which, translated into terms of the layman, is especially apt. It is as follows: "Architecture is putting into a building certain qualities—namely, logic, strength and beauty."

To make a five- or six-room house absolutely "logical" requires about as much concentrated gray matter as to design a state capitol. The house must be dimensioned, shaped, and planned so that every room is as big as it needs to be, but no bigger; so that stairs not only begin in the right place on the first floor, but end in the right place on the second; so that you don't bump your head going up those stairs; so that the front door doesn't admit the visitor directly to the family group around the hearth or dining table; to arrive at all these things without kinks and jogs and wriggles in partitions and roofs that complicate construction and increase costs—all that is what an architect means by "logic" in design.

Homes to stand up and give service must have "strength." That is why it pays to be sure that methods and ma-

terials specified are of substantial character.

"Beauty" means that quality of a building which gives you a feeling of pleasure when you look at it and live in it. There are many well-built houses without an atom of beauty to them.

The house illustrated contains all

these factors that make a house desirable. It is probable that no greater economy could be effected for the amount of space gained than in this plan. The design follows closely the Spanish type of architecture. The two porches add greatly to the living area of the house, particularly the sleeping porch, which is sufficiently generous for several cots.

Construction: Walls of cement or clay tile; exterior finish stucco; tile roof.

HOME BUILT FROM DESIGN *6-A-70*

SINCE HOUSES MUST BE LABELED

*We call this Italian, although it has been skillfully
adapted to meet American requirements*

Whatever you may please to call it, Spanish, Italian or Mediterranean, the plan of this house, design 6-A-70, is strictly American. The exterior is perhaps most nearly Italian, a modified Italian, an excellent design for a small home. Simplicity is the keynote of the domestic architecture of Italy, and walls and roofs glow with color. Its charms, therefore, are well adapted to our own needs, and considering the excellence of the architecture which these people have achieved with such extremely meagre means, it is no wonder that more and more we are designing houses after this style.

The plan is almost square, one of the most practical types for a six-room house. This permits all rooms to be corner rooms, well lighted and ventilated by windows on two sides.

In the living room double French doors open upon the side porch and upon the terrace in front. Beside the fireplace a wide doorway, with tall, narrow bookcases on either side, opens into the dining room. Both of these rooms have plenty of wall space for large pieces of furniture.

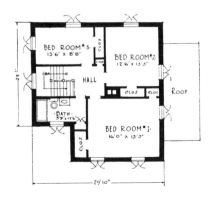

In the kitchen one long wall is devoted to cupboards, work tables and sink. The refrigerator, with its outside icing door, is located beneath one cupboard, so that everything necessary for the preparation of meals is close together and convenient. A built-in seat and table beneath one window may be utilized as a breakfast nook. At the side is a grade entry, and opposite the door to the basement is a broom closet.

Upstairs are three excellent bedrooms, one a double room with two closets. Of the four other closets, two are for linen.

Structurally, this house is of a type which architects call "masonry bound," meaning that the outside walls are of masonry. Here the walls are of hollow tile, the surface finished with stucco. The tile roof adds a lively note of color, and full length shutters, painted in pleasing contrast to the light stucco walls, complete a fine exterior.

The house can be built on a 40-foot lot if the porch is built at the rear, otherwise a 50-foot lot will be required.

HOME BUILT FROM DESIGN *6-A-72*

IN TRUE COLONIAL CHARACTER

With all the restraint and dignity which characterizes
the best in this style

If it were possible to get all the architects of the land to vote on the question of what is the best plan for a six-room home, it is probable that the most votes would fall to the type in which there is a central stairway, with the living room on one side and the dining room and kitchen on the other. With such a plan, in even the very small house, it is possible to secure large, pleasant living rooms and to get these rooms with practically no waste of space.

Of course, a house with a hallway running from front to back is the typical arrangement, but such a hallway requires a wider house and can only be had at considerable additional expense. Since many believe that the convenience gained by the full length hallway is not proportionate to the added expense, this house has been designed without the center hallway.

The first impression upon entering is that of pleasant spaciousness—rarely found, much less expected, in so small a house. The wide plaster arches on each side of the hall, one opening into the living room and the other into the

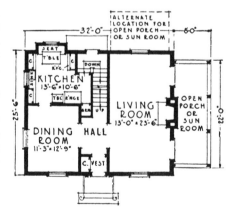

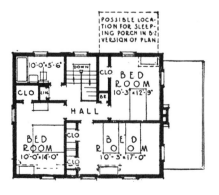

dining room, and the glimpses through these arches of well-proportioned wall spaces and windows, contribute in no small measure to the charm and beauty of the rooms. Add to this the sun room, which may be either at the end of the living room or at the side, and the result is a finished and livable piece of architecture.

A successful use of the Colonial design involves minute attention to details, such as the exact location of windows, the details of the doorway and cornice, the design of the windows, and more especially the shape and contour of the house itself. The designer has given these careful study.

The exterior of this design is not far removed from those of our Colonial forefathers. One will see that the effect is gained through elimination of extra details rather than through the addition of them. Yet, in spite of its simplicity, it is not severe. The whole effect is lightened by the wooden trim about the front door, the wrought iron railing and the Colonial stoop.

Construction: Brick veneer on wood frame, shingle or slate roof.

An Entrance of Classic Traditions

Entrance of design 6-A-72 illustrated on the opposite page

DESIGN 6-A-73

THE SMALL HOUSE ATTAINS THE IMPRESSIVE

Designed for a corner or a wide lot, with well-lighted
rooms cool in summer and sunny in winter

If you own a corner lot of which you want to make the best use, here is a plan made to order for your situation. Of course, it will be satisfactory for a wide lot also, but it would have to be a very wide lot, for the width of the whole house runs close to 60 feet. It is, you w i l l note, extremely shallow.

The style of this design is purely American, with details from our own Colonial period. Architects are more concerned with a house having a style of its own than they are with its following exactly the forms set by precedent. What is wanted is a building which stands on its own merits as a fine piece of architecture. T h i s design measures up to that standard.

As for the plan, there are six excellent rooms. If it is desired to omit the porch and the sleeping porch or child's room above, the size would be reduced thereby to five

rooms. This will allow the house to go on a 60-foot lot, with the broad side to the street.

One enters this house through a side lighted door into a generous hallway.

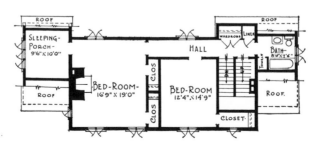

To the left there is a cased opening leading to the beautiful living room. To the right is the stairway to the second story and a door through a large coat closet to the kitchen. The stairway thus becomes accessible from both hallway and kitchen.

The handsome fireplace in the living room has a broad band of marble framing the opening and an exquisitely p a n e l e d mantel-piece of wood. Double French doors on one side balance a built-in bookcase on the other.

On the second floor there are three bedrooms, one for the owner in which a fireplace is provided and from w h i c h access is had to a smaller r o o m or sleeping porch. There is a generous attic reached by a stairway in the upper hall. Considerable closet room is provided, including a large built-in wardrobe and a linen closet in the hall.

HOME BUILT FROM DESIGN *6-A-74*

MAKING THE MOST OF ITS OPPORTUNITIES

*This plan offers a sewing room and a broad porch in
addition to six rooms and many closets*

Here is embodied the spirit of Colonial architecture, a house of quiet
dignity and lasting refinement and
charm. Although the architecture is
not spectacular, it is not for this reason devoid of life and interest. Had
it been so, the style would hardly have
retained its popularity so long a time.

Either siding or shingles
may be used for the exterior
finish. The plan, with its
large, well-lighted rooms,
speaks for itself. In the sewing room, which may be used
as a den or playroom, is a cupboard and a clothes chute.

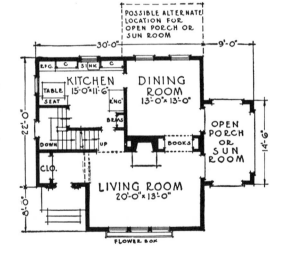

*The architect's
drawing of this
design. On the
house above a
simpler entrance
was substituted
for the small cov-
ered porch.
Otherwise the
drawings were
followed care-
fully. The en-
trance used is an
attractive stock
design*

DESIGN *6-A-75*

ANOTHER VARIATION OF DUTCH COLONIAL

*The exterior is desirable for its fine proportions. The interior
is roomy and conveniently arranged*

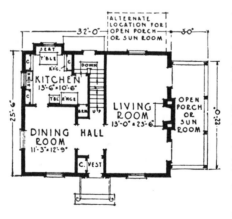

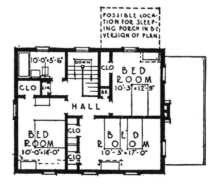

Every residential district and newly built-up subdivision has its quota of Dutch Colonial houses. Some of them are good, a few rather bad, and the greater percentage midway between. The general design is one which has been used for several hundred years, although the old Dutch settlers along our eastern coast might not recognize the present-day Dutch Colonial home —so called—as a descendant of their own picturesque dwellings.

The chief modification of the style, of course, occurred with the addition of dormer windows, and on them the beauty of these homes depends to a great extent. Another thing that may mar their beauty is the high foundation, which gives the house the appearance of trying to get up in the world. The Dutch Colonial house is a lowly, cozy affair, at its best when tied closely to the ground and surrounded by shrubbery, trees, and the flowers and vines which give to any house a more homelike aspect.

The house presented above is a charming version of the Dutch Colonial. The entrance is simple, but the wrought iron hand rails at either side make it distinctive. The roof is well proportioned and gracefully curved; and the arched dormers, delicately designed, serve their purpose of admitting light and air to the upstairs bedrooms without being of that undue size which makes some appear to weigh heavily upon the roof.

The plans are of the convenient central stairway type. The first floor plan is identical with that of design 6-A-72. The second floor is also the same, with the exception of the dormer windows.

Among the many desirable features of the plan is the large porch. The drawings present alternate details for an enclosed sun room. Arched openings separate living and dining rooms from the hall. The fireplace has a Colonial mantelpiece of wood.

Corner cupboards would be charming in the dining room. Provision is made for a breakfast nook in the kitchen, only one of the many conveniences in this room. There are commodious cupboards, and beneath the counter space to the right of the sink are seven drawers and a flour bin.

DESIGN 6-A-79

A HOUSE FOR A NARROW LOT

*Deep rather than wide, here is a design to fit a
special need*

Changes in materials are not always suitable but, on the other hand, a design may sometimes be developed in different m a t e r i a l s with equally pleasant and effective results. An excellent example is the design shown here in brick. With few changes it is the same as design 6-A-51, which shows a house finished in stucco.

If the sun porch is located at the rear, opening from the dining room, the house may be placed on a lot with a 30-foot frontage. On a wider lot the porch may be built at the side and open from the

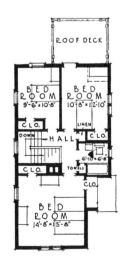

living room as indicated. Not only the color and texture of the brick walls, but the arched entrance and the two small gables at the side, contribute to the exceptionally distinguished appearance of the house.

The r o o m s are so arranged that each may be shut off from the others and complete privacy attained. The side entry opens into the hall. Circulation between rooms is direct, eliminating unnecessary steps for the housewife.

Construction: Brick veneer on wood frame, roof of shingles or slate.

DESIGN 6-A-76

NEW DRESSES FOR A WELL-PROVED PLAN

The room arrangement is compact and convenient, the
houses economical to build

What a difference in appearance the small things about a house can make. Here we have two exteriors of exactly the same size and almost the same contour, but each has a different spirit. The stucco house is formal and stately— as stately as a small house can be. The frame house is less formal, though it seems to be larger.

Design 6-A-76 is the kind of house home builders come to after they have gone through and discarded the romantic, illogical designs that cannot be built without waste, that do not give useful floor areas or sound and lasting architec-

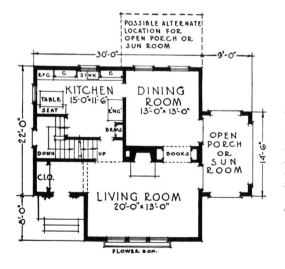

The simplicity of this entrance is in keeping with the unpretentious style of the house, yet it does much to beautify its appearance. The simple brackets and pilasters which support the hood and the wrought iron rail at the side of the porch make an attractive combination

DESIGN *6-A-77*

tural appearances. One of the most worth-while features of this design is its honesty. It does not pretend to be a castle, a picturesque bit of European peasant hovel, or any other type of building. It is straightforward American style without fuss or furbelows, the kind of architecture that gives good space at reasonable cost. It is at the same time attractive in appearance. The exterior finish may be either siding or shingles.

In design 6-A-77 the line of moldings, instead of being at the top of the lower windows, is placed at the bottom of the second story windows, which gives this house an appearance of greater height. The windows, too, seem taller and more stately by reason of the recessed arches above them. The smooth, fine texture of the stucco finish carries a dignity and feeling of permanence in keeping with the formality of the design.

Both houses are built on the same plan, one which is practical and efficient in arrangement. The rooms are of good size, brilliantly lighted, yet retaining fine wall spaces. The way in which they turn upon each other means simplified construction, one of the principal ways to keep down costs.

Among the items that make this plan desirable may be mentioned the following: A generous coat closet; an inside fireplace, for which the cost of construction will be less than for one on an outer wall; beautiful plastered arch between dining room and living room, with recesses for books; French doors from both living room and dining room to the open porch. The porch itself, if necessary, may be enclosed to make a sun

room. A completely equipped kitchen and three excellent bedrooms complete the major portion of the plan.

If the porch is located at the rear as suggested, these houses may be accommodated on 40-foot lots, otherwise 50 feet will be required.

Construction, design 6-A-77: Wood frame, stucco exterior finish, tile roof. A shingle roof may be substituted.

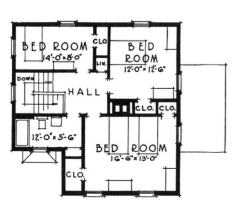

This sketch brings out the various features of this entrance and the general effect. The wrought iron railing above and at the side of the porch, the simple lantern, and the brick steps stand out to advantage against the light stucco of the walls

HOME BUILT FROM DESIGN *6-A-78*

A COMBINATION OF MATERIALS

*Stucco and shingles are used in this house
suitable for either a broad or a narrow lot*

Versatility. That is the word which best describes this plan. The illustration at the top of the page shows how well it may be accommodated to the narrow lot, even one as narrow as 30 feet. T h e lower illustration, the architect's drawing, s h o w s it appearing to equal advantage w h e n turned sideways on a lot of wide frontage, one of 60 or perhaps 75 feet. In either case it appears to be deliberately designed for that particular lot. The single dif-

DESIGN *6-A-78*

ference is in the location of the steps to the little entrance porch. As shown in the block plan, also, a rearrangement of porches accommodates it either to a 40- or 50-foot lot, with entrance either on the side or front.

Light-colored stucco covers the wooden frame w a l l s for half their height. F r o m second story level to the narrow eaves are shingles of a somewhat deeper tone.

Shutters u s e d at strategic points add interest to wall spaces.

rooms—excepting kitchen and dining room—open into one another. Both living room and dining room can be shut off from the hall so that as much privacy as is desired can be obtained.

The living room, one of the square type which lends itself well to furnishing and decoration, has outside exposure on three sides. A handsome fireplace and built-in shelves for books at one side give character to the room.

In this plan a large formal dining room is provided, and beyond it is an open porch, or, if desired, an enclosed sun room. In this location the porch has all the privacy possible, besides overlooking the garden, as our porches are doing more and more. An alternate location off the living room is suggested, however.

Although provision is made for meals in the kitchen, this room is compact and efficiently arranged. The built-in seat at one end, before which a table may be drawn up, takes the place of a breakfast nook. This serves equally well, and is more economical in cost and space. The bedrooms are all corner rooms with cross ventilation, all of sufficient size for practical purposes.

Construction: Wood frame, exterior finish stucco with shingles or wide siding above, shingle roof.

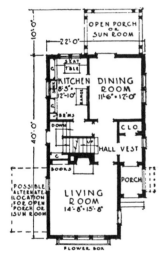

The attractive exterior in no way belies the pleasant interior of this house. Many windows—casements are indicated in the plans—make the rooms as bright and cheerful as any sun-loving home owner could desire. Closets, numerous and varied in use, will appeal to the most exacting housewife. One other thing not to be lightly overlooked is the fact that none of the

A sketch of the dining room window showing the heavy batten shutters used. Windows throughout are of the casement type

HOME BUILT FROM DESIGN *6-A-83*

FOUR EXTERIORS WITH ONE FLOOR PLAN

Each designed for an exterior finish of a different material

Taking a given floor plan and making it speak in four or five different languages is an American trick. On these pages there is a single plan with four exteriors.

Of course, it is futile to say that one is English and another is Colonial, but it is futile only in a historical sense. It is practically necessary to give these houses some sort of a label so that we shall be able to describe them at all. The labels that describe them by the nationalities from which the details were taken are as good as any other. But these are modern American homes, full of the vitality which our American manner of living has brought about. In this respect, then, they are not dead architecture, as they might be if we were blindly to copy what an older generation had done, and use it because we enjoy its fine exterior appearance. If we call these houses by their ancestral names, then, it is done with the tongue in the cheek.

One of the things which give character to the small house, in fact, to any architecture, is the material used. Unless the architect recognizes the particular nature of the material and uses it so as to bring out its beauties, he misses much of his opportunity. In these four houses the exteriors have been developed in different materials and the details adjusted to make the most of the best qualities of each material.

The materials change the detail of moldings and corner projections; they also necessitate a readjustment in the massing of the house. Brick, stucco, and shingles are more flexible than siding and lend themselves to the irregular and picturesque massing of the walls in the English designs. On the other hand, the Colonial design, finished with long boards, responds to the more formal handling required by this less flexible type of finish. This design, 6-A-80, is similar in both plan and appearance to design 6-A-48 found on another page. The plain gable roof of the latter and its single long dormer across the front constitute the chief difference between the two designs.

Construction: 6-A-83, frame with shingle finish; 6-A-80, frame with siding finish; 6-A-81, frame with stucco finish; 6-A-82, brick veneer on frame.

DESIGN *6-A-80*

In the house finished in shingles the sun room has been omitted, but this might easily have been added. In form the porch would correspond closely with that of the brick or stucco design. The use of a porch, particularly if it is glazed, increases considerably the livable area of the houses

The plan is of the type in which living and dining rooms are located at the front. Kitchen, downstairs bedroom, and toilet are at the rear, providing bungalow equipment on the first floor. The roof comes down low, breaking pleasantly into the second story ceiling and giving the bedrooms the quality of intimacy. This is true of the three English houses shown, and is indicated on the plans. The dormers of the Colonial design are of different shape, and in this respect alter slightly the second floor plan. Large storage space is provided under the roof at the rear.

HOME BUILT FROM DESIGN *6-A-81*

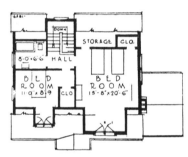

The entrance has been handled in a slightly different manner in three of the houses, and, of course, in the Colonial house in a distinctly different way. In each case the entrance seems particularly well adapted to the material of which the house is built, making of each a pleasant, picturesque feature

HOME BUILT FROM DESIGN *6-A-82*

DESIGN 6-A-84

THE LUXURY OF LARGER ROOMS

The living room is generous in size, no other room is small

The architect who designed this home was interested in giving it a somewhat different expression than is usually found in homes we know as Colonial. Most present-day Colonial houses were inspired from homes built by our forefathers in Connecticut or New York.

There are, however, other delightful forms of Colonial architecture. One of the most interesting was developed in the James River Valley, in Virginia. These houses have a high degree of stateliness and bigness about them. They reflect the elegant and luxurious way of living that distinguished the more free-spending Virginia planter from his thrifty New England neighbor. The mild climate called for large rooms, large windows, and a sense of openness. Almost always they had big hip-roofs.

In the house illustrated here, the architect has adapted to his use some

of the features from one of the most famous of the James River Valley houses. The original of the house was of brick. Here, however, the detail is all worked out in wood. Wood mold-

ings enrich the openings. The entrance is dignified by wood pilasters and cornice. A white latticed porch is harmoniously related to the general scheme of the house. The high stately appearance has been emphasized by the corner pilasters.

Since its interest depends on those very qualities of height and formal simplicity that make a house look well in a row of other houses, it avoids the danger that low, widespread houses tend to run into, that of looking misplaced on a narrow lot. It can be built easily on a lot 50 feet wide, and if the porch is placed at the back, a lot as narrow as 40 feet will be sufficient in most cities.

The plan of the house will be found to be a version of the center hall type. This has been arrived at through many years of experiment and research by architects as giving beyond any question the maximum of accommodation for a minimum expenditure. The stair arrangement gives three generous bedrooms on the second floor without wasteful hall space, cut-off ceilings, or jogs in partitions.

DESIGN *6-A-85*

GETTING THE MOST FOR THE LEAST

A house which has been designed for economies of construction

Are you, like many another home builder, faced with the problem of getting much room into your house yet keeping costs down as low as possible? If so, here is a design which merits your serious interest. It has been designed deliberately to cut out frills. It eliminates practically all items of excess cost, leaving the necessary walls and openings. These, however, are so well proportioned that appearances are fine.

There are, as everyone knows, two ways to reduce costs. One is to buy less of what is wanted. The other is to take a lower quality. In working out this design the idea has been to make use of the first of these methods particularly. Reduction in quality follows to the extent that the materials selected are not expensive or extravagant.

With framing lumber made in multiples of two feet as to length, it is manifest that if a house can be laid out so that there will be no cutting of these members as received from the lumber yard, there will not only be a saving in labor but a saving in the material itself. So the architect here started out to design rooms that would

use stock lengths of joists, and this pretty much determined the size of the house. The hall is wide enough to take care of the stairway and allow closet space. It is made a definite size

so that ordinary 14-foot joists cut in two will span across without waste. The rooms at the side use 12-foot lengths, and the house from front to back is arranged so that the spacing between joists is uniform throughout. There is thus no framing lumber wasted. In the second story are three excellent bedrooms arranged so that their size is approximately the same. The framing of the ceiling joists above is also in stock lengths.

Getting all this accommodation and three excellent bedrooms in a house which is only 30 feet wide and 20 feet deep is something of an accomplishment. The porch shown may be eliminated to reduce costs. There is no fireplace shown for the same reason, although this may be added if desired. Another saving is in the plumbing, as the bath immediately above the kitchen means short runs of pipe.

HOME BUILT FROM DESIGN *6-A-91*

THE RAMBLING HOUSE IN TWO STYLES

One plan serves both the Colonial and the Spanish bungalow

This house, design 6-A-91, is typically Colonial. The porch harmoniously combines square columns, pilasters, and a latticed railing. The roof may be of shingles stained green, and to carry out the color scheme effectively the blinds and also the doors should be green. For the exterior walls wide siding may be used as in this case, or shingles stained white or gray and laid twelve inches to the weather.

The two views shown of this house afford a clear idea of its extreme simplicity and fine proportions. Ornamentation is chiefly in the shuttered windows, the attractive entrance, and the beautifully handled cornice, so that building costs are kept to a minimum.

Design 6-A-92 is very different in appearance. Essentially of the South and West, the house has a charm which is retained even in the more severe climate of the North. In neither section does it appear out of place. The roof should be of

tile in variegated shades of red, the stucco preferably of gray or white, while the brackets of the hooded entrance and the cypress beams above the porch openings should be stained a weathered gray.

The plans of these two designs are identical, although in design 6-A-92 that portion which includes the living room, dining room, kitchen, and rear hall is two steps lower than the remainder of the house.

As the plan shows, the living and dining rooms have double exposure, and are so arranged that either room may be enlarged by an open porch or sun room.

The kitchen is located so that cross ventilation is afforded, with the sink under one window, and under the other a breakfast nook composed of seat and table. The room is compact and efficiently arranged, replete with cupboards, drawers, and work tables. The re-

frigerator is placed in the kitchen, with a cupboard of several shelves above it. The rear hall opening from the kitchen leads to the rear porch and to the basement stairway.

A sharp right-angle turn in the main corridor is an effective way to give the bedrooms privacy—a factor often sacrificed in one-story dwellings. Each of the three bedrooms has sufficient unbroken wall space to simplify the arrangement of furniture. Besides the closet in each bedroom,

there are two linen closets in the hall, another for towels in the bathroom, and one for coats close to the front entry.

Of the two closets in the hall, that between the two bedrooms has five deep shelves which will be found quite sufficient for linen. The second, beside the bathroom, has four shelves convenient for bedding. A basement is provided under all but the two rear bedrooms. Construction of design 6-A-92: Wood frame, stucco finish.

DESIGN 6-A-92

A DESIGN FOR A FARM HOUSE

*That combines as far as practicable the
ideas of 882 farm women*

What kind of a farm house would you like to build for your family to grow up in? Or for yourself to round out your years in? What kind of a farm house do you think that upstanding farmer lad who is courting daughter ought to prepare for the family circle that is to be? And when son is grown how should he build and outfit for his bride? What kind of woodwork do you want for such a house? How about built-in equipment? How much, how little, where and why? What about a washroom for the farm hands? What other provision for steady helpers? What kind of furnishings?

These are a few of many questions which 882 farmers' wives answered in response to an invitation and eight cash prizes ranging from $50.00 to $5.00 each.

After the 882 letters had been carefully studied and edited for requirements, the data was turned over to the Architects' Small House Service Bureau, which developed the farm house plan illustrated on these pages.

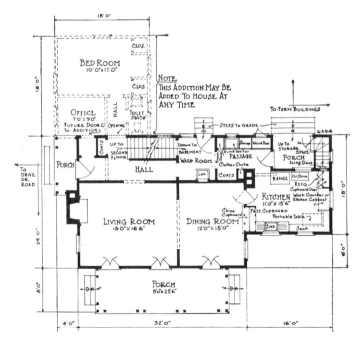

Of course, other farm houses have been designed, many of them, but none with such a wealth of information available about what farm women really want in a house.

In a single farm house not all of the suggestions offered could be incorporated nor could the architects possibly make one plan fit north, west, east, and south alike. But out of this data a home was developed which is clearly of rural life and for rural life. It suggests the strength, the soundness, the stability, the freeness, the genuineness, the independence, and the closeness to the soil of the rural home. It is truly American in style, just as rural life itself is truly American. It looks like a good place to live, to work, to rear a family, to enjoy life.

As to the type of house described in the contest letters, the plain square house still leads any other type in popularity because it is the most economical type to build. Other types are rapidly gaining favor. The bungalow and the story-and-a-half house both received many votes from farm women who feel that they save much time and strength which has in the past been spent in climbing stairs. Many mentioned the fact that the house which is low seems to fit better into the farm landscape than one which stands higher and on a smaller foundation.

It is the consensus of opinion that the farm home should have at least one bedroom downstairs for the reasons that the farm mother must be nurse as well as housekeeper and that there are often either old people or small children in the farm family and the downstairs bedroom saves much time and strength.

The location of the laundry is a question on which there was much disagreement. Of the women who expressed themselves, 56 per cent felt that the laundry in the basement was practical; 23 per cent wanted it on the same floor as the kitchen; 3 per cent ask for it in a building separate from the house. Those who favor the basement feel that it takes the "mess" away from the living floor; those who wish it on the first floor locate it near the kitchen so they can attend to the many other things a farm mother has to do while she is doing the washing—watch the small children while working and avoid carrying clothes up and down stairs. A place under cover for the drying of clothes in winter is considered essential.

The laundry room, these practical folk point out, whether in the basement or on the first floor, can also be used in canning and butchering seasons and the laundry stove should be of a type adapted to these needs. There should be in the room a table with a heavy top on which meat can be cut and so forth. Several women specified an extra range or cookstove in this room, the top to be used for laundry purposes and the oven for baking on hot summer days. They suggest that baking can be done here while the fire is going for laundry work.

An almost unanimous demand was for a special washroom for the men as they come in from their outside work. This washroom should be in connection with the laundry and so arranged that the men can go straight from it to the dining room or living room without having to go through the kitchen. It also provides a place for outside wraps, overshoes, mittens, where they will be dry and warm and—out of the kitchen.

Farm women are practically one in realizing that the farm home is—must be—the business center of the farm. Many of the contributors to this contest suggest a small office for the farm man so that he can transact the business end of things in a business-like way and further suggest that it should be possible for him to take his business guests straight to this room or office from either the front or back hall without taking them through the kitchen or the living quarters of the family.

Study of these plans indicates that the house is designed for future enlargement to include an office, bedroom, toilet, and attic space. The house can be well built without this wing, but in the development of a modern farm house the architects did not want to overlook the requirements of an office from which the farmer may conduct his business affairs.

In the first floor plan the working quarters of the house are separated from the living section. The kitchen has been designed to save steps and labor. It has been developed according to the latest theories of household economics. There are four principal elements in farm kitchen planning. One is the cleaning center which includes sink, drain boards, and place to store china. Another is the cooking center where the stove is, and storage for pots and pans. The third is the work center, a table for the preparation of food and storage space for small supplies. The fourth is one peculiar to farm kitchens. This is the rest center. You may sit here between meal preparation times with full view of the surrounding fields and roadway, and of the downstairs as well.

The rest center in this plan has been placed in the outer corner of the kitchen where there is a wide bench and table. Pull chairs up and there is a seating space for six. The rest center thus serves a double purpose.

All of these units have been set in proper relation to each other, so that one should find at the end of the day accomplishment of more work for the goodly amount of energy than would ordinarily be possible.

The dining alcove or the separate dining room—this subject was discussed thoroughly. More than 81 per cent of the women entering the contest said that the farm home needs a separate dining room large enough so that the table can be spread to accommodate guests and extra hands such as threshers and silo fillers. And they said the dining room should be big enough so that children need not wait until the second table or eat in the kitchen when friends and relatives gather for holiday celebrations. This problem is solved here by having an opening between the dining and living rooms sufficiently large to permit the table to be extended into both rooms.

Abundant storage space in the basement provides for furnace, drying area, vegetable cellar, laundry, etc. The second floor provides three excellent bedrooms and bath. The man's bedroom is reached by a stairway leading from the first floor porch. There is plenty of closet area.

This house is not intended to be a model farm house by any manner of means. It is just one farm house that has been developed by a group of architects working together on a problem laid out by data supplied from 882 letters by farm women.

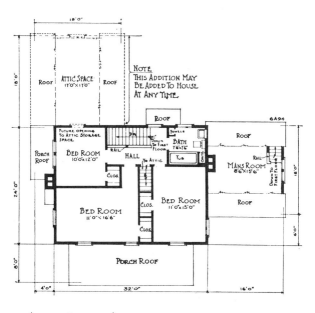

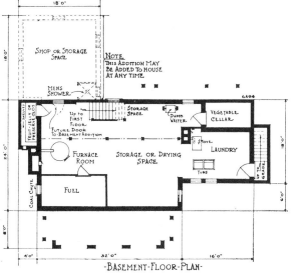

-BASEMENT-FLOOR-PLAN-

HOME BUILT FROM DESIGN *6-A-93*

OF BRICK ROWLOCK CONSTRUCTION

*Here are six rooms, a sleeping porch, and a sun porch
all on a single floor*

Common brick, whitewashed, was the material used for this charming bungalow. Whitewashing or painting brick may seem a good deal like gilding the lily, since one of the arguments in favor of brick is the fact that it does not run up an annual painting bill. Nevertheless, the rough brickwork showing through the whitewash gives a texture greatly admired. The working drawings for this design call for brick walls laid "rolok."

To increase the usefulness of this design it has been developed in both brick and frame. The design calling for frame with an exterior finish of stucco and, in the gable ends, stucco and half timber, is number 6-A-6 shown elsewhere in this book.

The plan has been so arranged that the living quarters occupy the front of the house, while the sleeping rooms are placed at the rear. This is an exceptionally fine arrangement for a bungalow. The accommodations it offers are three sizable bedrooms, a sleeping porch opening from the hall, a living room with a broad window seat and fine fireplace, a sun room, dining room,

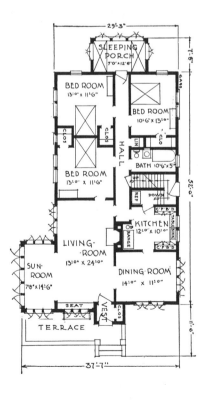

kitchen, and up-to-date bath. The kitchen, let it be said, is as practical in arrangement and equipment as architectural skill could make it.

There is additional space under the roof that can be finished off into two sleeping rooms and a bath. Three dormer windows, one on each side and one at the rear, will provide these with sufficient light and ventilation. The division of this space has been left to the home builder, but a stairway is provided on the plan.

The sun room is so placed with cased openings connecting with the living room that these two rooms practically count as one large room. French doors might be used and the opening made narrower if it seemed desirable to provide a more definite enclosure for the sun room. A vestibule takes the place of a hall. A grade entrance at the side leads to kitchen and basement. This is only partially excavated, but provides ample space for heater and fuel rooms, laundry and drying room, also a large storage closet for preserves.

Construction: Brick walls, slate or shingle roof.

HOME BUILT FROM DESIGN 6-B-1

A HOUSE IN THE GEORGIAN STYLE

*The entrance, the first-story windows with recessed arches above,
dormers breaking the cornice line, are characteristic touches*

A highly refined entrance detail which shows clearly the skill of the trained architect

Whether in the carefully restricted suburb where only beautiful and distinctive homes are permitted, or in the closely built-up section of the city, this house will make an excellent appearance. It is designed in the Georgian style, with all the dignity and stateliness this term connotes.

The plan is of the central stairway type, the usual hallway being given over to the pass pantry and coat closet. Spacious openings into the living room and dining room from the entry increase the apparent breadth of the interior. It is possible to provide even greater breadth and another room by enclosing the porch.

The living room is made inviting by a charming Colonial fireplace with red brick facing and bookcases on each side. The dining room is connected with the kitchen by a pantry containing cupboards, ice box, and broom closet. The bath, which opens from the larger bedroom as well as from the hall, gives the effect of a suite.

Construction: Tile or brick walls, brick trimmings, stucco-floated finish, shingle or slate roof.

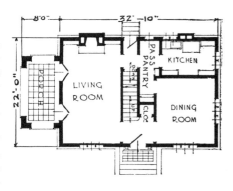

In the basement is a large billiard room with a fireplace. Directly under the living room, it is readily accessible and is approximately the same size, 12 by 20 feet

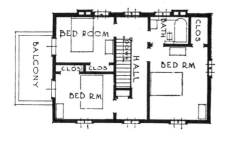

DESIGN *6-B-3*

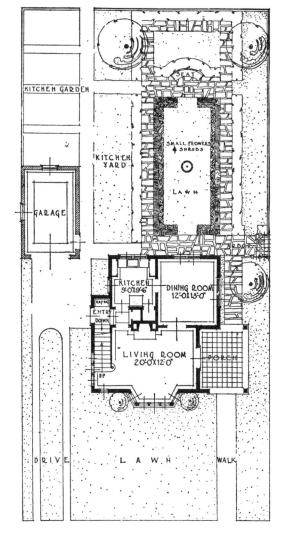

HALF TIMBER AND BRICK

*Bay window, open stairway, and fireplace—
add distinction to the living room*

We venture to say there will never be an excess of small homes that are well planned, compact, and of a pleasing and interesting exterior. At any rate we are always glad to present one that comes as thoroughly under this description as does the house above. Essentially English in character, it has been designed with a view to economy. The living room bay window, the treatment of the porch, and the quaint half timber work in the gable have been tied together in one picturesque, harmonious whole. It is also possible to enclose the porch, which will increase the living area.

An open stairway leads directly from the long living room, so that none of the beauty of this really charming feature is lost. The living room is accessible from the porch, from a door at the opposite end, and from the side or service entry which leads also to the kitchen. The garden for this house is beautifully designed, and its relation to the house is such that it is really as much a part of the house as the house is of the garden.

Construction: First story solid brick walls, second story stucco on wood frame, slate or shingle roof. This should be stained a light brown, the exterior woodwork light weathered oak.

The second floor contains one large, beautiful bedroom ample for twin beds, and two others of more moderate size. In the hall is a broad linen closet. The bathroom is placed directly above the kitchen, thus insuring minimum plumbing costs

HOME BUILT FROM DESIGN *6-B-4*

ARCHED OPENINGS PERFECTLY BALANCED

*Individuality marks this exterior both in general form and in
the arrangement of the openings*

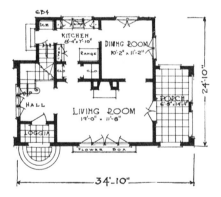

The modern well-designed small home is a wonderful combination of fine appearances and efficient planning. If anyone has any doubt about this, let him look critically about him. Nearly everywhere there exists the architectural products of the post-Victorian era—houses built thirty or thirty-five years ago, full of gingerbread, bric-a-brac, meaningless ornamentation, balconies, and cupolas round and otherwise. For the greater part these ideas are a thing of the past.

It is amazing, also, to find how generous that former generation was of space; how they did not hesitate to waste valuable floor area, how apparently unimportant they found it to have the rooms turn on each other so as to make the arrangement convenient.

The modern small home, of which the one above is a good example, shows how fine architecture may be achieved by direct methods. The design has the appearance of being quite effortless, with none of the straining for effect common to former years. Walls, openings, cornices, and the general massing of the house—that is all there is, but

the whole has a beauty which will endure.

The plan, arranged without waste spaces yet with every accommodation the small family of moderate means might within reason desire, shows what the skillful American architect of today can do. A large living room with a fireplace where the family may gather, a shady porch at the side, a kitchen where meals may be prepared with a minimum of labor, and three excellent bedrooms: these are only a few of the accommodations offered. Between kitchen and living room is an area which, beside affording direct communication between the rear of the house and the front door, is the location of two commodious closets.

Two features worthy of note are the beautifully proportioned stair hall and the many windows in all parts of the house. The living room and also two of the bedrooms have great batteries of windows.

Construction: Wood frame, exterior finish stucco; brick base course and trim; roof of shingles or slate. The porch is paved with cement.

DESIGN 6-B-5

THREE BEDROOMS AND ATTACHED GARAGE

Here are the requirements of many present-day home builders.
The rear porch meets another

This six-room home is of the story-and-a-half type—as are all good homes of Dutch Colonial adaptation—developed in a combination of brick and wood. The first story walls are of brick, while wide siding covers the gable ends and dormer windows. As may well be imagined, this will give a quaint, old-fashioned effect very charming in this sophisticated era. Finish the walls with red brick laid with white mortar joints, stain the roof a soft green, paint the woodwork white and the blinds turquoise blue, golden brown or green, and the result will be a house both decorative and individual — provided, of course, the proper shades are selected.

The direct connection to the garage through the side entry will carry a great appeal today, but this feature may be omitted without affecting the architectural balance of the house. As shown, the house can be placed on a lot from 55 to 60 feet in width. If the garage is omitted, it will go nicely on a 40-foot lot. As indicated, the garage has wide doors at both front and rear. This, of course, is not entirely necessary, but on some lots car owners would find this arrangement a great convenience.

The entrance porch opens into a recess or loggia, which may well be converted into a vestibule for regions of excessive cold. The porch, which opens directly from the living room, greatly increases the living space. This may be either screened or glazed as preferred.

As to the bedrooms, visualize the luxury of that large room extending the depth of the house; the possibilities for furnishing and decoration and the enjoyment of the comfortable chair and the sewing table it will be possible to provide space for. The other two bedrooms while of more moderate size are by no means cramped. Two of the bedrooms have each two generous closets. In the third a shallow wardrobe may be installed which will solve the closet problem very satisfactorily.

Construction: Solid brick walls first story, shingle or slate roof.

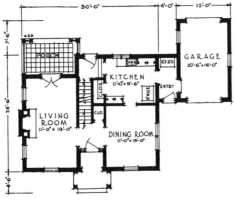
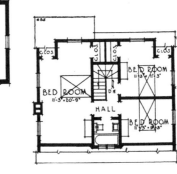

DESIGN *6-B-9*

BRICK FOR THE LARGE SMALL HOUSE

*Distinguished appearances and maximum accommodations
account for the popularity of this design*

Many houses are merely a protection against sun and weather. We say "merely" advisedly, for while it is the business of every house to offer protection from the elements, there are also other functions for them to perform. Should not even the somewhat inexpensive house encourage pride of possession in the family under its roof? Should it not appeal to the æsthetic as well as take care of the physical needs of this same family? Should it not through sheer beauty, and this not at the expense of sound construction, make the proud owner appear a lucky fellow in the eyes of his less fortunate neighbors?

In direct contrast to the great horde of houses which do none of these things, which are little more than four walls and a roof, here is a fine appearing little house that should possess for almost anyone all of the qualifications mentioned above.

The house can best be described as a modern interpretation of the English Tudor style. The high-pitched roof, with its corbel supports and its long sweep, is interrupted by the sharp peak

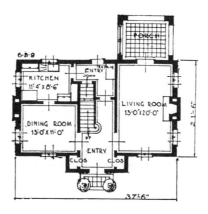

of the front entrance gable and by the well-proportioned dormers at either side. It is a home that might be built on a much larger scale without making any changes in either proportions or details.

The plan possesses all the sterling qualities of the center hall type, a plan that has proved popular for several hundred years. This made possible a living room running the depth of the house, with outside exposure on three sides, and a long, unbroken expanse of wall space that will eliminate any difficulty in furniture arrangement.

For those who desire a formal dining room, here is one of splendid size, well lighted and with plenty of wall space for the required furniture. The kitchen is conveniently arranged.

The second floor plan is indeed a jewel. Merely to think of that larger bedroom makes anyone yearn to possess it. The other bedrooms are both comfortably large, and the sleeping porch affords space for several beds. Closets are numerous and of good size.

Construction: Solid brick walls, roof of slate or wood shingles.

DESIGN 6-B-10

EMPHASIS ON THE LIVING ROOM

*Not only for its size but for its many windows
is this room unique*

This is a design of the Colonial school adapted to present-day conditions. The design has been made delightful with a close cornice, an interesting dormer treatment, and a refined and chaste doorway. It should prove especially popular with home builders whose means are limited.

On account of the fact that the plan is rectangular—is, in fact, nearly square—real economy in building has been gained, for this type of plan requires less materials and labor in the outside walls and in the roof. The principle of reducing costs of building has guided the designer throughout, yet this six-room house possesses a really practical arrangement of rooms, and an exterior that is exceptionally fine.

To the right of the hallway is the dining room and beyond this is an enclosed porch, beautifully designed and proportioned, and with many casement windows. The opening between the dining room and porch is equipped with French doors. This porch would serve excellently as an outside dining room.

The service portion of the house is also thoughtfully designed. There is a pantry with a deep recessed china cupboard and with a convenient space for the icebox, above which there is a window. The kitchen has been made inviting to the housewife with thoroughly modern equipment, all of which

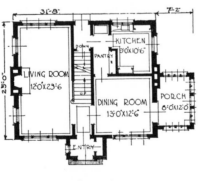

is well placed in relation to the light and the general working requirements of the house proper. The stairs to the basement are located in the grade entry adjoining the kitchen.

The second floor contains three rooms and a bath. The largest chamber is of generous dimensions, and contains two closets. It also has the advantage of direct communication with the bathroom. Each of the other two bedrooms is provided with a large closet. Additional closet space is provided in the bathroom.

The basement is fully excavated, and contains the usual laundry, heater, fuel and storage rooms.

The suggested color scheme for this house is as follows: The brick should be of variegated colors and of fairly rough texture laid in a white mortar joint cut off flush with the brick. The roof also should be of variegated colors and the woodwork painted white. A soft cream-colored floated finish for the stucco work in the dormers will combine well with the balance of the color scheme.

Construction: Exterior walls of solid brick, roof of slate or shingles.

DESIGN *6-B-14*

AN ARISTOCRAT AMONG SMALL HOUSES

*Its handsome exterior prepares one for the originality which
marks the interior*

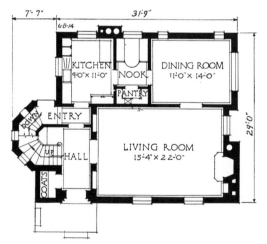

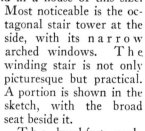

Although it contains but six rooms, this house will make an impressive appearance even among larger and more expensive homes. English in spirit, it is substantial in construction and handsome in design. There is a large recreation room in the basement, which has the added attraction of a fireplace. There is also a fireplace in the living room and a third in the front bedroom.

The plan has several features seldom found in a house of this size. Most noticeable is the octagonal stair tower at the side, with its narrow arched windows. The winding stair is not only picturesque but practical. A portion is shown in the sketch, with the broad seat beside it.

The breakfast nook, pantry, and recessed bookcases in the living room should not be overlooked, nor the size of the bedrooms and the commodious closets. The front bedroom is connected with the bath, and two closets in this room make it convenient for two people.

Construction: Solid brick walls, shingle tile roof.

HOME BUILT FROM DESIGN *6-B-11*

MASONRY FOR THE DUTCH COLONIAL

*Brick and stucco combined give this design an individuality not
often found in houses of this style*

Houses of the same general type as this one won the approval of our great and g r e a t e r grandparents; similar houses—this one, to be specific—will be as worthy of admiration a generation from now as they are today.

The house is of masonry construction, brick walls with a broad stucco dormer above, so that if it is well built repairs will be few and far between and upkeep slight. The design of the exterior is absolutely balanced in arrangement, which gives the house an air of dignity and repose. Two of the prettiest features are what we are inclined to look upon as minor details. These are the flower boxes beneath the dormer windows and the simple trellis which frames the front entrance. With all the emphasis that has been placed upon the use of shutters where called for, it might not be amiss to add a word or two in defense of trellis work also. Certainly it often plays no small part in the charm of the small house.

A study of the plans reveals many desirable features. They are, of course, of the type we find again and again in this book, in all cases equally fasci-

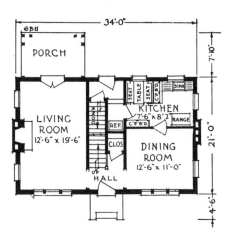

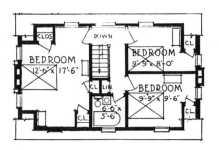

nating. The living room is delightful; bright, cheerful, and spacious. With a fire crackling on the hearth, books, lamps, and furnishings disposed about the room, it will be a popular gathering place. The fireplace, by the way, is entirely out of the line of traffic, so that the group around it will not be disturbed by people passing in and out of the room.

In addition to a handsome formal dining room, there is also provision for a dining alcove in the kitchen. Its location makes the working space in the kitchen somewhat smaller and quite compact, so that the greatest efficiency is possible in the daily work.

The bedrooms are as satisfactory in every way as the rooms on the first floor. There are three of them, and in addition six closets have been provided. The larger bedroom is exceptionally well provided, having three of them. Several closets will seldom come amiss even if the room is occupied by only one person. Many windows also feature this room.

Construction: Solid brick walls, roof of slate or shingles.

HOME BUILT FROM DESIGN *6-B-13*

GABLES AND CASEMENTS

*Clever planning makes possible this
effective exterior*

The many steep gables and groups of casement windows of the exterior suggest the English cottage and make an unusual and interesting treatment for this bungalow. The house is most efficiently planned. It has the privacy of a two-story house and the compactness of a bungalow. The living facilities are commodious. The design provides for three bedrooms, a large well-lighted living room, a delightful dining room as well as a dining alcove, and a complete kitchen. The basement has an extra finished room, as well as a large den with a fireplace.

The living room fireplace is well located at the end of the room where the group around it will not be disturbed. The well-lighted entryway, t h e coat closet off the living room, and the extra closet space in bedrooms and hall add additional values.

A bungalow possesses certain advantages which are not held in common with other types of small houses. One of the most

important of these is gained from its low-lying character. This gives it an air of hominess. It relieves the design of pretentiousness. Two-story houses are often less expensive to build, but when they are of small size, the shallow depth makes them seem unreasonably high. This, of course, is difficult to overcome since ceiling heights must be maintained. A bungalow such as this one lies close to the ground, and

Against a background of white stucco the color of the brick, forming the quoins about the entrance and in the low, rounded platform, stands out vividly

properly relieved with planting, may seem to be a part of the site itself. When selecting a plan, the home-builder should visualize the completed house in its setting. He should get the picture of trees, terrace, and garden; of the arrangement of rooms which affords the best views from the windows. Then his choice will be a wise one.

T h e construction provides for exterior walls of brick. Tile may be substituted for that part of the wall for which the exterior finish is stucco.

HOME BUILT FROM DESIGN *6-B-16*

A COMMON PLAN UNCOMMONLY HANDLED

Houses built from this strictly rectangular type of plan are frequently commonplace. The homes shown here, however, because of the high-pitched roof, good proportions, and careful working out of small details are distinctive and will hold their own for years to come.

Construction: The original drawings call for hollow tile, stucco exterior, brick veneer to first floor window sills, tile roof. Solid brick walls may be used as shown.

Bricks are laid here without gauge lines, and in keeping with this the roofing is of shakes. An uneven and harmonious texture results in both cases. Fine effects are possible by disregarding building traditions, but one must remember it takes a master to break the rules successfully

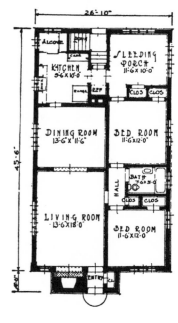

HOME BUILT FROM DESIGN *6-B-16*

HOME BUILT FROM DESIGN *6-B-15*

A DESIGN OF FINISH AND RESTRAINT

Details and ornament are in good taste. Windows are numerous

There is always the greatest economy in building a square house, for there are no angles, no breaks in the rooms or walls to eat into valuable floor space and the building budget. The square house also seems to have a larger amount of room, for every foot of area can be utilized to advantage.

As this home is very nearly square, it enjoys these advantages to a great extent. With its well-balanced window arrangement and arched doorway the home has a quiet dignity that is well suited to its location on a narrow city lot.

The interior is roomy. The living room is indeed so large that if an entrance hall is desired, that end of the room containing the stairway and the coat closet might be partitioned off with a broad archway separating the two areas.

In the dining room practically one whole side is glass, for double French doors provide access to the terrace, and high side lights on either side open casement fashion. In the dining alcove built-in furniture is specified: the benches with decorative end profiles, the table with prettily turned legs. The alcove is large enough for a small table and chairs, however. The storage cupboard here has glass doors, those in the kitchen wood. The alcove really serves all the purposes of a pantry.

Two of the bedrooms are exceptionally attractive, one as to size, one as to the number of windows lighting it. The group at the rear of this room is similar to that in the dining room below, with both side lights and French doors. A wrought iron railing serves as a protection when the doors are open and gives the effect of a balcony. In the upstairs hall is not only the usual linen closet but also a convenient broom closet for cleaning materials. In the ceiling of the hall is a scuttle which permits access to storage space in the attic.

The rear elevation is as attractive as the front, with not only the broad window groups mentioned, but a smaller one, with a recessed arched panel above and window box below, lighting the breakfast nook. The drawings show an alternate front entrance, a Colonial doorway with a pediment.

Construction: Solid brick walls, slate or shingle roof.

S. S. Beman, Architect

WALLS, ROOFS AND OPENINGS KEYED IN TUNE

*In this inimitably picturesque home the
informality of leaded glass and skintled
brickwork produces a beautiful effect*

HOME BUILT FROM DESIGN *6-B-17*

SIX ROOMS AND SOME EXTRAS

Such as porches, two fireplaces, and a second lavatory

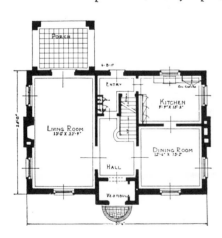

There are "Colonial" houses of every description in this era of strife for individuality. Modern methods of building and planning have wrought changes in this style which cause architects sometimes to ponder over what is really meant today by "Colonial."

When you think of "Colonial" you may have in mind a rectangular dwelling, with wide white clapboards and green blinds. Then again you may visualize some handsome house built in the early Colonial days of field boulders and slate roof. Perhaps a pilgrimage to Mount Vernon settled this question of Colonial architecture for you.

There is one characteristic of all Colonial homes—they have simplicity and dignity. We regret not being able to show the coloring of the modern Colonial presented here—the freshness of the mossy green tile roof with the harmonizing green shutters, combined with red brick, laid with wide white mortar joints. Every care has been taken in the house to carry out the Colonial spirit.

In plan arrangement this home is similar to that of countless old Colonial houses. But whereas in the old houses there was generally a back and front parlor, our modern Colonial homes have one fine, undivided living room. There used to be a butler's pantry between dining room and kitchen, but modern efficiency now uses this space to increase the size of these two rooms and builds plenty of cupboards.

This home provides six good rooms with an open porch to the rear and sleeping porch above it. There is space under the roof for a commodious attic. An open stairway in Colonial design forms an attractive feature of the hall.

Construction: Solid brick walls, tile, slate or shingle roof.

A DESIGN OF GRACE AND BALANCE

*The exterior, beautifully designed, has a simplicity
that bespeaks low cost*

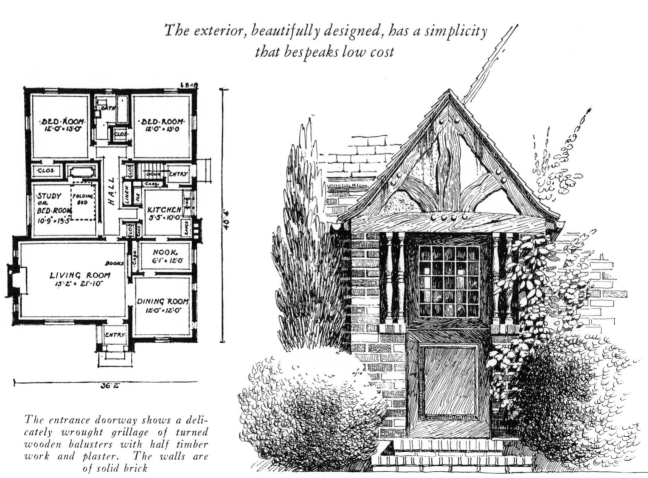

*The entrance doorway shows a deli-
cately wrought grillage of turned
wooden balusters with half timber
work and plaster. The walls are
of solid brick*

DESIGN *6-B-23*

A PORCH WHICH PLAYS A MAJOR PART

*Not only is it an essential and integral part of the design, but
its size greatly increases the living quarters*

When an architect speaks of what is known as balance, he does not mean the kind of balance the scales bring forth—one weight on one side and exactly the same weight on the other. The architect balances unlike things, but he gives them such relative importance that a stable effect is gained. Balance that is not symmetrical is the most difficult to get, and the most interesting after it has been worked out. One of the problems is to see that the main idea will not be carried away by a heterogeneous collection of minor ones.

This house shows admirably the point in question. It not only achieves balance by repeating the arch of the main entry in the front wall of the porch, but each arch accentuates the other merely by its repetition. The effect is sound architecture, which is simply another way of saying that it will be interesting to everyone who sees it, and mighty livable.

The entry vestibule is set one step down from the living room, an ideal protection in stormy weather. There is not only a coat closet in the vestibule, but another on the landing at the

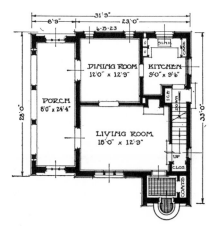

foot of the stairs. The fireplace is set within the partitions in such a way that it does not utilize otherwise valuable space.

Cupboard space in the kitchen is generous, and includes a cooler for keeping food fresh by means of a current of outside air.

The second story is an exercise in geometry. With the shape of the roof as it is here, it requires a real knowl-

edge of planning—of what the architects call the section of building—to get the accommodation we have here. The rooms are of good size with generous closet space. Halls and passages have been reduced to the minimum.

The construction is of hollow tile, with the exception of the dormers, which are of frame, and the entire house is finished with stucco. It is suggested that the stucco be left light, white or cream color, and stippled.

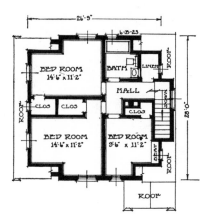

HOME BUILT FROM DESIGN *6-B-20*

BUNGALOWS OF BRICK OR STUCCO

Both appearance and plan are fine in character

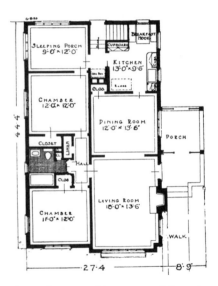

Living room, dining room, kitchen, breakfast nook, and porch; two bedrooms and a sleeping porch, to say nothing of a bath—that is the formula for most of our small homes. Juggling these units around to make a home out of a formula is an architect's job. If he succeeds in getting architecture into it, there is a fine, livable plan and beauty of all the parts. If at the same time with this usefulness there comes about economy of building, pretty nearly everyone is interested.

The small homes illustrated here are desirable for this reason, because

HOME BUILT FROM DESIGN *6-B-19*

t h e y have architecture. The plan, walls, window openings, and roof all belong to each other. The same plan serves both houses illustrated here, and it is a fine, workable one with all the conveniences that home builders demand.

The ordinary way to roof this plan would have been to put a gable over it running from front to back. That would have been commonplace, and probably ugly. Here, by the simple device of bringing the living room forward slightly, the architect obtains a reason for the roof's distinctive treatment.

One house, design 6-B-20, has hollow tile walls stucco finished; the other, design 6-B-19, solid brick walls.

HOME BUILT FROM DESIGN 6-B-22

A House of Architectural Distinction

Gables, chimney, and close-clipped eaves are consistently English

This interior is planned with thought for beauty and hospitality as well as comfort and convenience. Beside the handsome fireplace in the living room is a wide window seat. The dining room is large, the kitchen efficient and provided with ample storage space in cupboards and pantry.

In the bedroom over the living room is a second fireplace and a built-in dressing table which balances the broad wardrobe.

Closets are numerous. In the basement is a sizable recreation room. The house shown is built reversed from the plans.

Construction: Solid brick walls, roof of slate, tile, or shingles.

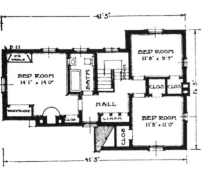

The beamed entrance porch is unique in design. Beyond is a hall of good size, with access on the one hand to the long living room and to the dining room on the other. The stairway, generous in width, is in keeping with the fine character of the interior

Photograph by Mattie Edwards Hewitt

Bringing the Outdoors into the Sun Room

*Use a bright, cheery scenic paper and woodwork
painted to harmonize, for if sunshine gleams
from the walls what matter if the weather sulks
without?*

HOME BUILT FROM DESIGN *6-B-25*

MAKING THE MOST OF GARDEN FRONTAGE

All living rooms open upon the beauty and privacy of the garden

This design incorporates much of the distinction and homelike qualities of the English style. The informal massing of the walls, the stair tower, and the closely clipped gables are typically English features. The roof, woodwork about the windows, and the brick trim afford opportunity for the interesting use of color and variety of texture.

The most arresting deviation from the standard room arrangement is the position of kitchen and stair tower. Increasing street traffic is making living rooms at the rear desirable.

Construction: Stucco over wood frame, shingle roof.

HOME BUILT FROM DESIGN *6-B-26*

WITH A BAY WINDOW IN THE KITCHEN

A dining alcove and a sleeping porch are other pleasant features

The low rambling effect of this cottage exaggerates its real size, for it is in reality a small house. There are six good rooms, although one has been called a sleeping porch. The connection between dining room and living room may be enlarged if the owner desires a more open, spacious effect. The lower illustration shows the open terrace screened and covered with a gay awning, which greatly enlarges its scope of usefulness.

In the kitchen light for the sink is assured, for this fixture is located in the bay with light from three sides. There is also provision for a broom closet and an additional kitchen cabinet. A dining alcove large enough for a separate table and four chairs completes the kitchen. The large attic is

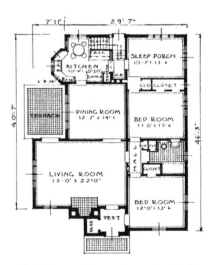

reached by a stairway from the kitchen.

The bedrooms are all arranged along one side of the house, and thus are provided with almost as much privacy as second floor rooms. Each bedroom has a generous closet, with two additional ones in bathroom and hall.

Construction: Hollow tile walls, stucco finish, and brick trim. Solid brick walls may be used. Roof of shingles, slate or tile.

HOME BUILT FROM DESIGN 6-B-27

BEAUTY WROUGHT IN TILE AND STUCCO

Contrasting materials afford vivacity of color and texture

Here is an expression of the alchemy of architecture by which gross materials of wood, brick, and stone have been transmuted into pure beauty. Only a skillful architect could have produced it. See how well the plan elements are disposed, how direct the communication between rooms.

To this six-room house, four on the first floor and two on the second, have been added breakfast room, terrace, ingle nook with a charming fireplace—shown below—closets in profusion.

Construction: Hollow tile walls, stucco finish, brick trim, tile roof, casements metal or frame.

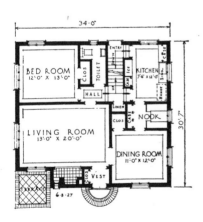

DESIGN 6-B-29

A BUNGALOW WITH A MANSARD ROOF

*A porch, breakfast room, and shower are among the features
provided in addition to the six main rooms*

The style of this house really is American, although in the roof over the main portion of the house may be seen the influence of the French Mansard style. It has the pitch on all four sides that is characteristic of the Mansard roof and terminates in the same type of flat deck. Especially pleasing details of the exterior are the entrance doorway, and the group of casement windows that light the living room.

About the first floor there is an agreeable air of spaciousness rather remarkable for a house of this character. There are six main rooms: living room, dining room, kitchen, and bedroom on the first floor. In addition to these, however, the plan provides a porch, a breakfast room about seven feet square, first floor lavatory with shower, a second bathroom and a large storage room upstairs.

These are the general features of this design, but after all the comfort of the family living in a house is not only dependent upon the number and arrangement of the rooms, but also upon the perfection of many small details. Really successful small homes often de-

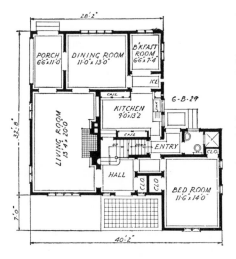

pend enormously on the proper working out of things which at first might seem of minor importance. Many conveniences are arranged here.

The stairway is of the combination type; that is, two steps lead from the kitchen to the common landing, as well as from the entrance hallway.

Perhaps one of the modern conveniences that women appreciate more

than anything else is a breakfast alcove in the kitchen itself, or a breakfast room in connection with it. This design provides such a room in a sunny corner and it is large enough so that it can accommodate a small breakfast set.

The first floor bedroom is accessible from both the kitchen and the front hall. The downstairs toilet is equipped with a shower bath.

Construction: Wood frame, exterior finish siding, shingles or stucco.

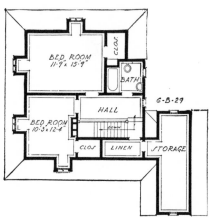

FIVE MAJOR ROOMS OR SIX

Two plans for essentially the same exterior

Formal houses are comparatively simple to design. Their orderliness is such that a good many problems about the massing of walls and roof are easily solved. Of course, even in this type of building architecture does not result unless the parts bear proper relation to each other. It is not a job for an amateur.

Picturesque houses are more difficult to design. Their organization follows no definite form, and the massing of the plan elements greatly influences external appearances. The sizes and shapes of the rooms must have an interrelation if the exterior is to be fine. Architects call this "composition." It is a process of modeling by which

forms are arranged so as to achieve the best results both in plan and in exterior.

Because of the exceptional charm of this design it has been developed with two different plans, one for five rooms, one for six. From the front the appearance is the same. The house illustrated is design 6-B-30. The sixth room is a bedroom on the second floor. The first floor plan is shown at the bottom of the page. To the left above is the five-room plan, design 5-B-36.

The plan is straightforward, easy to build, essentially economical. While it is necessarily a little more expensive than an absolutely rectangular house, the difference in cost is by no means commensurate with the greater difference in appearance between the two types.

The walls are laid with 24-inch tan-dipped shingles. The roof is of plain brown shingles. The chimney, chimney pots, and small brick platform before the door are dark red. The trim is twilight blue, while the awnings are tan and brown. The door is brown like the roof, with big strap hinges and

a thumb latch of dull bronze. The long window box matches the walls in color.

There is no waste space. Communication between rooms is direct, with a minimum of hall space. There are numerous interesting details.

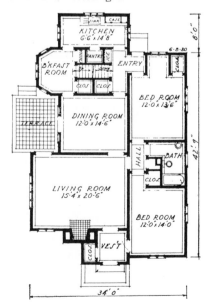

ENGLISH WITH AN L-SHAPED PLAN

This permits the living room, porch, and the bedroom above
to be set off from the rest of the house

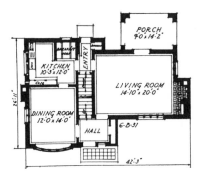

Among the many attractive qualities possessed by English houses is that of informality, and perhaps this is its most striking characteristic. This is particularly true of the English small home. It possesses a certain modesty, a lack of forwardness, which, however it may have come about, distinguishes it greatly. In these houses the architectural composition, which is the name the architect gives the arrangement of all the parts, often has a balance not gained by the simple formula of having windows and walls of equal number and expanse on each side of a central doorway. One of the ways by which this quality is attained is in the use of the L-shaped plan. This is definitely an English characteristic, and, more important, it has certain virtues which are uncommon.

Design 6-B-31 illustrates how much may be done with a plan of this sort. Even the most casual study of this design makes evident the fact that emphasis is laid on the living room. It will be seen that with this room occupying one entire wing of the house, a remarkable area of useful space is gained, as well as an extensive frontage for the room upon both street and garden. This is the most important room of the house and

this importance is emphasized by its position in the plan. It bears a certain detachment from the dining room and kitchen. For many this is an extremely desirable feature.

In the second story are three bedrooms and bath. Here seven closets are made possible by the low swing of the roof.

The exterior will carry its own message. The walls, made beautiful in themselves by well-chosen brick work, are enlivened by a variety of other materials well in keeping with the type of architecture and with good taste and discernment. The heavy wood beam spans a wide window in the front wall of the living room. Half timber work with stucco inclosure gives a touch of intimacy to the doorway. The roof, for which it is hoped the home builder may afford a covering of large and heavy slates, is designed with its importance to the whole impression given by the house well in mind. The "swept" valley, with its slates uninterrupted by any showing of metal work, is a thoughtful detail. The timbers about the entrance may be adzed.

Construction: Solid brick walls, with stucco between half timber work and in dormers, roof of slate.

A REPOSEFUL HOUSE

*With broad, open, beautiful rooms
overlooking a terrace*

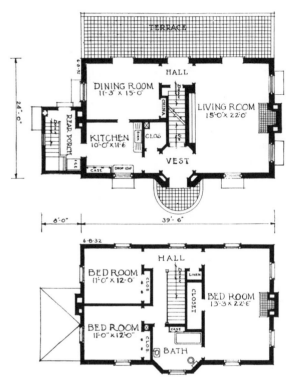

Traveling up and down the streets of newly built sections of almost any city one wonders at so many frenzied houses—grotesque little things, cheaply and gaudily built.

Now contrast these with this design, a quiet, unassuming house without pretensions to showiness. Here there are no bits of stone floating around throughout the brick work, no stucco rash, no projecting rafters nor artificial roof curves—just the beauty that goes with simplicity, honesty, good taste, and sound construction.

The sketch shows the modest entrance. Beyond is an entrance hall octagonal in shape. In the living room, opposite the fireplace, is a long length of recessed book shelves with cupboards below. In the basement, reached through the rear hall, is a large recreation room with a fireplace. In the large bedroom is a third fireplace.

Construction: Solid brick walls, roof of shingles or slate.

DESIGN 6-B-32

HOME BUILT FROM DESIGN *6-C-5*

WITH GABLED ROOF AND DINING PORCH

*The exterior is made interesting by an arched entrance, numerous
windows, and the large bay*

This house may or may not have a dining room, for the dining
porch shown may be used exclusively as a porch. The breakfast
nook will serve the purpose ordinarily. If the porch is omitted,
the house will be admirably suited to a narrow lot. The architect
visualized the needs of the small home owner down to the minutest
detail. All through the house will be seen numerous conveniences,
simplification of construction, and devices to make the house attractive without added expense.

The kitchen is intelligently planned, with cupboards for the
storage of food, linens, china, and near the range two others for
pots, pans, and cleaning equipment. The smaller of the three
bedrooms might also be used as a sewing room.

Construction: Wood frame, stucco finish, shingle or slate roof.

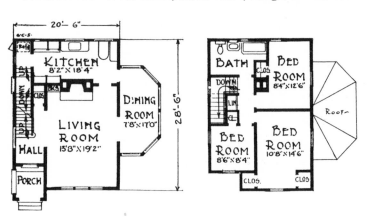

HOME BUILT FROM DESIGN 6-C-7

A LESS FORMAL DUTCH COLONIAL HOUSE

The floor plan is orderly, compact, and convenient.
The exterior has an engaging simplicity

This design has that rare quality which comes from a proper balance of formality and irregularity. The doorway, with the protecting hood above it, the domestic touch of the bay window, and the form and location of the chimney stack partake in a certain mild sense of the picturesque. By such means individuality is lent to architecture. Small houses having these qualities are much desired.

In this design, the long living room running across the front should be an especially beautiful one as it has a fireplace at one end with book shelves at both sides, with also the charm of a projecting bay window. The room is 18 feet long by 13 feet wide; the dining room approximately 14 feet by 13 feet. Both rooms are light and airy.

There are six rooms in all with, of course, the usual basement and bath. Access is provided to the front door from the kitchen without the necessity of going through the rest of the house.

Observe how well the kitchen is equipped with work and storage space and how pleasantly the dining room

is lighted with four windows of good size. In the second story there are three bedrooms. An alternate plan locates the closets at the outer corners of the rooms, making use of the space under the roof and adding the closet space as shown to the area of the bedrooms. The ceilings of the rooms are slightly cut off at the outer wall.

Many people who engage in the study of house plans will recognize in this a type often used with other exteriors. It is indeed a favorite with architects, and this comes about because they appreciate the logic and orderliness of this arrangement. So far as costs are concerned, it partakes of all the advantages which come from a rectangular plan, for with such houses the labor of construction tends to be less. So far as convenience and even luxury is concerned, it has the former quality through the common-sense arrangement of the plan, and possibilities for luxury to any extent to which the home builder may wish to carry it. As a beginning a porch may be added to the rear opening off the dining room.

WHERE SUNLIGHT HAS FREE PLAY

Every room has windows on at least two sides. Living room
and one bedroom get light and air from three

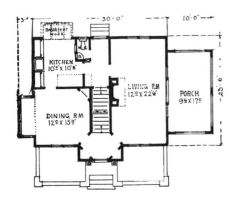

A breakfast nook may be added off the kitchen at little additional expense. Dotted lines indicate the location and size of the proposed nook

There is an old story that everyone will remember. It starts like this: "There was a crooked man, and he built a crooked house ——"

The story did not tell how much extra the house cost because it was crooked. No matter what he spent, if the crooked man had built a square house with the same accommodations, it would not have cost him so much. The square house is economical because it is compact. It takes less roof, less excavation, less foundation wall, than the picturesque and interesting rambling house. Perhaps the most important factor in lower cost for the square house is in the labor bill. For the rambling house there must be a great deal of measuring, cutting, fitting, and adjusting of parts. This takes time, and when time is computed in terms of wages for high-class mechanics, the cost runs to a high figure.

The design shown here is not a square house in the absolute geometrical sense, but its rectangular outline certainly distinguishes it from a house of rambling character and puts it in the square house group. It will achieve all the economies that go with that type of building.

Another advantage of the square house of this type is its convenience.

The rooms are close together. Several may be thrown together to make the house seem larger than its actual size.

This plan is exceptionally well provided with the extra conveniences that make a home a delight to live in. The rooms in general are large and airy. There is an abundance of closet space. The downstairs toilet is highly desirable.

The living room is an inviting place with a fireplace, and double French doors leading to the open or enclosed porch. The dining room has an interesting plan to which a great deal of variety and much glorious sunshine is added by the projecting bay window. A corner cupboard is indicated to balance the angle at the entrance from the hall. The straightforward stairway, enclosed between walls, eliminates the extra expense that goes with elaborate millwork.

Of the three bedrooms one is plenty large enough for twin beds. The smaller room would serve excellently as a study or child's room.

A sleeping porch large enough to accommodate several beds or cots could be built above the porch, thus greatly increasing the sleeping accommodations.

Construction: Wood frame, exterior finish stucco, roof of shingles.

DESIGN *6-C-20*

DESIGN 6-D-3

GEORGIAN HOUSE OF EXCEPTIONAL PLAN

The location of the stairs increases the amount of floor space available for use

The particular architectural family of which this pleasant house is a member is relatively unimportant. We might say it is a modern adaptation of the Georgian. Certainly it has some of the characteristics of Georgian English architecture.

If the plan is viewed in detail, taking into account all the equipment—the grade entrance, sun porch, fireplace, and in the second story, besides the usual three bedrooms and bath, six closets and a dressing room—it will be seen that a great deal is afforded in the way of convenience and livability. The type of plan is not new, but this arrangement of it is unusual, for the stairway has been brought back to the rear of the house in such a way as to interfere to the least extent with circulation between the rooms. The actual useful area in the house is larger than it would be if the stairs were located farther to the front.

The details of the exterior that attract the eye particularly are the entrance, the wrought iron balcony above it, the ornamental dormers, and the low-pitched roof. The ceilings in the second story are broken slightly by the

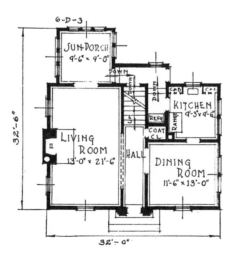

roof, but by the use of dormers full length windows have been made possible. The height of the wall is still sufficient for the reception of standard bedroom furniture. Yet by bringing the roof down in this way the desirable quality of apparent low height of the walls has been obtained. This is a result toward which architects bend their efforts in small house designing.

The plan is somewhat flexible in ar-

rangement as the sun porch at the rear may be placed at the side. The dressing room in the second story may be shared by both the flanking bedrooms. A vestibule may be accommodated to the front hall and doorway. Also a sleeping porch may be built above the sun porch.

The upstairs hall is unusually pleasant; attractive in form and well lighted from the windows on the stair landing.

Construction: Stucco on frame.

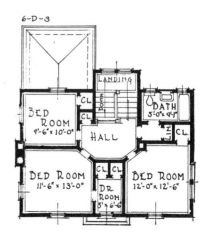

HOME BUILT FROM DESIGN *6-D-1*

A PLAN WITH A CENTRAL HALL

*A broad front porch and the long dormer
have been skillfully designed*

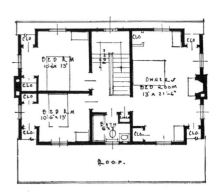

Many of the so-called Dutch Colonial homes do not rightly deserve the name. They get this classification principally from having a gambrel roof or the appearance of one. Many of them are actually two-story houses with lines of gambreled gable ends running down the sides. This, of course, is false as well as ugly. Even in true gambrel roofs too often we see the results of overheavy cornices, projections that cast heavy shadows out of proportion to the size of the house.

Here, though, is a house that is essentially Dutch architecture in all respects excepting perhaps that of the dormer. This has been added to make the second story rooms more livable. It is an improvement on the original form.

The porch shown here is truly a part of the house, being bound into it by the overhanging roof. For the people who must have a porch, the generous dimensions of this one will have an immediate appeal.

The details of this house conform to its general style and quality. The shutters at the sides of the windows

add a play of color and texture. Painted or stuccoed common brick is used for the chimneys. The front wall of the house enclosed by the porch is plastered, as were many such walls in old Colonial days. The front doorway is a side lighted affair, an expression of hospitality as well as an assurance of a well-lighted hallway.

The plan itself is a typical central hallway type with a balustraded stairway mounting to the second story. All of the rooms are well lighted, two of them having windows on three sides. There is a coat closet in the hall and a broom closet in the kitchen. In the upper hall there is a linen closet and each of the bedrooms has two closets, in fact, the owner's bedroom might have two additional areas of this kind. They are indicated on the floor plan. The fireplace in this bedroom is a pleasant feature that might be included. Because of the additional expense it would entail, it is not indicated on the working drawings. Except for its closets, this room is as large as the living room.

Many have raised objections to the

Dutch Colonial house in that the low roof lines cut into the second story rooms. In certain types of such houses this does constitute an objection—floor spaces are interfered with, rooms are made irregular, the broken ceiling lines are oppressive. But, when these roof planes are well handled, these objections do not arise; in fact, the bedrooms of Dutch Colonial houses may have an especially fine quality gained directly from the section, the way in which the roof comes down. It requires skill to do it correctly. This plan is a demonstration of that skill.

HOME BUILT FROM DESIGN *6-D 2*

A SIX-ROOM SQUARE HOUSE

*Simplicity of design promises economy of
construction and of upkeep*

The dignity and impressive mien of this house did not come about through accident. Every element of the design was developed with that end in view, even to the downspouts which are ordinarily considered a minor detail, an afterthought and left more or less to chance. Brick has been used here in such a way as to bring out all the beauty of this material. As a result the house has a distinguished air pleasant to see.

This house is another of the square type essentially economical in design. The practically unbroken planes of the hip roof make it well adapted to tile or slate, but shingles would also be an attractive covering. The w o r k i n g drawings show slightly projecting iron balconies, after the manner of French city houses, placed at the two outer second story windows. Instead of the shuttered windows shown in the house illustrated, French doors take their place, opening upon the small balconies mentioned. This arrangement gives an impression of even greater dignity to the design. The arched and recessed panels above the openings shown here

are omitted when the balconies are used at the second floor windows.

The appearance of the house gives a promise of comfort that is fully realized in the arrangement of rooms and the careful consideration given to all the small conveniences of modern living. The rear porch, opening as it does from both living and dining rooms, is almost a part of these rooms. It may be used either as an open porch or glazed as a sun room.

The first floor contains three generous rooms, and in addition there is the porch, a dining alcove, kitchen entry, and stair hall. The arrangement of the rooms is suitable for a setting in which the principal views and lighting are at the front. However, the location of porch and dining room is such as to make the most of a garden at the rear.

The hall provides direct communication between the kitchen and the front door. A grade entrance is also provided for entrance to the kitchen or basement. A coat closet on the first landing of the stairway is conveniently situated. There is a full base-

ment reached through the grade entry.

On the second floor are three bedrooms extremely desirable as to size, lighting and ventilation. Two closets in the larger room make it convenient for two people. The second front bedr o o m is connected with this room. This makes the smaller room suitable for a variety of purposes: for a study, sitting room, nursery or child's room.

Construction: B r i c k veneer on wood frame. This house was built reversed from the plans.

Hewitt & Brown, Architects

MAKING THE MOST OF THE ENTRANCE

The shingles on the roof have been laid without lines, but with restraint. The plaster surface has been made rough, but not with wild abandon. The stones are rough hewn, but naturally, as though the elements had softened their surfaces. Happily blended, the different materials look as though they all belong together

HOME BUILT FROM DESIGN *6-D-4*

FORMALITY IN THE ENGLISH EXTERIOR

*The plan has a central hall, large porch, and the commodious
rooms which make for comfortable living*

The early American builders developed a type of plan
with a hallway and stair at the center. For certain
kinds of homes it has never been much improved upon.
Here we have it with an exterior strongly dominated by
English forms—high roof, peaked gables, dormers that
break into eaves. But the side porch is an American
feature, a device which has possibilities for enjoyment which
no one who has ever been accustomed to it would do
without.

As for the plan, we have a hall that makes a clean sweep
from the front door to the back. The open stairway with
graceful spiral newel adds a fixed ornament to the house
and a constant source of pleasure. Archways lead to living
room on the right and dining room on the left.

The dining room has triple windows at the front and
two windows at the side set far enough apart so that a
buffet may be placed between them. Beyond is the kitchen
where all the equipment is in proper order for efficient
management. There is space for a dining table here with
the sink, food cabinets, china closet and refrigerator arranged along one wall.

The living room is unusually large, has a handsome fireplace, broad windows, and ready access to the porch.

In the second story there are three excellent bedrooms
each with generous closets. The large attic space is accessible by means of a disappearing stair ladder which folds
into the ceiling of the upper hall.

The decorative moldings about the door and over the
windows may be worked out inexpensively in stucco or in
cast stone.

Construction: Wood frame, exterior finish stucco. Roof
of slate or shingles.

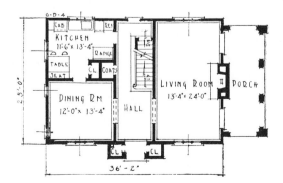

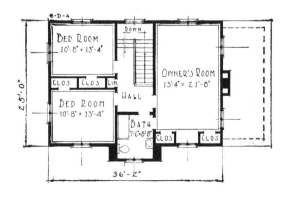

HOME BUILT FROM DESIGN 6-D-12

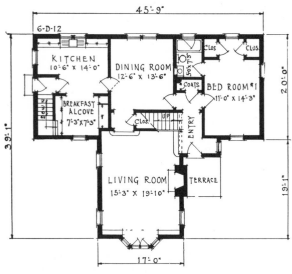

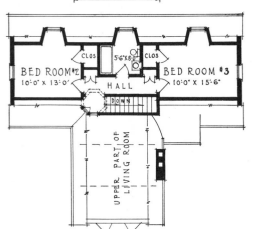

HIGH UP AND LOW DOWN

*This living room extends from below floor
level through two stories*

About no home can we say arbitrarily that it is the best, since what would be so for one family would be quite unsuitable for another. For some home builders, however, even the superlative might be applied to this house.

The brick walls display the attractive variations in color common to this material. The sharply pointed front gable, the long length of chimney, and the cupola which lights the stair hall within are all set off to advantage against the broad background of the main roof.

The living room may truly be called a handsome room, for it is not only large but exceptionally high. Set down two steps below the level of the rest of the house, it extends up through two stories. A full length bay window, a beautiful fireplace, and steps which lead up to hall and dining room give it character, while the stairs to the second floor are open and lend further distinction to the room. The balusters are elaborately turned. On either side of the baywindow are bookcases equal to it in height, and with enclosed cupboards below. There is a wainscoting of wide boards, with V-shaped joints between, about the room.

Not content with a large formal dining room, the designer has included a convenient breakfast alcove which opens off the kitchen. A double bedroom with a bath opening from it completes the first floor.

The plan is not the strictly rectangular affair most economical to build, but its rambling tendencies account in large measure for the picturesqueness of the exterior, also for the fact that many of the rooms have outside exposure on three sides.

Construction: Brick veneer, roof of shingles or slate.

HOME BUILT FROM DESIGN *6-D-21*

A COLORFUL AND UNIQUE HOUSE

Here also is a studio living room. A built-in
garage is included in the plan

Designed for a mild climate, this house has n o basement, although one may be arranged. The heating plant is on the first floor. Laundry space may be arranged in the garage near the kitchen.

The living room, with its g r e a t window, extends t h r o u g h two stories. On a higher level than the rest of the h o u s e, this room is reached by a short flight of steps from the hall. Stairs from the living room lead to the second floor. The fireplace is in keeping with the style of the house.

Cream or buff colored stucco, colored tile inserts, a n d a brilliant awning over the sleeping porch are suggested.

Construction: Stucco on wood frame.

THE OUT-OF-THE-ORDINARY HOUSE

Exterior and floor plan have been carefully modeled together
to achieve the finest qualities for each

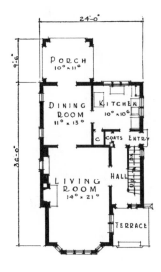

Six rooms and an open porch are two of the most common demands of home builders. Recently there has been added another—an English exterior.

This house has been designed to answer these requirements. It is a city type house, particularly for those cities where lots are narrow, for it can easily be accommodated on a 40-foot lot. Undoubtedly there will be an automobile. Even on a 40-foot lot there is plenty of space for the driveway.

This is an entirely modern house—not an adjustment of old forms to new requirements. The plan recognizes present-day costs of construction and the necessity of minimizing these, the problems of household management when a servant is not employed, and sound methods of construction to keep down the yearly expenses for repairs and maintenance. It is a modern house in every sense of the word.

But with this distinction it has qualities of Old World architecture that are attractive to home builders almost the nation over, particularly as to exterior. The forms are English. The whole appearance of the house has had somehow wrought into it the spirit of English architecture.

This house has comparatively few features of design. There is the doorway with its enhancement of stone, the great bay window with its tall lights, the low sweep of the roof about the dormers, the garage driveway gate. But it depends for its effect chiefly on the massing of the walls and roof. It is a type of architecture which never grows old.

As for the plan, it explains itself—a fine living room turning so conveniently on the dining room and upon the porch beyond that a vista of great length is obtained. The handsome bay window increases the feeling of spaciousness. The beautiful fireplace and comfortable seat under the window at the side give the intimate touches we desire in our homes.

The open porch beyond the dining room may serve as an outside dining porch in the summer with most convenient service from the kitchen. The kitchen itself is replete with modern equipment and with plenty of space for everything. A good coat closet is convenient to the rear entry, through which one steps to the automobile drive.

Upstairs there are two large bedrooms and a smaller one, besides a small space for sewing or storage, a closet for each room, and a linen closet in the hallway. There is also a clothes chute in the linen closet. A deep window seat, filling the space between the two closets, enhances the larger of the rear bedrooms.

Construction: Brick veneer on wood frame, casement windows with metal sash, roof of slate.

DESIGN *6-D-16*

DESIGN 6-D-25

COMBINED ECONOMY AND DISTINCTION

The straightforward plan and simple design of this house account for both

Labels are ordinarily applied to houses according to more or less superficial qualities. Generally these names mean only that in the matter of exterior silhouette and detail precedents derived from the architecture of certain countries have been drawn upon. The essential character of a house, however, is determined almost entirely by the plan, and this ordinarily being distinctly American, houses should fall more often under this heading.

The plan of this house is a variation of a type that most nearly approaches the ideal combination of economy and livability of any type that has been evolved. Its outstanding characteristics are a simple rectangular shape, a central stairway, and a living room across one end. These three features result in numerous advantages. The rectangular shape is cheap and easy to build, easy to roof, and automatically gives good proportions in mass. The single central stairway, turning back on itself, gives easy circulation between all stories, an outside cellar entrance, and a second floor landing that permits the maximum development of bedroom space. The living room across one end makes possible light and air on three

sides, an outlook on both street and garden, and a location for fireplace and chimney that results in the minimum of complications.

With this general arrangement and shape the total width of the house, even with the side porch, is such as to permit its use on a 50-foot lot. If the frontage of the lot demands another orientation of the rooms, the plan can easily be reversed.

The height of the roof is great enough to allow an additional room in the attic if needed, and a stairway can be arranged over the main stairs.

The size and proportions of the dining room are excellent. The kitchen has been skillfully arranged. Cabinets on either side of the sink make up one convenient working center; the table or cabinet to the right, another.

The exterior walls are to be covered with wood shingles. These should be of large size, with wide butts, and laid so that each course has at least 10 inches exposed. Wide siding could be substituted if desired, although it should be emphasized that any diminution in the width of the exposed courses of material will result in a certain loss of distinction.

DETAILED IN THE ENGLISH MANNER

*Stucco and half timber construction, a great bay window, and the
distinctive treatment of the roof differentiate this house*

The English people in long centuries past built houses with frames of heavy wooden timbers; these they fastened together with wooden pins. Between the great timbers they filled in masonry and plaster and called it "half timber" construction. This had picturesque qualities of a decided character.

Today we use half timber work, but not in the old manner. With us the wooden areas are commonly nothing more than boards that are put upon the wall after it is built. Even this construction, if it is well done, gives to the house the pleasant air of domesticity that is such an essential part of the English style.

Here is a design in the modern half timber style. One of its most distinctive features is the roof. This, as will be seen, is something more than an assembly of pitched planes with which we ordinarily crown our homes, for this roof expresses in an essential way the idea of protection from the elements, a shelter.

The management of the roof planes is something in which the English have excelled. They have excelled also in the management of windows. The Englishman likes to group windows

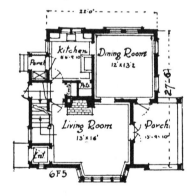

*The bedrooms are of good size,
well lighted, with adequate
closets, and each has cross ventilation*

together, letting in great floods of light and sunshine. By breaking up the glass areas into small panes he obtains privacy in the rooms. His windows are easy to see out of, not easy to see into. Often, as here, they project from the wall in a bay or oriel, accentuating the area of the room and affording greater breadth of vision.

In such respects this design follows English precedent, but the plan is American. The plan shows six rooms and a porch, but even a casual study shows that there is nothing common or stereotyped about their arrangement. The living room, dining room, and kitchen turn upon each other conveniently. The bay window adds to the roomy, spacious effect of the first floor, as does the porch also.

The kitchen is replete with conveniences that will effect economies in labor. There is abundant storage space, including a closet for pots and pans.

The three bedrooms are all corner rooms, with cross ventilation and an abundance of light. All of them are oblong, the most practical shape for bedrooms.

Construction: Wood frame, stucco and half timber finish.

Left—Detail of the porch. To gain more space in the living room the owner moved the end wall outward, thereby eliminating the door from the dining room and making the porch smaller than shown on the plan

Right—Detail of the entrance. In the old days wooden pins were used instead of nails to connect the beams. Such pins are shown here

This view of the living room shows the interior of the great bay window with its transomed casements. The window seat provides place for flowers and cushions, intimate things that contribute so greatly to the homelike air of a house. The French doors shown are those leading to the porch

HOME BUILT FROM DESIGN *6-F-3*

A COLONIAL HOME IS A REPOSEFUL HOME

And because the plan is rectangular it is inexpensive to build

Colonial houses are characterized by grace and delicacy of detail, many lighted windows, fine doorways, well-proportioned walls, accurately spaced windows.

The Colonial home illustrated above was built from design 6-F-3. The owner made some changes, however, the most conspicuous of which is in the exterior finish and the grouping of the windows across the front. The architect's drawing below illustrates the arrangement of the windows intended by the drawings.

The plans provide six main rooms, a dining alcove off the kitchen, six large closets, a porch at the side or rear, and an attic with full stairs.

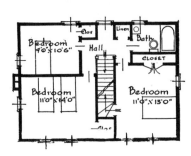

DESIGN 6-F-6

SERVICE AT THE FRONT

Permitting living rooms at the rear

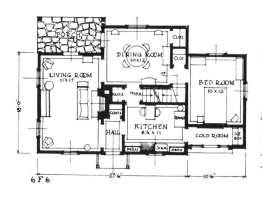

The rear porch, brought under the main sweep of the roof, becomes a part of the house. It is further enhanced by flag-stone steps and floor and graceful woodwork

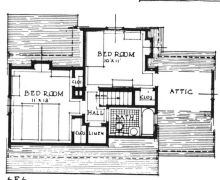

The little Dutch Colonial house here shown has quite a different air from the hunched-up so-called Dutch Colonial houses often seen, where the large second story has the appearance of pushing up through the roof. This has the same graceful lines that one finds in the old houses, with the characteristic deep overhanging eaves, but it is all house, not an inch of waste space anywhere. At the same time it has ample closets and space for storage. The sheltered walls are stuccoed, and the other walls of the house are covered with shingles or siding.

The house is homey, it is intimate, it is picturesque, all of the things which have caused this style to be admired for hundreds of years. In addition it has, at the hands of a modern architect, a full quota of the comfort, convenience, and efficiency of arrangement which has brought the American small home to its present high standard. Worthy of note are the kitchen at the front, large enough for table and chairs, the sizable dining room, and the pleasant living room. The downstairs bedroom is readily accessible to the stairs and to the bath on the second floor.

EARLY AMERICAN BROUGHT UP TO DATE

*After window openings covered with heavy oiled paper came
casements with diamond-shaped panes similar to these*

This house is in the early American style. It is designed after the manner of houses built before the Colonial style was developed. In it is reflected a great deal of the special character that our earliest builders wrought into their homes.

From the beginning, one of the characteristics of this type was an overhanging second story. It was usually placed in front, as it has been in the design shown here. It is said that the overhang was originally intended for purposes of protection from Indian marauders. However well this legend may be based on fact, it is evident that the overhang with its ornamental features is justified from a purely decorative point of view. The projecting overhang also has merit in the fact that it supplies extra space in the second story.

Another feature common to these earlier homes was the lean-to. Ordinarily this was an addition made as the needs of a growing family required more space. One side of the roof would be brought down in a long, graceful slope, sometimes nearly to the ground, to cover additional rooms in the first story. If the lean-to was placed on the windward side of the house, it bore the brunt of the fierce storms, and helped to keep the other rooms more comfortable.

The porch, which in this case occupies the position of the old time lean-to, serves perhaps no such utilitarian purpose as its predecessors, but it makes possible the distinctive outline characteristic of this style. It achieves, too, a pleasurable amount of privacy, and will be a delightful place in warm weather.

There is a quaint charm about houses such as this that the early builders gained through methods that are rather clear. They did not hesitate to put their windows off center. The early builders who had been skilled in the art of home building of old England brought with them the tradition of diamond-paned windows and leaded muntin bars. Bay windows they were familiar with from long usage. The ornamental drops under the projecting second story are reminiscent of the half timber architecture they knew of at home.

The design shown here has much of the quality of the old time architecture as to the exterior, but the interior is

HOME BUILT FROM DESIGN *6-F-7*

A house built from the same plans; here the exterior walls are covered with shingles. The most no-
ticeable change, however, is in the windows. Double hung windows with square lights have been sub-
stituted for the quaint diamond shaped panes specified, and heavy board shutters have been added. In
other respects the drawings have been followed carefully

a matter wholly modern. Perhaps there is an acknowledg-
ment to the old time architecture in the cavernous fireplace shown in the living room. A beautiful fireplace is
still one of the most decorative and attractive features of
the modern dwelling and here is one in keeping with the
style of architecture.

The plan is well organized, conforming in principle to
an arrangement that has become extremely popular. In it
will be found all those
conveniences with which
we have become familiar
in the strictly up-to-date
suburban dwelling.

The location of the
living room at the front
is such that greatest ad-
vantage can be taken of
views in front of the
house. The dining room
looks out upon the porch,
and through it to the
garden.

The kitchen is unu-
sually desirable in size,
equipment, and conven-

ience. At right angles to the sink—which is the combination type with a laundry tub in connection—is a wide
built-in cabinet with ample drawer and cupboard space in
addition to its work table. The large, many-shelved storage
closet will be welcomed by the housewife.

In the second story are three bedrooms, one of somewhat smaller size than the others, but with sufficient space
to include the usual bedroom furniture. There are five
closets in the second story,
thus insuring sufficient
storage space.

The basement called
for in the plans does not
extend under the entire
house, but where the cli-
mate makes this desirable
the basement could be
fully excavated.

The plans show a sug-
gested arrangement of furniture in each room, giv-
ing a very good idea of
their pleasant size and of
the wall spaces allowed
for the larger furniture.

HOME BUILT FROM DESIGN *6-F-8*

*The old Orton homestead of Revolutionary times is still an inspiration to us because of its
particular dignity and grace. Design 6-F-8, although smaller and adapted to modern needs,
has successfully caught the spirit of this pioneer house*

MODERN AFTER THE BEST OF THE OLD

*From the days when architectural taste was unerring
and grotesqueries were yet to come*

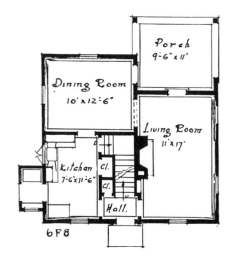

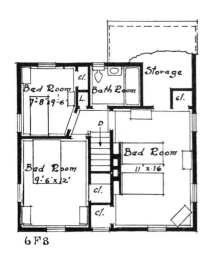

HOME BUILT FROM DESIGN *6-F-8*

The fine appearance of this New England Colonial home is gained through simplicity of detail, careful proportioning of the walls and roof, the proper spacing of windows with relation to each other and to the front door, and the dignity and grace of the Colonial entrance.

The long low roof which extends over the porch at the rear is after the manner of the old New England colonists, who, according to tradition, gave the northern exposure of their roofs this low sweep for protection against cold winter winds. But this was before the development of insulation. The side walls of the house shown here, if properly built, will afford ample protection in themselves against cold weather.

In the plan of this house, notice how the kitchen has been placed at the front with the dining room and porch overlooking the rear. This arrangement is particularly pleasant to those who dislike the activity and dust of the street.

This house is inexpensive to build. Its distinction does not depend upon the use of costly materials, nor do the convenience and pleasantness of its rooms depend upon an intricate arrangement of floor plan.

The architect's drawing above shows how carefully the drawings have been followed in the house illustrated, and what a fine effect may be obtained when this is done. No nicety of detail is lost

HOME BUILT FROM DESIGN *6-F-9*

AN OLD SOUTHERN HOME FOR MODERN LIVING

The two-storied column is truly Southern, while throughout New England may be found the corner porch with similar treatment

Here is a house inspired by the type made famous by Washington's home at Mt. Vernon. It is a small house, of course. As such it is without the pretentiousness of the home of the national hero. Yet much of the character of the old Southern mansion has been retained.

A recital of the elements that go to make up all that is best in the Colonial architecture of this type would take a great deal of space. It is sufficient to say that it is marked by delicacy of line and by simplicity. Even the larger houses have a quality of domesticity, which finds a sympathetic understanding among American home builders. One of the most striking features of the old architecture and of this home design is the two-story portico which here has been handled so expertly as to be well in keeping with the character of a small house.

The entrance is beautifully designed, with fan light and high, narrow side lights of leaded glass. The door is solid, divided into six panels, and a band of moldings surrounds the arched opening.

The plan is L-shaped. In the angle

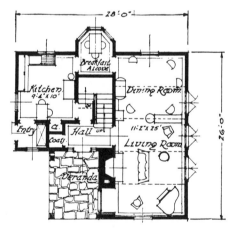

is placed the two-story entrance porch, giving the impression of a small forecourt.

The living room with its three long windows arranged on one side, and from which access is gained to a terrace or garden, occupies the space usually allocated to both living room and dining room.

Between this room and the kitchen is a dining alcove, which will serve for dining excepting when there are guests.

This dining alcove is not of the ordinary sleeping car type with built-in benches, but has space enough to include a small table and chairs. It will be seen that it extends from the main body of the house and is provided with three windows, which, opening upon the garden, make it a most delightful place in which to dine. When there are guests the dining alcove may serve as a pass pantry. There is an outside entrance to the basement.

Construction: Wood frame, exterior finish stucco, shingle roof.

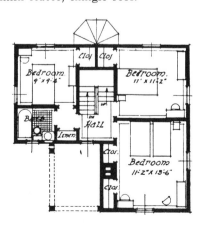

DESIGN *6-F-10*

SIX-ROOM ENGLISH GEORGIAN HOUSE

*Formality unusual in so small a house—yet nevertheless
appropriate and attractive*

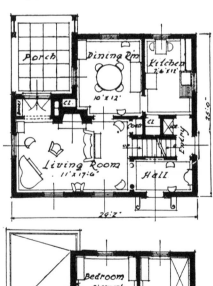

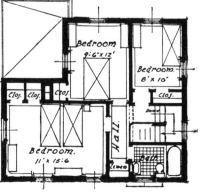

The house presented here has been developed in the English Georgian manner, with a formality quite out of the ordinary in a house of this size. The long windows, with their wrought iron railings in front, are extremely pleasing in effect, as is the beautifully proportioned entrance with its handsome lanterns and graceful iron railing at either side. The gambrel roof, broken with three slightly arched dormers, is an attractive feature, and the house as a whole is strikingly effective.

Because of the rather rich style of the period, the first floor plan is designed with a formality usually found only in homes a great deal larger. The door opens directly into a small reception hall. Immediately opposite, a narrow arched opening reaching to the ceiling affords a view of a portion of the stairway and the railing with its graceful, slender balusters.

The long windows which add so to the appearance of the house on the exterior, also add greatly to the beauty of the living room. Although double hung, they extend to within six inches of the floor in the true Georgian man-

ner. The fireplace is of simple design, somewhat on the order of our Colonial fireplaces, and quite in keeping with the formality of the room. French doors open onto the rear porch, and at one side of them are built-in bookshelves.

The furniture shown on the plans indicates clearly the comfortable size of the rooms. In the dining room French doors could be substituted for the window toward the porch.

Windows on two sides of the kitchen give light and cross ventilation. There is space at the end of the room beneath the second window and overlooking the yard for a small table and chairs to be utilized as a breakfast nook. The cupboards included are ample, but a closet at one end of the kitchen adds welcome storage space.

Ascending the stairs, which open directly from the living room, we find three bedrooms, all with windows on two sides; one a room large enough for twin beds and possessing two closets. There is also a linen closet conveniently located.

Construction: Brick veneer on frame, shingle roof, double hung windows.

DESIGN *6-F-11*

INSPIRED BY THE ENGLISH COTTAGE

*The bay-windowed dining room and downstairs bedroom
carry their own recommendation*

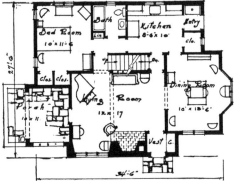

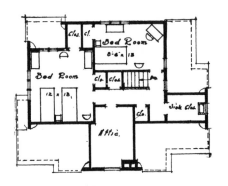

Many small houses can be catalogued. Depending upon the way in which the living room, stairways, and bedrooms are worked out, they can be put into one type or another. Thus, there is the central hallway type, the living room across the front type, and so on. Here is a design typical of the class of six-room houses with one bedroom on the first floor. It represents an extremely useful type of house, for which many people have preference, and it is a fine example of its kind. The style is English and yet it has been designed with so much consideration for American family life that it is practically as much at home here as on English soil.

The plan has many practical advantages. There is an entrance vestibule with a closet, a living room of fine proportions with a large fireplace, and a stone paved open porch opening from one side. In the dining room there is a charming bay window. In the rear, a kitchen, bathroom, and bedroom. The second story bedrooms are spacious and comfortable, and there is a real attic with no stairs to climb. When the bank account permits, the large sink closet may be made into a second bathroom.

The drawings indicate a long window seat beside the fireplace, a broad plaster arch over the recess. There is also an archway to the dining room.

The simple homelike loveliness of the exterior represents those qualities that make real architecture. The massing of the walls and of the roof, the contrast of the gable ends with the broad sweep of the roof, the chimney, doorway, bay window, the ballustraded porch, and other details of the house are all in keeping with the character of the architecture and an extraordinarily fine balance is maintained.

This little house enjoys its distinction partly from its informality, which is one of the finest qualities that may be possessed by small house architecture. The shape of the plan and the modeling of the roof have been arrived at by careful study. What seems informality is the result of careful planning.

Construction: Frame, exterior finish stucco with brick midway up the first story, shingle or slate roof.

DESIGN 6-F-12

FRENCH STYLE FOR AN AMERICAN SETTING

*A rambling plan makes possible much of the picturesque
beauty of the exterior*

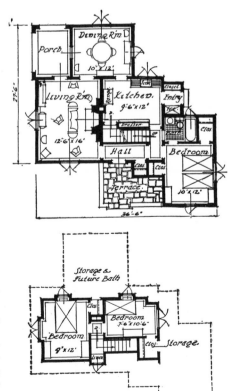

Our streets and countrysides would indeed be monotonous if everyone elected to build a square or rectangular house. It is fortunate that there are many who prefer homes of pleasantly irregular outline, houses that ramble picturesquely over the lot and are charmingly unconventional in their room arrangements. In the old country the houses which have inspired much of the recent small home building in America have gained their picturesque qualities often from having been built bit by bit as the years went along, a wing added here, a bay projected there. Such a house is represented here, though it is complete in itself. It has taken its character from the old chateaux and manor houses of France, but it is designed for an American setting and adapted to the needs of the American family.

High roofs are characteristic of this French type, but it would not do from the point of view of fine architecture for the architect to borrow this quality without its having some purpose in his design. The large space gained under the roof must serve a use. Here the high roof has been turned to advan-

tage so that it includes two excellent bedrooms with space for a bath should the owner desire to add this additional feature to the second story.

The main bedroom is on the first floor. This is a fine room with two closets and space for twin beds. The bathroom opens upon it. Thus the plan is a flexible one. It may be built as a bungalow with one bedroom, or as a two-story house with three bedrooms, and it may have either one or two baths.

The living room is a beautiful room lighted from three sides and possessing a handsome fireplace. Granted that it is but of medium size, there are pleasant views through the openings to dining room, hall, and porch, and ample room for even the larger pieces of furniture.

The kitchen is in a particularly advantageous position, for it is readily accessible to the living quarters, the first floor bedroom and bath, the stairs to the second floor, to the front hall and entrance, and, of course, to the rear yard by way of the side entry.

Construction: Wood frame, exterior finish stucco, shingle roof.

PLEASING FORMALITY IN THE ITALIAN

A rear porch and a second floor balcony provide outdoor comfort
conveniently for the occasions when this is desired

The house above, with warm yellow stucco walls and tile roof, is designed in a style much in favor, that is, the Italian. Almost every building today that has stuccoed walls and tile roof, and a bit of iron railing somewhere is carelessly called Spanish or Italian or just "Mediterranean." But the design shown here honestly comes by this name, for it is an attractive and practical adaptation of the Italian villa style to an American home of modest size.

Typically Italian is the stone quoined entrance doorway with its sturdy wooden door. And the second story loggia, or covered gallery, made so much of in many of the Italian palaces, becomes a small porch serving the second floor.

The low-pitched hipped roof over the main portion of the house and the irregular roof line of the rest of the house is another feature found in Italian

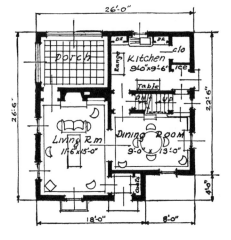

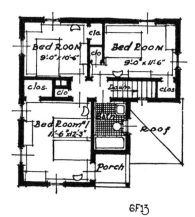

houses. Dormers or windows in the roof, so much used in this country, are practically unknown in Italy.

In the corner at the rear is a garden porch. This can be left open or enclosed as the owner may desire. A glazed door at the left of the fireplace leads to the porch thus providing the living room with light and air from a third direction. At the right of the fireplace is an arched recessed bookcase to balance the arched doorway to the porch. The partially open stairway has a twisted iron rail. This stairway is most conveniently located to serve as a combination stairway for it can be reached from both the dining room and the kitchen. A step from each of these rooms leads to a common landing.

The large storage closet in the kitchen will be convenient for pots and pans as well as for food supplies.

Construction: Frame, exterior finish stucco, tile roof.

DESIGN 6-F-15

A SMALL INFORMAL STUCCO HOUSE

Pleasing lack of symmetry seems to imply a house
that has grown with the needs of the family

The house illustrated here is designed to have stucco walls with weathered siding in the gables, steel casement windows, a roof of slate of green, gray, and mottled purple (but not too spotty in appearance), and a door stained a dark brown. It is suggested that the stucco be troweled to a slightly rough texture and contain enough ochre coloring to give it a warm tone. In order to realize the house that is here sketched, it is important that the details be carefully followed. The eaves, for instance, are close to the walls with practically no projection; the house is set low to the ground with the first floor but two steps above grade; the chimney is substantial and low, and the door is of sturdy design.

The plan is one of great convenience, with good circulation and no waste space. In the living room there is opportunity for several groups of fur-

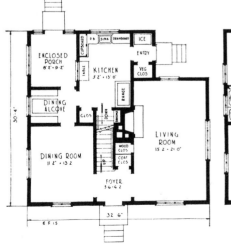

niture, and those pieces placed around the fireplace will have the seclusion they should, for the temptation to make an opening between the living room and kitchen, which would at once make of a large part of the room a mere passageway, has been avoided.

The service quarters need particular notice. As the basement is small, only large enough for fuel and heater rooms, a laundry tub is located in the kitchen beside the sink. The refrigerator and a capacious vegetable closet occupy the entryway. Broad windows light the room from two sides. The dining alcove, enclosed porch, and another storage closet are accessible.

The bedrooms are all of advantageous size. In the larger room two shoe closets occupy the space under the slope of the roof.

Construction: Wood frame, stucco finish, shingle or slate roof.

DESIGN *6-F-16*

IN THE SPIRIT OF OLD SPAIN

Its beauty lies in its perfect proportions and mass, for of ornament there is little

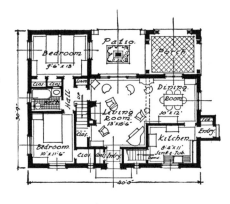

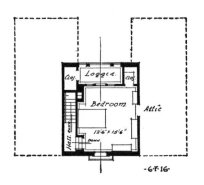

The atmosphere of Andalusia lingers in this Spanish Colonial home. In form it is not a bungalow, nor is it at all like the usual two story house. It has the long lines, the low gables, the entrance feature with the window above, the plain stucco walls, and the patio so characteristic of southern Spain and of the old Franciscan missions of our great Southwest.

Houses in Spain, great and small, are built around the patio. The name patio means something more, something different from the interior courts of other nations. It has a feeling and a spirit all its own; it is Spanish.

We of the northern and colder climes cannot have the open patio as a part of the house, but we can have out-of-door rooms, such as the porch and the patio shown here, or sun rooms, or regular rooms with many windows. Light, air, and sunshine must permeate them all. Too often the insistent porch cuts off all direct light from a room and is a positive detriment. The designer of this house has been careful to avoid that danger.

In studying the plans, one probably has an instinctive feeling that the patio

may be too expensive, but in spite of its patio this house is planned simply for economical construction. The whole arrangement of walls and roof is plain and straightforward.

It would lend itself particularly well to the requirements of a warm climate. In the South there need be no cellar. Special care should be taken for ventilation under the floors if the basement is omitted.

Although the living room proper may not appear large, any cramped feeling is entirely overcome by adding the dining room space to it without hint of partition between. Another thing which contributes to an effect of spaciousness is that practically one whole wall is of glass, affording a beautiful view across the patio and beyond. Access to the bedrooms is by way of a small private hall.

An attractive feature of this house is the second story room with a charming Spanish balcony overlooking the patio. It may be a sleeping room, a nursery, or a sitting room, as the household may desire.

Construction: Tile with stucco finish, tile roof, casement windows.

DESIGN *6-F-17*

A Six-Room Stucco Cottage

Shown lengthwise of the street, the house would look equally well
with the narrow sun porch end to the front

If this house were seen first in dim light it would at once appeal, for much of its charm lies in its massing and its low horizontal lines, accentuated by the use of wide siding under the eaves and by the long sweeping roofs. These horizontal lines give it a stability and well-established appearance that would be felt even though only the outline were visible.

The feature that would be next observed, if we may imagine ourselves viewing it in a gradually increasing light, would be its excellent arrangement of windows. The windows of the casement type are well placed.

With these fundamental elements—that is, the proportion and openings—found satisfactory, we should last note the detail to see whether it is in harmony with the character established. There is little exterior detail, as the house depends principally for its effect, as mentioned before, upon its massing. There is no wood trim around the windows and doors, and no elaborate cornice. The door itself is of extremely robust

design. Indeed, the only decorative notes are given by the wood lintels over the porch door and windows, by the wide siding at the top of the wall, and by the use of brick laid in checkerboard pattern under the porch windows. Since the detail of the house

is so straightforward, it will be even more important to have the color and texture of the stucco pleasing. The roof, which is specified as wood shingle, should be dark in tone. The lintels and siding should be weathered or stained a warm gray or a rich brown.

The stucco should be natural color or slightly tinted and finished with a moderate unevenness.

A study of the plan discloses at once its ingenious compactness. There is not a foot of waste space on either the first or the second floor. The small foyer serves as a convenient vestibule to the living room and as a link between this and the dining room. The stairs mount from a small passageway, separated from the foyer by a flat arch, straight between walls to the second floor. An attractive feature of the living room is the porch end, which is shown separated from the room by only a beam. If desired, a glazed partition could be used here.

Construction: Wood frame, exterior finish stucco, roof of shingles or slate.

DESIGN *6-F-18*

FOR THE LOT THAT FACES NORTH

*A house of stucco and shingles. A trellis screens the service
entry conveniently located at the front*

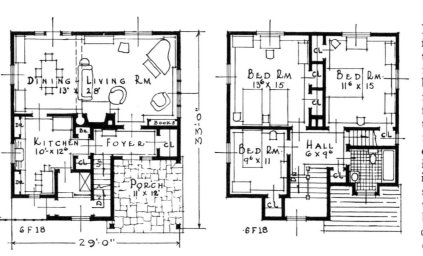

Almost a fourth of our houses must face north. To build for this exposure a house designed for a south-facing lot is to lose an opportunity to have the rooms most pleasantly situated. If you ask an architect how a house should face, he will say that the living quarters are most delightful with a southern exposure and that the dining room should have morning light. If prevailing breezes are from the south or west, as is usually the case, the cooking odors from the kitchen will not be wafted through the house if the kitchen is north and east. The living room, too, will receive direct breezes from the southwest in summer to cool it and be protected from the cold northeast winds of winter. So you will see that this house has been particularly designed for a north-facing lot.

There are numerous beauties and conveniences about this house that can be appreciated only from seeing it as built.

For example, the fireplace is of distinctive design with random width boards covering the front and sides from floor to ceiling. In the cement mantel facing is a metal door behind which is provided a warming oven. At the side of the door to the right are broad bookshelves with drawers below. The doors to this room are also of random width boards, recalling the chimney facing.

An inexpensive wooden molding where walls and ceiling intersect frames the ceiling and tends to make living and dining room one continuous apartment.

From the drawing of the furniture in the bedrooms, it is easy to see that these rooms are all of comfortable size, with sufficient floor area and unbroken wall spaces which permit the most logical arrangement of furniture.

Construction: Wood frame, exterior finish combination stucco and shingles or siding.

DESIGN *6-F-19*

A STUCCO HOUSE WITH INGENIOUS PLAN

*A handsome exterior, beautifully arranged rooms, all designed
to make the most of a narrow city lot*

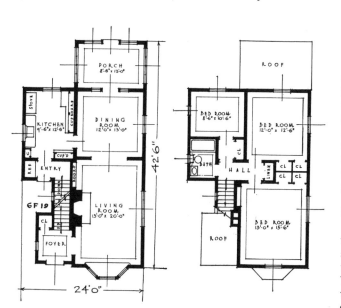

The working out of a design of a six-room house for a narrow lot requires real ingenuity. Of course, the exterior must be beautiful. No one wants to build a homely house. And yet what chance has the average narrow house to be beautiful? The restricted width of the front and the extreme depth of the side give a frame essentially of ungainly proportions. Yet since there are many narrow lots, narrow houses are inevitable. Here the designer, by the careful massing of the roof planes, and the insertion of dormers at just the right places, has given us a contour of striking individuality. He has given the house further vivacity by a happy use of contrasting materials. Such an effect could only be obtained by an artist.

In a house designed for a narrow lot, the plan necessarily must be somewhat long, with the rooms in line, one behind the other. Here a distinct advantage has been made of this necessity. Living room, dining room, and porch, placed in line, are separated by wide openings, forming one long vista, which at once increases the apparent size of the rooms and gives a most pleasant architectural effect. The feeling of spaciousness is further accentuated by the wide groups of casement windows and the glazed porch at the rear.

The kitchen has good cupboard space, well disposed.

As indicated in the sketch, the house is designed for stucco over wood construction with a brick chimney. The roof is of shingles and the casement windows of steel, though they may be frame. In the finish of the walls, the combinations of textures and colors of the various materials is of utmost importance. The stucco should have a fairly smooth surface, and it may have one of a number of tints—warm gray, light buff, or the faintest pink. The bands of rough sawn siding or shingles under the eaves should then be stained to match or in a contrasting color, not as dark as the roof. The door should be of oak, which may remain natural color, or it may be stained.

Construction: Wood frame, stucco finish.

DESIGN *6-F-20*

A BRICK AND HALF TIMBER HOUSE

With excellent roof lines and a well-placed, substantial chimney

There are certain delightful people in this world possessed of an indefinable quality that enables them to capture all hearts. Formerly we said of them that they had personality, or charm. Today we content ourselves by saying they have "It"—and everyone knows what is meant. And so we say of this house that it has "It." From its terra cotta chimney pots to the wrought iron hinges on the door it has the charm of Old England, yet in compactness and efficiency of arrangement it meets the requirements of modern America.

The house combines brick, stucco, and half timber, with a shingle roof laid in picturesque broken lines. The rough sawed edges of the siding above

the spacious open veranda make an equally effective detail.

Through the front door we enter a square hall, with a convenient coat closet at one side and a winding stairway beyond. The large living room has casement windows on three sides and an attractive fireplace at one end, brick faced and with a beautifully designed wood mantel. French doors in both living and dining rooms open onto the veranda which runs along one side of the house.

On such engaging features as the pergola, the little wooden service gate, and the delightful sweep of the wall at the front, there is not room to enlarge.

Construction: Brick and stucco on wood frame, shingle or slate roof.

This sketch shows more clearly the charm of the picturesque front entrance

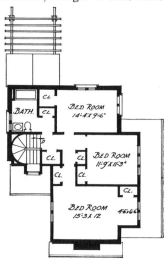

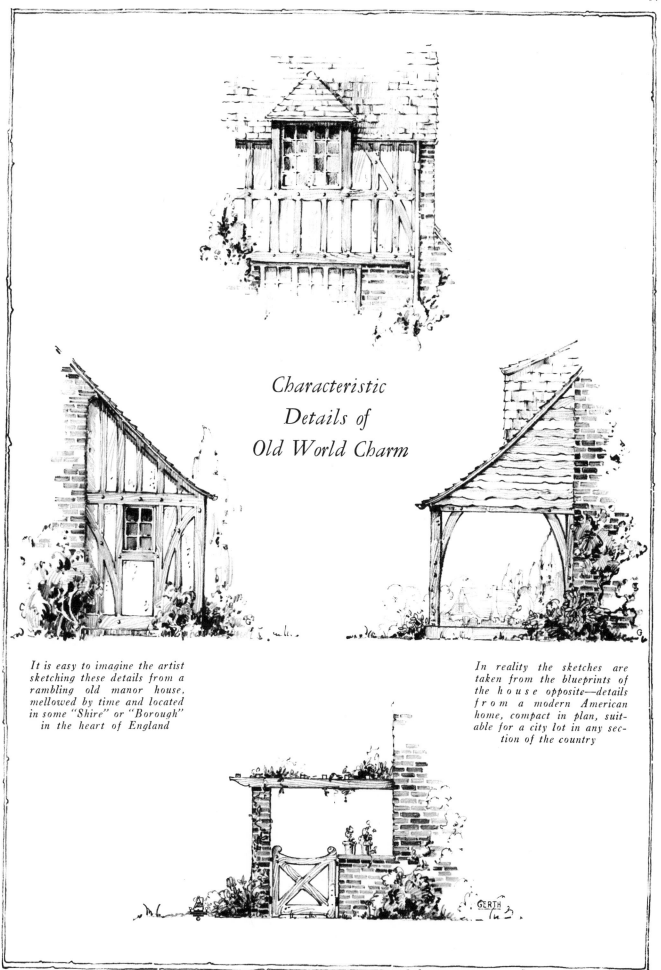

*Characteristic
Details of
Old World Charm*

*It is easy to imagine the artist
sketching these details from a
rambling old manor house,
mellowed by time and located
in some "Shire" or "Borough"
in the heart of England*

*In reality the sketches are
taken from the blueprints of
the house opposite—details
from a modern American
home, compact in plan, suitable for a city lot in any section of the country*

A STUCCO HOUSE OF SIMPLE DESIGN

*With a doorway to pique the interest and an
odd bay window for attraction*

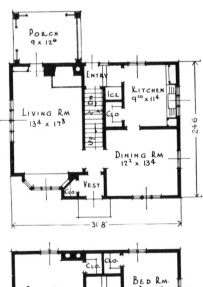

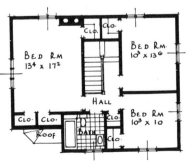

If the Colonial palls, if the English cottage no longer intrigues, and the Mediterranean styles have lost their allure, in short, if you are looking for something "different," we suggest design 6-F-21. It is not always easy to find a two-story house of such originality that embodies also real architectural distinction.

The doorway in particular attracts attention, with its oddly scalloped cornice and the sturdy simplicity of its pilasters. The flat surface of the door itself is marked off by deep V-shaped incisions, with wrought iron nail heads emphasizing each intersection, and the ever delightful knocker adds further charm.

Though the exterior wears a slightly foreign aspect, the plan itself is strictly American in its efficiency, the interior equaling the exterior in charm and interest. The rooms are all of attractive size, the windows numerous and grouped with an eye to their decorative possibilities within, as well as to the design of the house without. Entrance to the hall is by way of a small vestibule, the most suitable ar-

rangement for cold climates. The central stairway opposite is enclosed.

The bay window in the living room frames a wide, comfortable seat. The window at one end of the bay is balanced by a built-in bookcase at the other. The opposite end of the room, occupied by a plain brick fireplace, is sheathed with beveled pine boards of random widths. A sturdy batten door leads to an open porch partially enclosed by lattice work. Built-in bookshelves with a small cupboard beneath complete a composition with an old style Colonial atmosphere.

The dining room beyond the small square hall has wall spaces well adapted to the arrangement of furniture. The kitchen is a practical workroom including the most desirable built-in features. For good measure it adds a commodious, many-shelved storage closet. Windows on two sides give light and cross ventilation; the location of the sink is a particularly happy one from this point of view.

Construction: Stucco on wood frame, shingle roof, steel or frame casements.

"PERFECTION IS NO TRIFLE"

DETAILS FROM THE HOUSE ON THE OPPOSITE PAGE

Good books—a comfortable chair—a cheery fire on the hearth

Soft lamplight reflected from a background of wide pine boards.

HOME BUILT FROM DESIGN *6-G-1*

AT HOME IN NEW ENGLAND

*With a prim simplicity illustrating the best
in Colonial design*

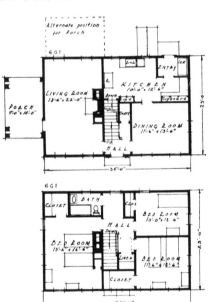

Anyone who has motored though New England will realize how suggestive this design is of the old towns and villages.

Formal in type, it has a few ornamental features handed down from the old c l a s s i c traditions, which give it an architectural quality and redeem it from any hint of the commonplace. Yet it does not depend upon ornamentation alone for its distinction. Its basic beauty lies in its fine proportions and well-spaced openings. One of the moldings of the cornice along the eaves is decorated by a simple sawed fret, which gives a sparkle in the shadow. The first story windows on the front of the house have molded caps.

Within, the house is entirely modern and carefully considered for comfort of living and saving of steps. On one side of the hall, with its attractive staircase and useful coat closet, is a living room extending from front to back. This has a fireplace on the inner wall with a beautiful Colonial mantel, and opposite it, wall space for a sofa.

The dining room, small but with good wall spaces, opens directly into the kitchen. Close beside it is an alcove which could be used as a dining nook, but which serves here as a pantry.

DESIGN 6-G-2

COLONIAL BROUGHT UP TO DATE

Narrow siding, molded drops, and second story overhang
are characteristic of early American homes

This small house design, while not belonging strictly to any one particular period, is a rather free version of the earlier Colonial seventeenth century house with the slightly projecting upper story characteristic of the time. Double hung windows have been used instead of the leaded casements of the original houses, as these are rather more convenient and usually better fitted to withstand the rather trying conditions of our New England climate. Actually, this design has much the appearance of most of the earlier houses which have survived to the present day, as the leaded casements were invariably discarded and replaced by the double hung sash when these came into general use. The molded "drops" under the projecting story were a characteristic detail of these houses, although as they became weather-worn, they were unfortunately often cut off and discarded. The partly enclosed porch, with its pitched roof, is an attractive feature adding another unit to the design, and giving additional interest to the simple front. A garage with a roof of the same pitch might

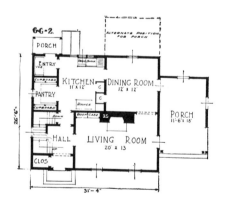

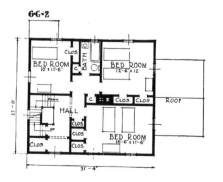

well be placed near the corner at the opposite side and connected with a trellis or pitched roof, thus adding further interest to the single central mass.

The house, as shown, has old-fashioned narrow clapboards and corner boards, and the whole, including sash and all exterior finish, should be painted white. An acceptable alternative would be to cover the walls with shingles which might be stained gray or left to weather, or large hand-split cypress shingles might be used to advantage. The blinds and doors would best be a cheerful shade of green. It would also be well to paint the chimney white with a black band at the top.

Besides six main rooms of generous size, the plan includes a large pantry, numerous closets, and a happy allotment of built-in features, among them the bookcases beside the fireplace in the living room. Upstairs are three excellent bedrooms, two of them with wall space sufficient for twin beds. Each of these rooms has two closets. A stairway in the hall, adjoining a large storage closet, leads to the attic.

DESIGN 6-G-3

THE CHARM OF NEW ENGLAND COLONIAL

Here is grace and repose found only in houses of fine proportions

A person studying house plans is not generally carried away by mere adjectives no matter how true they may be. A house must work. It must have a plan that can be lived with, an exterior that will keep the cost of building low, yet be fine appearing. Here is a design with these qualities.

Study of the plan will reveal what it offers. There is a coat closet where it should be, near the front door. The stairway is enclosed and inexpensive to build. The kitchen with its pantry is convenient. There is communication between the front bedrooms through a large closet.

The living room is long and broad with many windows. The fireplace is recessed and does not occupy floor space.

As for the exterior, it has the beauty of proportion and the grace that comes from skill. No amount of fanciful and extravagant building has ever displaced Colonial architecture from its position of leadership in our home design. This is an extraordinarily fine example of it.

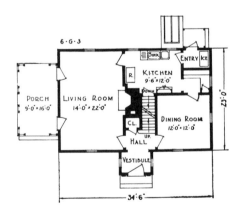

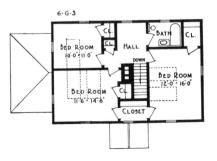

DESIGN *6-G-4*

IN THE GOOD OLD STYLE OF CAPE COD

The walls are shown of clapboards, but shingles would be equally characteristic

There need be no halfway measures in houses today, for with all the skill available it is quite possible to build a home, even a small one, both convenient in plan and correct in design. This design is a good example of both, for it is not only distinctive and picturesque in appearance but practical and well arranged as to plan. For the narrower lot the semi-attached garage may be eliminated and the porch placed at the rear.

The rooms are generous in size, even the hall is large enough to create an impression of hospitality. The Colonial fireplace and the treatment of the archway between rooms is shown below. Doors opening from both living room and dining room to the porch give ready access to this useful area.

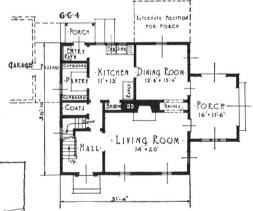

DESIGN *6-G-5*

GAMBREL ROOF AND GRACEFUL DORMERS

These make possible three bedrooms of generous size on the second floor

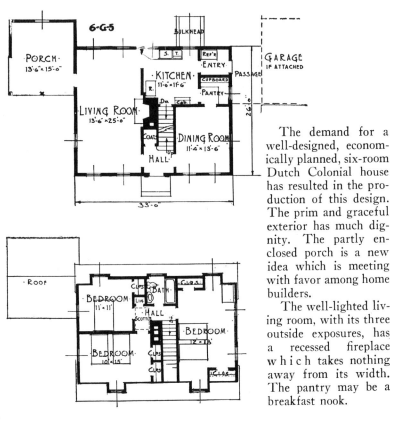

The demand for a well-designed, economically planned, six-room Dutch Colonial house has resulted in the production of this design. The prim and graceful exterior has much dignity. The partly enclosed porch is a new idea which is meeting with favor among home builders.

The well-lighted living room, with its three outside exposures, has a recessed fireplace which takes nothing away from its width. The pantry may be a breakfast nook.

DESIGN 6-H-2

A TWO-STORY HOUSE ECONOMICAL TO BUILD

Simplicity of form and materials results in worth-while economies
of construction

It is said that our American home building is pretty much in the hands of the woman of the house. If this is true, the mistress of the house will find in this plan a great deal to interest and attract her.

A study of the plan will show it entirely suitable for a narrow lot. All of the rooms, however, are generous in area, so that the limitations of lot width do not affect the house adversely in that respect. The fireplace at one end of the living room is flanked by bookcases on either side, and many large windows afford ample light.

The dining room will logically be the next place to engage the housewife's attention. Two built-in china closets—always a decorative feature when of well-chosen design—and the ever-desirable bay window make this room a charming place.

Out in the kitchen she will find an assembly of equipment distinctly modern in both choice and arrangement. The sink is under a window, the range immediately to the right. At the left is the kitchen cabinet and a clothes chute. The refrigerator may be placed where shown in the entry, convenient for

icing from the grade entrance, or, if it is an electric one, on either of the two inside walls of the kitchen.

The next thing to be noted is the position of the stairway. Opening directly off the living room, it is also accessible from the rear of the house through a door in the kitchen. The advantages of this arrangement are manifest to everyone. Combination stairways have been demanded by American housewives for years. Here is one without any elaboration of construction.

The porch carries its own message. Built in under the main roof of the house, it becomes an integral part of the architecture, and this is as it should be.

Each bedroom is provided with a generous closet. There is a linen closet in the hallway and a special closet for supplies in the bathroom, also a clothes chute. A stairway leads to the attic.

The style? No matter what the name, it is enough to say that it is well balanced, pleasant, a charming house to see and much more so to own. The exterior may be finished with siding or shingles. The shingle roof would be attractive in variegated colors.

HOME BUILT FROM DESIGN *6-H-1*

PARTICULARLY DESIGNED FOR THE CITY

*The arrangement of the stairway eliminates waste space and
affords rooms of comfortable size*

Here we have a house designed by city architects for city home builders. It has been designed for the typical city lot which often is not more than 35 feet in width. Having exterior walls of solid brick, it is especially adaptable to city building conditions.

The scheme of the planning depends largely upon the location of the stairway and here it will be seen that this is located at the rear of the house. The principal effect of this location has been to make possible unusual breadth for the living and dining rooms. The porch at the front increases the spaciousness of the first story.

The living room should be extremely pleasant. It is well organized. Large windows along the side wall insure adequate air and sunlight. The treatment of the end of the room with the fireplace flanked on one side by books and on the other by the stairway to the second story should make this space most interesting.

The arrangement of the kitchen will appeal to many, especially with respect to the location of the grade entrance and stairway to the basement.

In the second story are three good bedrooms and bath. A stairway in one of the closets leads to a spacious attic. All of the bedrooms are well lighted and have cross ventilation. Not many small houses can boast of so much closet space while still retaining conveniently large areas in the rooms.

The quality of the wall from the point of view of appearance may be made very fine through the use of common brick. Inexpensive brick used in this way and painted with a semi-opaque paint makes beautiful walls. If face brick is used it should be selected with an eye to its color and texture and laid in interesting coursing, the mortar joints handled intelligently. Beautiful effects may be obtained.

Construction: Solid brick walls, roof of shingles or slate.

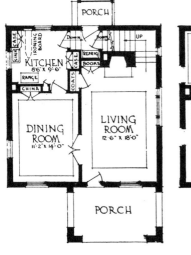

HOME BUILT FROM DESIGN *6-H-4*

MASONRY FOR THE TWO-STORY HOUSE

*The use of brick for the walls gives added interest to this
attractive design*

Here is a bit of Colonial architecture that represents no dull following after older forms or misuse of parts that have been taken from the past. It is a beautifully modeled small home with a plan of a distinctive order and an exterior that we may call Dutch Colonial for want of a better designation. There are some of the Dutch features, to be sure, but it is a modern American home design fashioned to accord with the conditions among which we live today.

As one looks over the plan he may wonder how the designer managed to get such large rooms, especially in the living quarters. The trick is in the location of the stairs. Imagine the stair hall brought clear through to the front of the house—see how this would cut out space in the dining room. As it is, no useful space is taken from the kitchen; in fact, here we have an arrangement that the modern housewife is demanding with louder and louder voice—that is, a combination of proper equipment within a small space. The kitchen is not too small, neither is it overlarge. Located as it is, the stairway is immediately accessible to the

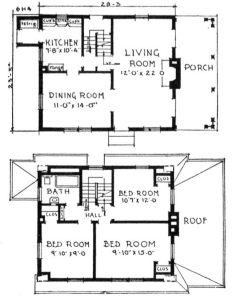

kitchen so that the housewife does not have to pass through other rooms to reach it. The stairs to the basement and to the rear entry are next to the kitchen.

There is a flue in the kitchen for a coal burning range. This can be omitted where gas is used. If an electric refrigerator is used, it may be placed on the inside wall. It would then be possible to utilize as a breakfast nook the space taken up by the side entry. The grade entry would then give the necessary access to the outside from the kitchen.

A sun room could be built in place of the open porch if the home builder prefers. Glass enclosed, faced so that it would be in the sunlight, this would greatly extend the usefulness of the house in the wintertime. The porch might also be placed at the rear for a lot that would otherwise be too narrow for this design.

Construction: Brick facing on hollow tile, or solid brick. Roof of slate. The original drawings call for dormer walls of siding. They should be of brick and slate in districts where fire laws require this type of construction.

DESIGN 6-H-5

CONCRETE BLOCK HOUSE FOR A NARROW LOT

Two china closets, a recess for the buffet, and French doors
add interest and variety to the dining room

The closely built-up districts in many of our cities present certain problems to the home builder with which he who dwells in the country or suburbs does not have to cope. All of them, of course, result from the original problem of the narrow lot. Not only is there the question of getting the necessary living quarters within the confines of the lot lines, but the problem of achieving an attractive exterior within these same limitations. In many cities, too, there is the problem of fireproof construction required by ordinance, which definitely limits the materials to be used.

In the aggregate these requirements p r e s e n t a serious problem for the architect, and a design that deals successfully with them all is a real achievement. Throughout this book will be found a number of such houses, and it is with pleasure that we present here still another.

In the first place, this house has been especially designed of fire-resisting materials. It is constructed of concrete block on masonry foundations, and the roof is of slate or some other fireproof roofing material. It is suggested that some special

texture block be employed, of which there are several on the market. Another alternative is the use of brick or hollow tile instead of concrete block. In either case the wall may be stuccoed.

A rectangular, almost square plan such as this one is the height of efficiency and economy. Here those accommodations such as the stairway and fireplace which take up valuable wall space have been placed at one side. This side may be placed as close to the property line as possible, which gives the other side of the house, which has more and larger windows a n d greater living area, the advantages of more light and air.

The living room is lighted from three sides, assuring light and air even though the house be built on an inside lot. Direct passage from the front of the house to the kitchen is another desirable feature. There is a grade entrance at the side, as well as an entrance from the back porch into the kitchen.

For greater economy, the addition containing the convenient breakfast nook and rear porch might be omitted, and a small, uncovered platform substituted.

DESIGN 6-H-6

ARCHED OPENINGS FOR THE FRONT PORCH

*For home builders who require a porch at the front, here is one
of picturesque and distinctive treatment*

Whether the porch is placed at the front of the house or at the back is a matter of taste and judgment. Perhaps it is an American trick to put it at the front. The Englishman puts it at the rear. He prefers it looking out on the garden. But the Englishman's house is somewhat more private than the typical American house. The Englishman is inclined to hide his house behind a high hedge, and, if he can afford it, behind a wall. But our front lawns are open. We like to see the view from the front porch. Whatever we may think about this, for the home builder who desires a front porch here is an excellent design with veranda nearly nine feet wide and more than twenty-five feet long.

Not every house has a porch in this fashion as well designed. A porch that is simply an adjunct, something added, retains that quality and the architecture suffers in consequence. In other words, in order to get good results from an architectural point of view in a house with a front porch, the porch m u s t seem to belong to the house, a kind of outdoor living room, a part of the house itself. This principle is well observed here. Without the porch the house would have a wholly different character.

As to the plan, it is an interesting variation of the type with living room across the front, dining room and kitchen across the rear. It varies from the usual plan of this type by having a fireplace at the stair end of the living room. In this location it serves a double purpose in that it screens the stairway and thus avoids expensive millwork, balusters and hand rail, and plaster work below. And it also preserves for the other end of the room a window of standard size. The top of the bookcase at one side of the fireplace is level with the mantel.

To the rear through French doors is a dining room of generous size. If desired, a garden porch could be built beyond. A stairway to the kitchen leads to a grade entrance and the basement. In the entry is a refrigerator convenient for icing. If an electric refrigerator is used location for it can be found in the kitchen. The space thus gained in the entry may serve the useful purpose of storage for tools.

Construction: Brick on hollow tile; shingle or slate roof.

INTERIORS FROM DESIGN *6-G-1*

Interiors from a house built from a Bureau design. One wall, simply paneled from floor to ceiling, frames the lovely Colonial fireplace. The *dining room is sheathed with wide pine boards in natural finish. Narrow moldings cover the edges, accenting also the beautiful grain of the wood*

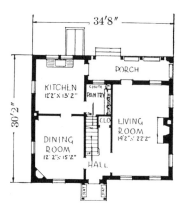

DESIGN 6-H-7

AVAILABLE IN BRICK OR WOOD

Two exteriors adapted to the same plan

This small house design, which may be had either in frame or masonry construction, is not a passing fancy but will remain in style long after old age has overtaken its builders. It has those qualities of intimacy and charm that bespeak the successful small home.

The plan has, through long years, proved to be one of the most satisfactory yet devised for the small dwelling. For a house of this size the central entrance and central hall is ordinarily an excellent arrangement. On account of the fact that the plan is rectangular—in fact, nearly square—real economy is achieved in building. Such a plan requires less materials and labor for the outside walls and roof. The principle of reducing building costs has guided the designer throughout, yet the room arrangement is eminently practical and the exterior, in both cases, exceptionally charming.

Double French doors may separate living room and hall if desired. The dining room is a beautiful room of good proportions, with a built-in china closet provided in one corner.

In the pantry off the kitchen are storage cases, a clothes chute, and stairs to the basement. Both kitchen and living room open onto a rear porch, a pretty place with slender wooden posts, flower boxes, and a brick-bordered concrete floor. This porch may be enclosed as a sun room for the width of the living room and the remaining space used for an entrance porch to the kitchen. Located at the rear as it is, the porch provides privacy as well as

an excellent view of the garden. It may also be utilized for dining, as there is immediate access from the kitchen.

There are three excellent bedrooms, with an abundance of closet and storage space. A window seat, clothes chute, and linen closet feature the second floor hall.

Construction: Design 6-H-7, solid masonry walls of brick or tile faced with brick, shingle or slate roof. Design 6-H-8, wood frame finished with wide siding or shingles—stucco may also be used; shingle roof.

DESIGN 6-H-8

DESIGN 6-H-10

MORE HOME FOR LESS MONEY

Livable and homelike without affectation

The Old Woman Who Lived in the Shoe might have found this house to her liking, for the four large bedrooms will accommodate a sizable family—or enable the younger members to gratify that most cherished desire, "my own room."

In spite of the large area of living space afforded, the house is economical in cost, being constructed of texture face hollow tile, a modern material which makes either stucco or brick facing unnecessary. It may be had in either plain or textured surfaces, and in a variety of colors.

The exterior reflects the straightforward plan. Unbroken roof lines, elimination of fireplace, and reduction of built-on features to a single porch make for economy in both cost of building and maintenance, yet the flower box beneath the front windows, and, if desired, on the porch, gives a gay, luxurious touch.

A breakfast nook takes the place of a dining room, an economy that will be appreciated by the man of the household in the building cost, and by the housewife in the elimination of many steps in the daily routine. While the plan is as compact as possible, yet the size of the rooms is such that the family need not feel cramped.

The kitchen incorporates many desirable built-in features; kitchen cabinet, ample cupboard room, and that most appreciated of all—the built-in ironing board. Win-

dows on two sides make the room light and cheerful, and provide cross ventilation.

Any woman who has at some time or other endured a sink placed by some unimaginative builder in a far corner of the kitchen, poorly lighted and ventilated, will appreciate this layout. The sink, placed beneath a double window, affords an outlook over the yard and garden, and in summer a breath of fresh air.

There is ample closet space throughout the house.

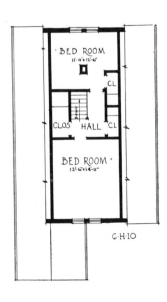

DESIGN *6-H-13*

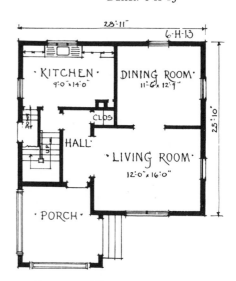

WALLS THAT WILL MELLOW WITH THE YEARS

Built on a compact, square plan, this is a dignified, substantial home in which the family may take pleasure for years to come. All six rooms are large and well lighted, with windows on two sides giving the desirable cross ventilation. A fireplace, eliminated for reasons of economy, could be included if desired and located on the long inside wall. In this case the opening to the dining room would be smaller and at one side. The second floor, like the first, is arranged to make good use of all floor space.

Construction: Texture faced structural tile, roof of slate or shingles.

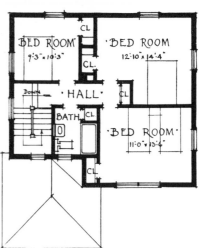

This sketch of the rear wall of the kitchen shows the convenient arrangement of refrigerator, sink and cupboards, with the door to the dining room in close proximity

Dwight James Baum, Architect

SHIPSHAPE AND AMERICAN

*The overhang, typical of many an old New
England home, was not to keep off marauding
Indians, but to add essential beauty*

HOME BUILT FROM DESIGN *6-K-10*

WITH ATTACHED GARAGE

Balanced by a broad porch on the opposite side

One of the most decorative features of all Colonial houses is the doorway. It is the hall mark of this type of architecture, varied in form yet always unmistakable in its marked dignity. In the entrance to this house we find the most typical Colonial elements: fan light, side lights and a projecting canopy, pyramidal in shape.

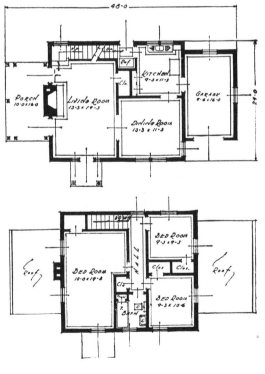

On the second floor one double bedroom, suitable for twin beds, and two smaller rooms. These will be found quite adequate in size, and windows on two sides make them bright and cheerful

The door opens directly into a large living room running the depth of the house, with an open stairway at the farther end. French doors on either side of the fireplace afford access to a large porch, and a wide cased opening opposite leads into the dining room, so that from practically any point in the room one gets a long vista. This, too, is typical of the old Colonial homes. The coat closet off the living room is large enough to include a closet bed. The sink, with broad double drain boards, is beneath the window in the kitchen. Built-in cupboards occupy the long recess on the left wall. The garage opens directly into this room.

DESIGN 6-K-16

FROM SUNNY MEDITERRANEAN SHORES

Stucco and tile give a wealth of color and texture

Design 6-K-16 combines the picturesque with the purely practical. Walls of masonry construction throughout permit deep window reveals. The rooms are all large. The studio living room is an unusual feature. Between this and the dining room is a group of three narrow arched openings with slender twisted columns. Opposite these columns in the living room is the fireplace shown in the "closeup" sketch. Note the number of windows in breakfast nook and kitchen, and the ingenious arrangement of the kitchen, the first floor lavatory and toilet, and the commodious closets. Of the three bedrooms one is a double room. Here the two closet doors and the panel between are of mirrors

Terra cotta chimney pots, richly colored tiles, and a metal ship ornament are effectively combined. The wrought iron stair rail is noteworthy for its distinctive simplicity. The moldings around the entrance, the heavy door of wide matched boards, the narrow barred windows, show discriminating use of detail

The tall narrow windows at the end of the living room present a real problem in decoration. The drapes in this case are hung against the wall at the side of the window on poles of regulation length, thus softening the severity of outline yet obstructing no light. The chimney breast forms an admirable background for a tapestry or painting

DESIGN *6-K-18*

PERMANENCE AND BEAUTY IN A SMALL HOUSE

With a rear elevation as interesting as the front

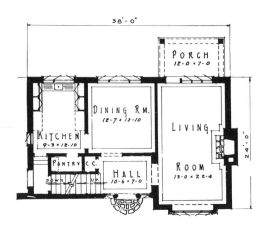

The oblong plan of this house affords six large, pleasant rooms, in addition to an attractive reception hall, which adds a touch of formality in keeping with the design. Arched openings lead from this hall to dining and living rooms. As it is reached through the hall and not the living room, the dining room has the virtue of comparative privacy. The housekeeper will appreciate the compact arrangement of equipment in the kitchen.

The construction is of concrete masonry, finished with stucco, with precast concrete forms about the entrance and stoop. The roof is of tile, slate or shingles. Casement windows of either metal or wood are used.

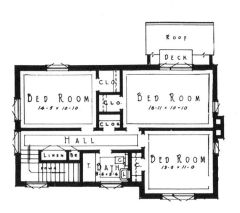

A small open porch ties house and garden together. This is located at the rear of the living room, a room delightful for its size and proportions and its ample fireplace of masonry construction

DESIGN 6-K-19

NEAT AND TRIM IN DESIGN

With a quality of style that is ageless

Describing this house from the point of view of what you cannot see in the drawings, we begin with the vestibule, which has a concrete floor laid off in tile patterns with variegated colors. Beyond is a beautiful plaster archway with vaulted ceiling. At the left and right of the hall are graceful French doors to the dining room and living room.

The cryptic designs in the kitchen are cases and cupboards. At the left of the sink is counter space with cases above and two flour bins and six drawers below. About the kitchen table, the rectangle marked T, is plenty of room for four chairs. On the right hand wall is a broom closet, with space for the refrigerator beside it and cases above.

Construction: Concrete masonry, stucco finish, roof of shingle tiles.

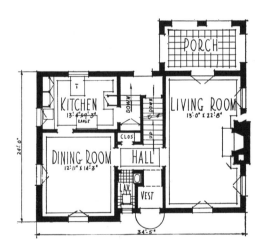

Not the least desirable feature of the house is this rear porch opening from the living room, its plastered arches framing enticing views of the garden. It is shown quite open, but may be either screened or glazed as desired

DESIGN 6-K-20

MANY CONVENIENCES

A house with the wanted things

All about this house are countless details which have been handled with minute care—little things which might have been missed were it not for the long and careful study put into the drawings by the architect. One immediately appreciates these things when they can be seen in the completed house. It is more difficult to visualize them from the drawings, but if we go through the plan carefully we will discover some of them. First there is a vestibule with a convenient closet at the right and a lavatory at the left. A third door leads into the hall where an open stairway mounts to the second floor. An archway at the right leads to the living room.

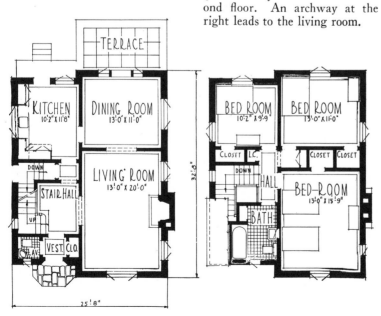

This room is well proportioned, with finely arranged windows and a handsome fireplace which has a commanding location directly opposite the entrance from the hall. Beyond we have the dining room, which has been so arranged that there is a beautiful vista through to the open terrace. Thus a fine view of the garden may be had from either living or dining room. A pleasant kitchen efficiently arranged, three fine bedrooms, and an up-to-date bath complete the plan.

Construction: Concrete masonry walls and basement partitions. Reinforced concrete has been used for the first floor slab, although other materials may be used. The finish of the walls is stucco, with cast stone trim used effectively about the windows and doorway.

DESIGN *6-K-21*

OVERLOOKING THE GARDEN

*Here the principal rooms look
toward the rear*

Most plans of small houses are a compromise; one wanted feature has to give way to another of lesser importance. For example, supposing it is desired to have both living room and dining room facing on a garden. Most small house plans do not provide this. A choice has to be made. Here, however, the most has been made of this very desirable feature.

Here, too, many other requirements of home builders are met. There is a downstairs lavatory; a beautiful fireplace that does not encroach upon useful floor space, but is nearly flush with the wall; a breakfast room in conjunction with the kitchen; a commodious coat closet off the front vestibule; fine bedrooms with many closets; and a pleasant stairway in an open stair hall at the front. A closet bed may be arranged for any of the bedrooms, thus converting that room into an upstairs den or library.

French doors from living room and dining room open out directly on the garden. These doors are protected with heavy wooden shutters. Gracefully designed plaster arches separate dining room and living room and lead from the latter into the hallway.

The fine plan is combined with a beautiful exterior. The walls of concrete masonry, finished with stucco, which is treated like stone at the corners, and with precast stone for the trim around the doorway, are not only substantial in construction but beautiful in scale and mass.

Construction: Concrete masonry, first floor slab of concrete, exterior finish stucco, roof of cement shingle tile. Casement sash of steel or wood.

DESIGN 6-K-22

A HOUSE OF MANY SURPRISES

With a wealth of odd and unexpected detail

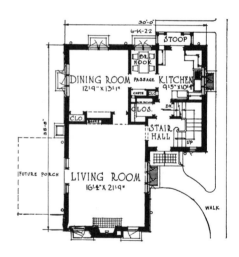

Another example of the beauty and charm that can be worked into the English style home. The shape of the plan permits an exterior of exceptional interest and variety, from the lines of the roof broken by dormers to the gable ends enhanced by well-designed windows. At the side half timber has been used effectively.

The construction is of masonry throughout, with consequently deep reveals at the windows. Precast stone blocks at the corners and on the chimney add a pleasing touch of informality. At one side of the entrance is a decorative wrought iron balustrade. The door is of heavy matched planks.

The illustration at the left shows the rear portion of the side elevation. It includes the dining room windows and those of the bedroom above, as well as the little dormer which lights the bathroom. It also shows the manner in which the stoop outside the kitchen door is handled, with the sloping roof and the trellis

DESIGN *6-K-17*

A HOUSE ON THE SQUARE

*Where architectural management yields
fine results*

An architect must be a good manager to create a thing of beauty out of a square house using practically only the basic elements of construction. This design is a particularly happy example of the fine results which may be obtained when the walls are of good proportions, the openings put in the proper locations and themselves well proportioned, the roof something which strives to be nothing more than a proper finish for the top of the building. The only additional details are the shutters—which are inexpensive, and a bit of ornamental work about the door. The design has been devised with an eye to economy throughout.

The plan is old and well established, one that thousands of home builders have tried and found entirely satisfactory. The six rooms are all of adequate size, and turn on each other conveniently.

Enumerating the accommodations supplied by this house, we have a vestibule with a coat closet, a beautiful open stairway, an archway between stair hall and living room, a decorative fireplace with bookcases in the archway beside it, a handsome dining room, a thoroughly equipped kitchen. In the rear hall is a large storage closet, and the grade entrance to basement and side yard.

On the second floor are three excellent bedrooms, bath, and seven closets conveniently disposed. All the bedrooms are well lighted, two having three windows, the smaller room double French doors protected by an ornamental railing.

Construction: Concrete masonry, exterior finish stucco, roof of cement tile.

STATEMENT

The Architects' Small House Service Bureau is constantly at work enlarging and improving its selection of designs for small homes. During the process of preparing this book several beautiful new designs have been completed. As they have features that should carry a strong appeal, the Bureau felt it desirable that prospective home builders be given an opportunity to see these designs. They have therefore been added in the pages which follow.

DESIGN *4-K-18*

FEW ROOMS

But these of good size make for comfortable living

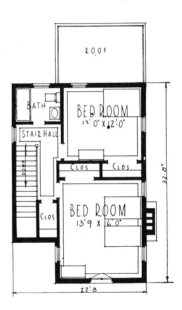

How can we live with such great comfort in so much less space than our grandfathers considered necessary? In this design we see the answer—by facing the problem of what our needs are as to space and equipment, supplying these, and eliminating the rest. For example, here we have a four-room house, yet there are actually three bedrooms, two upstairs and another one downstairs. The modern closet bed in the living room gives us the third bedroom.

Again we save costs and retain useful space for other purposes by omitting the dining room. However, we do not draw up our chairs around a table in the kitchen in the old-fashioned way. We have a dining alcove which affords plenty of space for the family and for intimate guests. For more formal occasions the dining table may be set in the living room. Windows on two sides of the alcove and on still a third side in the kitchen make this portion of the house bright and sunny.

The house is efficient throughout, and so narrow that it will go on a 30-foot lot. The rear porch is shown in the small sketch.

Construction: Walls of concrete masonry, stucco finish, roof of cement tile.

DESIGN 5-G-3

TWO BEDROOMS OR THREE

A flexible plan with large and
varied accommodations

The designers of this charming English cottage have succeeded in achieving a gracious informality within and without. The lower half of the house is of stucco over frame. The gables are finished in rough siding of random widths, a pleasant contrast of materials.

The plan is eminently practical. One end of the long living room may be used as a dining room as shown in the sketch. The downstairs bedroom or den opens from both front and rear halls, and is easily accessible to both kitchen and downstairs lavatory. If desired it may serve as a dining room. The kitchen is convenient and planned to save steps. Attractive bedrooms of irregular shape afford interesting opportunity for decoration and arrangement of furniture, and their lighting and ventilation is excellent.

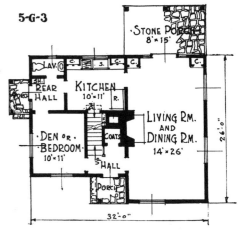

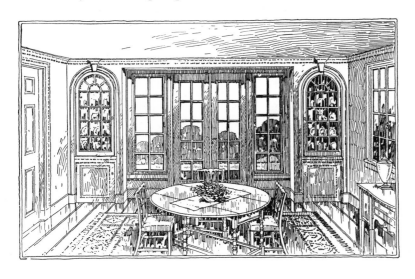

DESIGN 6-B-34

THE ENGLISH COTTAGE ATTACHES A GARAGE

*A convenience that adds still another decorative
feature to the design*

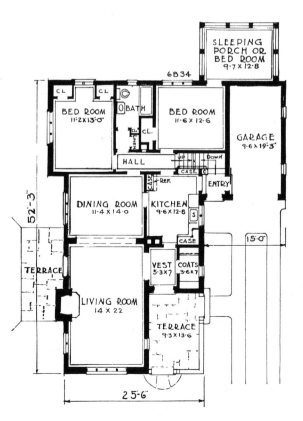

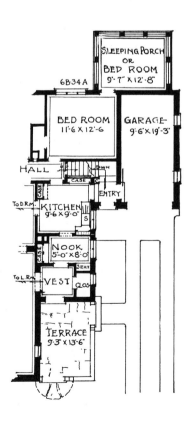

Home builders looking for a six-room bungalow of the least expensive type will forego this design unless they are willing to eliminate a great many factors which give it distinction. Although not an extravagant house, it is more complete than the usual inexpensive six-room bungalow

The plan at the right repeats the left hand section of the full floor plan at the left, and illustrates how a breakfast nook may be added by taking a little space from the kitchen and vestibule

DESIGN 6-F-22

SIX ROOMS WITH ATTACHED GARAGE

Common specifications uncommonly interpreted in this house of interesting design

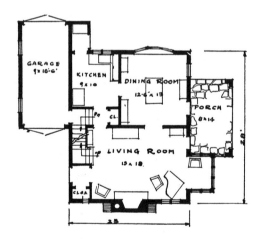

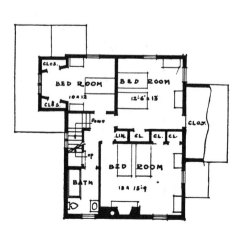

Above is the side porch and the glass-enclosed alcove at the end of the living room. Both exterior and plan merit study for the many desirable features they reveal. These include the special grade entrance to the garage, and the use of planking on the garage doors which brings this difficult element into complete harmony with the house. Construction is of frame, brick veneer about the living room, stucco elsewhere

DESIGN 6-G-7

FROM NEW ENGLAND

A charming possibility for the inexpensive house

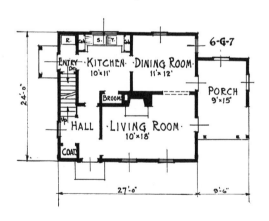

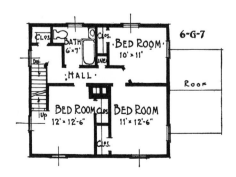

Houses like this, with an overhanging second story ornamented with wooden drops, were fairly common in the early period of our national existence. Considering their very real beauty they are seen far too seldom today. The design has a romantic character without extravagance; it is picturesque without the slightest affectation. The pitched roof over the half-enclosed porch recalls the lines of the main roof and becomes part of the whole composition. Narrow siding finishes the walls.

The architects have not missed the opportunity to make the best use of all floor space and to provide the facilities that are necessary for modern home making.

If a larger living room is desired, the wall between hall and living room may be omitted. The fireplace is of Colonial design, with a wood mantelpiece. A stairway from one of the bedrooms leads to the attic. Closet space is ample, including one for linen and another of large storage capacity located at the head of the stairs.

DESIGN 6-G-6

ECONOMY THE KEYNOTE

Developed on a square plan using inexpensive ornamentation

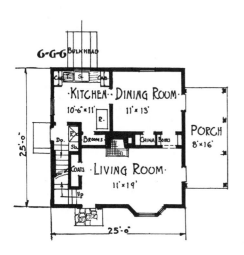

The purpose of the architects who designed this attractive house was twofold: to keep the cost within reach of persons of moderate means by planning a six-room house of the smallest dimensions compatible with comfort and, at the same time, to have a house of good design and convenient arrangement.

Although the outside dimensions are only 25x25, the compactness of the plan makes possible rooms of ample size and eliminates nothing that makes for convenience. There are closets for every need both upstairs and down.

The attractive bay window, the well-proportioned doorway, and the wooden quoins used instead of the cornerboards usually found on clapboarded walls give the house distinction and relieve what otherwise might be the austerity of the design.

In spite of the idea of rigorous economy which guided the designers, the house has decorative properties within as well as without. There is a pleasant Colonial mantelpiece, an archway connecting dining room and living room, with a place for books, and pleasant vistas from both rooms through the French doors to the open porch. Although the house is designed to be built of wood, it would look equally well if built of brick with white stone quoins.

Choosing the Plan for Your Home

Study the plans first. Remember that the plan is far more important to your comfort than the exterior

More than two hundred designs from which to choose your future home are presented in this book. No doubt somewhere included in the collection is the plan that will best meet your requirements combined with the exterior most pleasing to you. Among such a large number of designs, however, you may have difficulty in making your selection. To simplify the matter, and to make sure that you will not make any mistake in selecting your plan, the Architects' Small House Service Bureau offers several suggestions. If you will follow them, it will require only a short time to find the most desirable design to fill your needs.

Presumably you have already decided whether you want a three-, four-, five- or six-room house. Your next decision will be, of course, as to whether your home will be a bungalow or a two-story house. The needs of your family, the character of the site, the type of building in the locality must guide you here.

When you have determined the number of rooms you want, you automatically eliminate a large number of designs. Suppose you have decided on a six-room house. The exteriors of some of these are of wood, some of brick, and some of stucco. For the time being do not let this fact influence you at all. It would be much better if you do not consider the exterior until after you have selected the plan.

At this point eliminate the plans for which you do not care, then the houses which cannot be accommodated on your lot. In this connection perhaps the setting of your house is such that a living room across the front with a stairway at the side will be more satisfying than a plan wherein the living room runs from front to back with the stairway in the center of the house. If this seems to be the case it is possible to drop out further plans. The outlook from your different windows is next in importance. Some plans will give you better views from your living room windows than will others. By this time you have left perhaps eight or ten designs which provide in general for the things you most wish to have.

When you have limited your selection to a reasonably small number with the most desirable room arrangement, then is the time to start comparing the exteriors to see what combination of exterior and interior plan you like best.

CHANGES IN PLANS

It will help you in reaching your final decision if you will remember that the Architects' Small House Service Bureau is prepared to make minor changes for you in any plan that may fall short in some way of meeting your needs. For example, such changes might be the re-location of a door, porch, pantry or breakfast nook. Many houses shown with siding exterior may readily be finished in stucco, brick or shingles. The charge for making such revisions depends upon the amount of time required by the draftsman. All changes should be made by the Bureau or a practicing architect.

Remember also that many of the houses are so designed that they can be enlarged. Provision is often made for a room or rooms under the roof which may be finished off when you build, or at some later time.

It may be that you will find a plan which meets your requirements in all respects except that it is too large for your lot. In such cases it is often possible to adjust the house to the lot by putting the porch at the rear instead of at the side, without seriously injuring the design. Perhaps the end of the house may be turned to the front. Such changes can almost always be made without difficulty.

REVERSING THE PLAN

As to facing: if your lot faces north, it is obvious that a plan designed for a lot facing south will not give the best exposure. The Bureau will send you an additional set of blue prints printed upside down showing the reversed room arrangement if you require this change. There is no extra charge for the first set of reversed prints.

In selecting the house you wish to build there are thus four definite steps to consider. First determine how many rooms you want. Second, study only that group of designs which has the desired number of rooms. Third, eliminate from this group those plans which you do not wish to consider. Fourth, select from the finally retained plans the one which has the exterior you most prefer. To put it another way—read the plans first and choose the exterior afterward.

In considering the style of your home, remember that good design is always conservative. A house is a permanent thing. It will be well, therefore, to disregard the vogue of the moment, the bizarre and the freakish, choosing rather some interesting modern example of a style whose popularity has lived for centuries. Choose also a home whose well-planned interior gives a practical explanation for every gable or dormer, every sweep of the roof.

THE COST OF BUILDING

With a definite amount in mind for the building of your home, the cost of any selected house plan becomes the final determining factor. In conclusion, then, it should be pointed out that the final cost is largely determined by the specifications, the decision as regards the selection of materials resting with the owner after consultation with some reliable local architect, contractor, or advice from the Architects' Small House Service Bureau. If the owner specifies the highest grade of materials and finishes, the cost will necessarily be high. If he adds expensive equipment, it adds to the ultimate cost. By using moderate or low priced equipment the final cost of the building will in turn be materially reduced.

It should always be remembered, however, that the cheapest is not always the most economical in the end. On the other hand, the highest priced materials are not always necessary. Every care should be used in determining in each case the most economical material to use. Again be it said, the final decision as regards the quality of materials and therefore the cost of building rests with the owner.

What the Bureau Plan Service Includes

*Architectural help secured at very small cost insures the
building of extra value into your home*

Few people appreciate the vital importance of adequate documents to the success of a building. Many even feel that they may "borrow" a design that they have seen published somewhere, change it around a bit, and be quite safe in letting some contractor or builder guess at the dimensions, the specifications, the interior details, and the exterior elevations that do not appear in the perspective. It should be perfectly obvious, however, that such a course can result only in higher costs and the risk of a much lower standard of construction.

Architects' Small House Service Bureau documents will be welcomed by everyone with whom you come in contact in the building of your home. Contractors will give you a closer figure because guesswork has been eliminated and construction can proceed rapidly. Banks and real estate mortgage companies will allow a more favorable loan since the value of the completed house can be definitely and surely appraised. In addition, Bureau documents call for a high grade of workmanship and the use of materials that will insure long life.

Your purchase covers three complete sets of detailed blue prints, three sets of specifications, three quantity surveys, and two forms of contract agreements, documents which if followed closely will assure you a full measure of value for your investment.

HOME BUILDING DOCUMENTS

The contractor must have working drawings to follow in building a home. The more accurate and complete these drawings are, the more efficient will be his work. A contractor can bid much more closely on a set of Architects' Small House Service Bureau plans because he can be sure that there are no omissions or duplications and that he will be able to handle the construction at a considerably lower cost to himself.

The working drawings and details give the contractor the complete instructions which are needed in his work. They are drawn accurately by competent architects and every detail has been carefully checked and rechecked. Wherever possible the plans are designed to permit the use of stock lengths of lumber and standard sizes of other materials. Every effort has been made to eliminate waste and reduce the cost of good construction. If Bureau plans are closely followed, you may feel sure that your home has been soundly built and has the greatest margin of value that your investment could secure.

Few people realize the difference between an ordinary "cheap" set of blue prints and a set of complete detailed working drawings such as the contractor should have to guarantee economy and eliminate extras. Few understand how easily a pleasing architectural effect may be destroyed by a minor change in the plan. Purchase the best documents obtainable and follow them closely.

Included in the service of the Bureau is another document called the Quantity Survey, in which are shown the sizes and quantity of the various materials required in the building of the house you have selected. It enables different contractors to figure on essentially the same basis, and protects the owner against excessive allowances. In other words, the contractor knows, with this list, the quantities of each material needed to complete the job; therefore he does not find it necessary to add an amount to protect himself against the possible contingency of his estimate being too low.

The specifications supplement the working drawings and are, in fact, your written instructions to the contractor covering the various materials and equipment which he is to use and the character of workmanship that you will require in the building of your home. They eliminate the possibility of later misunderstandings or disputes and are your protection in securing exactly the home which you are asking your money to buy. Of necessity, with so many local conditions controlling, these specifications as first sent you cannot in all details be complete. They are made open, leaving the brand name or type of product or material to be specified either by the owner himself, or preferably by the owner in consultation with a local architect. Direct questions, addressed to the Bureau, regarding competing brands of merchandise are answered from an unbiased professional viewpoint in as fair and complete a way as possible. Through the use of complete specifications, the owner knows exactly what to expect in the way of materials and workmanship and the contractor knows just what he must do to fulfill his contract.

The fourth document, the form for the "Agreement Between Contractor and Owner," is based on the standard legal forms used by the American Institute of Architects. It is the printed agreement that you sign with your contractor by which he promises to deliver your completed house in accordance with the specifications, and by which you promise to pay him an agreed-upon sum. It is a carefully prepared legal instrument and is a necessary safeguard to both parties. This agreement finishes the whole scheme of the Bureau's document service, and makes it complete, accurate, and dependable in every way.

SPECIAL SERVICES

Throughout the period during which your home is under construction the Architects' Small House Service Bureau is at your service. Puzzling problems and difficulties of one sort or another are bound to arise. What a satisfaction it is to know that they may be referred to this professional body for a practical solution! No charge is made for this technical advisory service by correspondence—it is yours to use to the best advantage.

Should your individual requirements make necessary some minor change in your plan, such as the re-location of a door, pantry, lavatory, breakfast nook, or the addition or elimination of a fireplace, porch or sun room, you are entitled to the services of our expert architectural draftsmen at a nominal rate for the time involved. Changes of this kind should not be made arbitrarily, however. Here again you have the advantage of professional advice. In the long run you will find this cheapest.

If you desire personal assistance from an individual architect, this can be arranged on an hourly basis through one of the Regional Offices of the Architects' Small House Service Bureau.

Divisional Bureaus are maintained for the convenience of home builders in the following cities: Boston, Chicago, Denver, Indianapolis, Milwaukee, Minneapolis, New York, Pittsburgh, Seattle, and St. Louis.

PLANS ON APPROVAL

Your final decision regarding any plan will, of course, be influenced by the cost of building the home. Although the Bureau can give you a general idea of the price range into which any of their designs would fall, it would be impossible to give an exact figure. Variations of as much as 30 per cent sometimes occur in the cost of houses built from the same plans in the same town. This would be due to the difference in finishes, grades of material, and equipment selected. Local prices for materials and labor greatly influence costs.

To allow you to secure accurate cost estimates the Bureau will supply complete sets of documents for any of its houses on approval. You may then submit them to different contractors for bids and thus learn what the exact cost would be to build the home in your own city, furnished and equipped as you wish it.

The approval service is handled in this way. You place your order for plans of a certain design and send in your check for the full amount of the service fee, according to the established rate. A 15-day period is allowed, after you have received the plans, for you to secure whatever bids you wish to have made.

If the approval privilege is exercised and the plans returned, a service charge of $5.50 will be deducted from your deposit, and the balance will be returned to you. If drawings or other documents are worn or soiled, a small replacement charge would be also deducted at the following rate: Blue prints, $3.00 a set; Specifications, $1.00 each; Quantity surveys, $2.00; and Forms of Agreement, 15 cents each.

If drawings are kept, your original deposit is considered payment in full for the service and no charge is made for the approval privilege. Should costs run higher than you expected, or should you encounter any other difficulties, submit your problems to the Architects' Small House Service Bureau.

SUPERINTENDENCE OF CONSTRUCTION

One of the principal services performed by the individual architect for the home builder is known as "superintendence of construction." Many architects believe this to be of greater importance even than the making of the drawings, for the drawings alone are no guarantee that fine building will be achieved. Even where the most faithful and intelligent contractors are employed errors may creep in, which, however, do not pass the trained eye of the architect.

There are many other services performed by the architect in superintending construction. He selects the contractors who shall bid, he reviews their bids, makes arrangements for proposals contemplating alternate types of construction and the installation of a variety of different mechanical devices. He checks the specifications to see that they are complete, that the proper materials are selected, so that the home builder is protected against every eventuality. He advises the home builder about costs of construction and the merits of the many kinds of materials now offered by the markets. He recommends from among those who bid the particular contractor who is best able to do the work. From his experience he is able to judge which of the bids submitted is actually the lowest, all things considered. Then all during the construction of the house he is in constant attendance, watching the work, making sure that the materials and equipment are in accordance with the specifications, and seeing that the workmanship is of the high order required. During this period of building, it will be necessary to pay the contractor from time to time for materials and labor which he has worked into the house. The architect indicates the times at which payments are to be made and the amounts. He reviews the contractors' bills to make sure that money appropriated by the owner is used against bills for labor and material, so at no time will there be basis for mechanics' liens or any other unpleasantness for the owner.

It is impossible in this short space to detail all the services rendered by the architect during the home building. In short, however, the architect is the professional advisor with whom the home builder may consult at any period of the construction and through whom all his negotiations with the contractors are carried on. It is a service worth many times what it costs. The Bureau strongly urges every purchaser of Bureau plans to employ an architect to superintend the construction of his home.

An Outline of Service Costs

The modest fee charged for Bureau service entitles the home builder to expert direction and advice of marked value. He receives all the necessary documents for a well designed home; the privilege of consulting by mail with the technical service departments of our Regional Bureaus; the privilege, at a fair hourly rate, of having revisions and alterations made in the working drawings by Bureau architects; personal advice, also by Bureau architects and at a fair hourly rate; and finally, assistance in obtaining an architect to supervise the construction of the building.

The Fee

The regular fee is based on the rate of $6.00 a principal room, with 50 cents more for packing and postage. By principal rooms is meant living room, dining room, kitchen, and bedrooms. Halls, porches, sewing rooms, and bathroom are not counted. Thus the charges are as follows:

3-room house............$18.50
4-room house............ 24.50
5-room house............ 30.50
6-room house............ 36.50

Extra Blue Prints

Ordinarily the number of documents supplied with the original service is all that will be required. Extra copies, however, may be had at the following rates:

Blue prints on paper....................$3.00
Blue prints on cloth..................... 5.00
Specification forms 1.00
Quantity surveys 2.00
Forms of agreement, each................. .15
Revision sheets, each.................... .50

General Index

PLANS FOR NARROW LOTS— HOUSES 27 FEET OR LESS IN WIDTH

PLANS WITH LIVING ROOMS ACROSS THE FRONT

* With porch at rear or without porch.   † Narrow end toward front.

PLANS WITH LIVING ROOMS AT THE SIDE

LIVING ROOMS IN MISCELLANEOUS POSITIONS

PLANS WITH BEDROOMS OR SPACE FOR THEM ON TWO FLOORS

PLANS WITHOUT DINING ROOMS

* Alternate Plan.